Backyard Woodland

THE COUNTRYMAN PRESS
A division of W. W. Norton & Company
Independent Publishers Since 1923

Backyard Woodland

JOSH
VANBRAKLE

How to Maintain and Sustain
Your Trees, Water, and Wildlife

THE COUNTRYMAN PRESS

www.countrymanpress.com

A division of W. W. Norton & Company
500 Fifth Avenue, New York, NY 10110
www.wwnorton.com

978-1-58157-509-5 (pbk.)

10 9 8 7 6 5 4 3 2 1

DISCLAIMER

Throughout this book, company and product names are included with project ideas. These are for example only and do not imply endorsement.

All uncredited photos were taken by the author. All photos other than author photos or those credited to staff at the Watershed Agricultural Council are in the public domain and not subject to copyright.

While the activities described in this book are generally chosen as safe, there is inherent risk in any outdoor activity. Consult your doctor before engaging in any outdoor exercise program, and be sure you have the necessary skills before engaging in any potentially hazardous outdoor activity.

This book contains numerous links to websites that provide additional resources such as videos, applications, and fact sheets. Although these links worked at the time of writing, websites change often, and you may encounter dead links.

CONTENTS

CHAPTER 1

Private Landowners Rule!

If you go off into a far, far forest and get very quiet, you'll come to understand that you're connected with everything.
—Alan Watts

Late in the summer of 2007, my coworker and fellow forester Tom Foulkrod stood before a group of high-ranking diplomats from several southeast Asian nations. They had flown halfway around the world in suits, dress shoes, and heels to learn about how we care for the forests where Tom and I work, in the Catskill Mountains of upstate New York.

I'm not sure what the diplomats expected when their bus arrived at the site of Tom's woods walk, the Frost Valley Model Forest. I'm certain they did not expect Tom. He was twenty years younger than the youngest among them. Instead of a suit, he wore Carhartt's, a t-shirt, and hiking

OPPOSITE: *Because most US woodland is privately owned, landowners like you are essential for sustaining the many values of woods, including wildlife habitat, rural scenery, and water quality.* Photo credit: public domain

boots. To top it off, he sported a red beard that would make any Viking proud.

Tom could not have come from a more different life than those of the group he was now to lead, but he didn't let those differences bother him. He set off on the hike with his typical gusto, pointing out challenges New York's woodlands faced and ways we were trying to overcome them. He talked about how we protect trails from washing away during storms. He talked about invasive species, some of which the group knew from their home countries. He talked about deer pressure on the young trees and shrubs.

None of it was sticking. The group—all English-speaking—followed along with uninterested expressions. "It was a pretty boring conversation to start," Tom told me later. "I was talking at them, not with them."

He still doesn't know what made him mention

his 12 acres of fields, woods, and swamp in nearby Stamford. Maybe it was desperation as he grasped for anything that would help these bigwigs feel like they hadn't wasted their time coming here.

At once the group's whole manner changed. Hands flew up. Tom was surprised, but he gestured to one of the diplomats.

"What's the deer pressure on your land?" the man asked.

Tom answered, and more hands rose. "So you manage 12 acres?"

"No, I own 12," Tom corrected. "We saved up and own it outright."

Another hand. "What did you pay for your property?"

And another: "Do you have to keep paying for your property?"

As fast as Tom could answer one question, two more hands went up. The formerly reserved diplomats now waved their hands like schoolchildren.

"I kept figuring the next question would be the last," Tom told me, but the questions just kept coming.

When the time came for the group to leave for the next site on their tour, Tom led them back to their bus. They asked him questions the whole way there. They invited him to the next stop, a farm an hour up the road, and Tom was so happy that he accepted. The group kept right on asking him questions about his 12 acres the rest of the day.

That night Tom went out on his back deck and looked over his land. A grin blossomed on his face. He'd owned this property for two years, but he'd never thought of it as anything unusual. For him it was a nice few acres to see deer, birds, and the occasional coyote. After that day, though, Tom saw his property in a new light, as something rare and special.

And it is. The fact that an everyday, middle-class guy like Tom can own woodland is unusual around the world. Our planet has about 9.6 billion acres of forested land. Of that, governments own more than 85 percent.[1]

In countries like those from the delegation that visited Tom, the percentage is even higher. China owns all its nation's forests. So do Russia and Indonesia. Brazil and Canada both own 90 percent.[2]

America is different. We're unique among countries with large forests in that most of those woods are in private, not public hands. Private citizens own 56 percent of US forests.[3]

Who owns these private forests? Big corporations? Wealthy land barons? The 1 percent of the 1 percent?

Nope. Families like yours, mine, and Tom's hold the largest share. In total, more than 10 million family owners control 260 million acres of US forests.[5]

Just as Tom didn't think his 12 acres were anything impressive, it might be hard to think of your wooded land as a "forest" or something important to the broader landscape. But make no mistake. Even if you only own a few acres of trees, you own a forest,

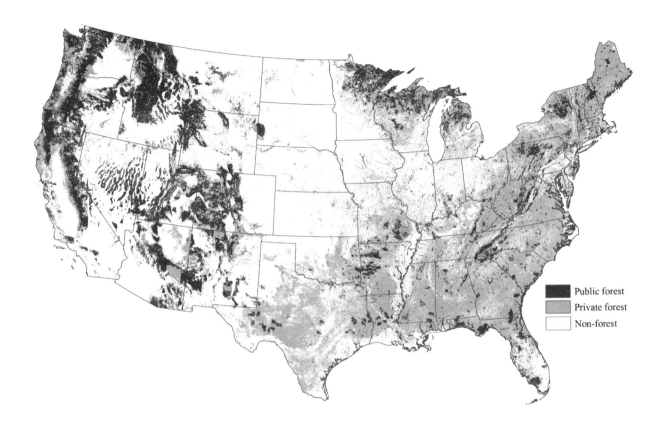

The United States is unique among countries with large amounts of forestland in that most of its forest is privately owned, especially in eastern states.[4]

Public forest
Private forest
Non-forest

or at least part of one. Together with your neighbors and the other millions of woodland owners like you across this nation, you and your land provide the rest of us with enormous value.

Wherever you're reading this, take a moment and look around. You'll see the contributions of pri-vate woodland owners. The wood floor, furniture, and framing of the building you're in probably all came from private woods. 92 percent of US lumber production comes from trees on private land.[6]

How about that glass of water or cup of cof-fee? 88 percent of all rain and snow in the United

Large mammals like the endangered Florida panther have wide ranges, making them especially dependent on private lands. These animals need vast areas of open space uninterrupted by development to survive, so they cross both public and private lands often throughout their lives. Photo credit: John Hollingsworth, US Fish and Wildlife Service

States falls on private land.[7] From there it flows into streams, rivers, groundwater, and ultimately through your faucet.

The birds chirping outside your window, as well as a host of other wildlife, need private land too. Colorado State University biologists estimate that private land provides habitat for 85 percent of United States wildlife.[8] And according to the Fish and Wildlife Service, half of all threatened and endangered species in the United States rely on private lands for 80 percent or more of their habitat.[9]

Private forests are also among our nation's best climate change fighters. Together they store more than 100 billion tons of carbon dioxide, 58 percent of all US forest carbon storage.[10]

Finally, there are the jobs. Private forest management directly or indirectly employs 2.4 million Americans.[11] Another 6.1 million have jobs in outdoor recreation, which often relies on private land.[12] About a quarter of wildlife-watchers and 84 percent of hunters use private land.[13]

Whether you own 5 acres or 5,000 (or any amount in between), your woodland is part of providing these diverse values in American life. The actions you take on your land influence—for better or for worse—the lives of those in your community, state, and country.

You're a private landowner, and that means you rule. It's both a great honor and a great responsibility. When you do right by your land, you not only help yourself and your property but all those, human and nonhuman, who depend on it.

But what does it mean to "do right by your land?" Does that mean leaving it alone, letting nature take its course? Are there ways you can use your land without harming it? And, most exciting, are there opportunities for you to make your land even better?

The purpose of this book is to answer these questions.

How Do I Use This Book?

Most landowner guides focus on growing and harvesting trees, but there's so much more to woodlands than that. Odds are you don't own your woods solely to log them. This book is for landowners like you, people who own woods for lots of different reasons and as a result have lots of different questions. I'll talk about timber production, but I want to focus on other topics too, ones you wouldn't normally see in similar books. I picked these topics by drawing on landowner surveys, interviews, forums, and woods walks. I wanted to know what keeps landowners like you up at night. What excites you about your woods? What worries you about them? I hope to give you some tips to get the most out of what you love and some answers to put your concerns to rest.

Throughout the book you'll find "Try This" sidebars with DIY ideas that can make your woods healthier and more enjoyable. Also look for "Watch Out!" features that highlight common pitfalls land-owners face and how to avoid them.

A NOTE ON EXAMPLES

I'm a forester in upstate New York, so a lot of my personal examples will come from the Northeast. If you own woods in another part of the country, please don't let this be a turnoff. While forests do vary from place to place, many of the same issues and solutions apply regardless of the location of your woodland.

That said, there will be nuances that differ from state to state, particularly when it comes to financial and legal questions. In these cases, it's worth connecting with your local extension office, forester, attorney, or tax accountant for information specific to your area and situation.

To help you find these folks, I've included a "State Resources" appendix in the back of this book. It includes links to forester lists, landowner organizations, woodland property tax reduction programs, and more, all organized by state.

The book is organized by topic, so if you know what your interests are, feel free to jump to those chapters. If you're new to woodland ownership, or if you just want to explore, it's worth at least skimming each chapter to find out what options are out there and to get ideas for activities you might like to do.

Whatever your background in woodland ownership, I recommend reading Chapter 2, "Where Do I Start?" Caring for your woods is as much an art as a

WATCH OUT!
FORESTER, LOGGER, ARBORIST . . .
WHAT'S THE DIFFERENCE?

Throughout this book you'll hear me refer to three different professions: foresters, loggers, and arborists. With their similar-sounding names, these professions often confuse people. Which is which? Who should be used in a given situation?

Let's start with arborists. They specialize in individual tree care. They often work in urban or suburban areas and handle yard and street tree maintenance and removal. While their skills are exceptional, arborists often lack knowledge for dealing with large numbers of trees in a natural setting like a woodland. Since this book focuses on woodlands, arborists won't come up much.

As for foresters and loggers, let's explain their jobs with an analogy. Say you're having a new home built. An architect draws up blueprints for what the house will look like and provides instructions on how it goes together. A construction team then uses those plans to build the house.

Foresters are architects for the woods. College-trained, usually with a Bachelor's Degree in forestry, foresters develop the plan for how to care for a forest over time. When logging takes place, they indicate which trees to cut and which to leave to meet the landowner's and woodland's needs. They supervise the cut to ensure it follows local, state, and federal laws. There are also educational foresters—I'm one—who teach others about forests and how to protect them.

If foresters are the architects, loggers are the construction team. When a forester's plan calls for cutting trees, loggers carry out that work. They specialize in the safe, efficient removal of trees from the woods.

Even though foresters and loggers have separate jobs and require different training, both are valuable when caring for your woodlot. A forester has knowledge that can help you navigate the complexities of woodland ownership, while a skilled logger provides on-the-ground expertise to help make your woodland dreams a reality.

science, and there are lots of ideas about how to do it. Chapter 2 explains what I believe it means to do right by the land.

It's my hope that this book won't be an end to your learning about your woods, but a launching pad for a lifelong adventure. Woodlands are amazing places, and there's always something new to learn about them. To help you on your journey, I've included a "Beyond the Book" section at the back of this book. There you'll find web addresses for fact sheets, videos, professional contacts, and more to help you take the next step on topics that grab your attention.

I hope this book motivates you to seek out more information, connect with other landowners, and find professionals who can help you. Most important, though, I hope it inspires you to get outside and interact more with your land.

CHAPTER 2

Where Do I Start?

Conservation means harmony between men and land. When land does well for its owner, and the owner does well by his land; when both end up better by reason of their partnership, we have conservation. When one or the other grows poorer, we do not.
—Aldo Leopold

A lot of books put inspirational quotes at the start of each chapter. I hate to admit it as a writer, but I usually skip them when I read. I'd rather get to the substance of the chapter.

If you're like me and skipped the quote at the start of this chapter, go back and read it. It's the substance not only of this chapter, but of this entire book. Those three sentences by the late renowned forester and landowner Aldo Leopold sum up what I believe it means to do right by your land.

OPPOSITE: *The options for what to do in your woods are virtually endless, and many landowners are concerned about doing the wrong thing. By following six simple rules, you can make changes to your land while still doing right by it.*

I find two parts of Leopold's quote striking. The first is his condition of conservation: Both land and landowner wind up better. Certainly, if you damage your land, you aren't doing right by it. But if protecting your land damages you, that isn't doing right by it either. Land and landowner should both benefit through their interactions with each other.

That leads to the second and even more powerful part of Leopold's quote. It's the word he uses to describe the relationship between land and landowner: partnership.

It might seem strange to think of your land as a partner, but I encourage you to see it that way. Leopold championed the idea of a "land ethic," a mindset where we view the land as part of our com-

WATCH OUT!
"I'LL NEVER CUT A TREE!"

Something curious happens when you talk to landowners about logging. If you ask them whether they own their land to produce timber, only about 1 in 5 will say that they do. But if you ask them whether they have harvested timber, about half will say that they have.[1]

A lot of landowners have told me, "I will never cut trees on my property." Then life happens. The tax bill comes. A spouse gets sick. A tornado hits the property. When an unexpected cost appears, I've seen landowners who thought they'd never harvest timber scramble to get a logger into their woods as quickly as possible.

The end result is usually bad. Since the harvest is rushed, the landowner often skips steps to ensure the land is looked after. Trails wind up rutted, streams are polluted, and the woodlot's future value becomes lowered through damage to the trees that remain. Adding insult to injury, the income is typically less than what the landowner would have received had they planned the harvest in advance.[2]

Because these landowners believed they would never log, they never bothered to plan for what they would do if they had to. They weren't aware of the steps to go through to get the best harvest, and they didn't have time to learn after a crisis hit.

I believe careful, well-thought-out timber harvesting can benefit both you and your land. But even if you don't accept that view, I still encourage you to be aware of the harvest process . That way, if you find yourself in a situation where you have to log, you'll be prepared to get the income you need while still respecting your partner: the land.

munity. I believe that that mindset is the starting point for all wise decisions about actions you take in your woods. By adopting a land ethic and by considering yourself and your land partners, working together to make each other better, you'll open up all kinds of possibilities. More importantly, you'll forge a respect for the land that will carry into everything you do on it and to it.

Isn't It Best to Do Nothing?

Respect the land. See it as a partner. Do right by it. These ideas all sound good, but isn't the best way to carry them out just to leave the land alone?

A lot of landowners have that opinion, and on the surface it makes sense. After all, forests have been around a lot longer than people. For millions of years they handled themselves without any interference from us.

But today's woodlands face challenges past forests didn't, like invasive pests, a changing climate, and soaring development pressure. Our woods often aren't prepared for these threats, and left to their own devices, they won't necessarily take care of themselves.

In fact, it's often threats that have nothing to do with nature that pose the greatest risk to a woodlot: property taxes, health care costs, and lack of interest in the property by heirs. Even if your woods would otherwise be fine on their own—by

no means a guarantee—these economic and social challenges can lead you or your heirs to make poor choices about your land's future. Doing nothing to prepare for them is a disaster in the making for your woods.

For this reason, a hands-off approach to your land isn't what's best for it. To be sure, doing nothing won't harm your woods in the short term, but in the long run, ignoring your woods leads to problems. If instead you play an active role in caring for your land, you can address threats before they harm your property. At the same time, being active on your land can create lasting connections, memories, and attachments. If you involve your children and grandchildren in your land and the decisions surrounding it, you can instill in them a value for nature and the outdoors. That's something younger generations today desperately need.

"An active role" doesn't mean you have to log your whole property. It doesn't mean you need to plant ten thousand trees. Even if you're just taking small steps, you're forming a relationship with your land. That's what matters.

Doing Right by the Land— Six Simple Rules

One of the most exciting—and frustrating—parts of working in forestry is that the science behind it is always changing. We're always learning something new about woodlands, how they work, and how to care for them.

Not surprisingly, then, you'll hear different recommendations about how to look after the land, depending on whom you talk to. Even as someone who works with forests every day, I have a hard time keeping all the ideas straight.

Regardless of the source, though, I've found the same overarching concepts seem to stick out. While the details vary, following these six rules will give you confidence that your actions, at least, are doing no harm to your woods.

RULE #1: PROTECT THE SOIL

When I say *forest* or *woods*, what image first comes to mind? Trees, most likely. But beneath all those trees is something even more important: the soil.

In the woods, everything starts with the soil. Soil stores the water and minerals that plants need to grow. Soil anchors trees to protect them from blowing over in storms. And when trees die, they decompose and return their nutrients to the soil, so new plants can grow. If you don't have healthy soil, you won't have a healthy woodland.

With few exceptions, you won't be improving your woodland's soil. It's unnecessary—not to mention prohibitively expensive—to fertilize or add other elements to it.

Protecting your soil is about safeguarding what's already there. The main way to do that is to keep soil from washing away through erosion.

There are lots of ways to reduce erosion on your land, and most of them have to do with actions you or your logger should take to keep your roads and trails intact. To learn more about these techniques, check out Chapter 7, "The World's Biggest Water Filter."

RULE #2: PROTECT THE WATER

In general, if you're protecting your soil, you'll also protect your water. That's because when soil washes away, it finds its way downhill and ultimately into streams, where it can foul the water and promote algae blooms. If you do what you can to limit erosion on your property, you'll be keeping your streams, ponds, and wetlands clean at the same time.

RULE #3: PROVIDE DIVERSITY

Not all woodlands are the same. Some are old. Others are young. Some are cold and wet. Others are hot and dry. Some have evergreen trees. Others have trees that lose their leaves.

These variations matter because different plants and animals prefer different conditions. A woodland that's great for eastern bluebirds will be poor for scarlet tanagers.

As we'll see in Chapter 6, there are ways you can make your woods more attractive to the wildlife you want to see more of. Recognize, though, that there are wildlife winners and losers with almost any change you make. As strange as it sounds, even leaving the woods alone will harm some species.

To create homes for as many species as possible, variety is key. Avoid actions that simplify your woodland, and work instead to make your property more diverse.

RULE #4: LEAVE SOMETHING FOR THE FUTURE

We love instant gratification. We see murders solved in a one-hour episode. We answer questions in seconds with an Internet search. We send money around the world with a click.

Forests don't operate on that scale. They change over decades, even centuries.

That's why it's so important to remember the future when taking action on your woodland. The trees you see today may have started when your grandparents were kids. It took that long for the trees to turn into the grown-up forest you walk around in.

When you plan actions in your woods, don't just think about this year or the next. Think about ten, twenty, a hundred years from now. What do you want your woods to look like then? What legacy will you leave for future generations who will own your land?

The last three chapters of this book delve into these long-term issues. They offer suggestions for actions you can take now to give your land its best possible chance for a happy, healthy future.

RULE #5: KEEP THE LAND INTACT

I grew up in central Pennsylvania, about an hour and a half west of Philadelphia. Back then, the area was mostly farm fields and woods with some small towns and cities.

When I visit my family there now, I'm stunned by how much the landscape has changed in my few short decades on this planet. Townhomes stand where corn and trees once did. Dogs and cats roam around, rather than cows and beavers. There are still a few farms, but they're harder and harder to spot.

Suburbia is creeping into our rural areas, and its effects on the land are devastating. As the land gets more developed, water quality declines, and the likelihood of severe floods increases. Wildfires become more common and more expensive to fight. Built surfaces, fences, and pets (especially outdoor cats) decimate wild animal populations.[3]

Nature is resilient. Given enough time, your woods will bounce back if you break the first four rules. But when you chunk up your land into house lots, that land will never again be woods. It has changed forever.

That's why I consider this rule the most important of the six. Whatever else you do on your woodland, if you want to do right by it, do what you can to keep the land undivided and undeveloped.

RULE #6: MEET YOUR OWNERSHIP GOALS

The previous five rules focused on making sure your land improves as a result of your actions. But you and your land are partners, so your relationship should enrich your life as well.

I don't mean enrich in a financial sense, although there are ways to earn income from your land while respecting these six rules. I mean that whatever your reasons are for owning your property, you should be able to fulfill them. Owning woods shouldn't be a punishment. You should be able to have fun. You should be able to have privacy. You should be able to earn income. These are all OK.

In fact, these reasons are essential. Owning woodland is expensive. Even if you do nothing with it, you're still paying property taxes on it every year. You and your family should get something for that investment.

That's why I've devoted the next part of this book, not to weighty topics like your land's future, but to simply having fun on it. Because the more you and your family get out and enjoy your property, the more excited you'll be to partner with your land for years to come.

TRY THIS:
DISCOVER YOUR INTERESTS THROUGH PHOTOS

Rule #6 is to "meet your ownership goals." But what are those, anyway? When I ask landowners about their goals, I get a lot of blank stares in response. Often folks have never thought about why they own woods. They aren't even sure what the options for goals could be.

If that's you, try out this activity. On the next few pages I've included a bunch of photos. Look through them, and then answer these three questions:

1. Which photo shows something you like about your woodland?
2. Which photo shows something you worry about on your woodland?
3. Which photo shows something you wish your woodland would have in the future?

Each picture corresponds to a chapter or chapters in this book. By picking out the photo or photos that answer these three questions, you'll figure out which chapters to focus on as you expand your woodland knowledge.

1

2

3

4

5

6

7

FOR SALE

POSTED
PRIVATE PROPERTY
HUNTING, FISHING, TRAPPING OR
TRESPASSING FOR ANY PURPOSE
IS STRICTLY FORBIDDEN
VIOLATORS WILL BE PROSECUTED

8

1040
U.S. Individual Income Tax

9

10

11

12

13

14

15

16

17

18

19

20

21

22

23

24

Photo credits: author photos (1–10). Heather Hilson, Watershed Agricultural Council (11). NPS (12, 22–24). Steve Hillebrand, USFWS (13). Jim Gathany, CDC (14). Yasunori Matsui, NPS (15). Pam McIlhenny, USFWS (16). USDA NRCS (17, 20). Jeff Schmaltz/MODIS Rapid Response Team, NASA/GSFC (18). Dr. James E. Zablotny, USDA APHIS (19). Jeff Vanuga, USDA NRCS (21).

If you picked photo number ...	Check out these chapters ...
1	Nature's Beauty (Chapter 3)
2	Wonderful Woodland Wildlife (Chapter 6)
3	Nature's Beauty; The World's Biggest Water Filter (Chapters 3 & 7)
4	The World's Biggest Water Filter (Chapter 7)
5	Wonderful Woodland Wildlife; Start a New Forest (Chapters 6 & 16)
6	The World's Biggest Water Filter; Start a New Forest (Chapters 7 & 16)
7	The Taxman Cometh; Keep Your Woods as Woods; Leave a Legacy (Chapters 9, 17, & 18)
8	POSTED (Chapter 10)
9	The Taxman Cometh (Chapter 9)
10	Timber! (Chapter 13)
11	The World's Biggest Water Filter; Timber! (Chapters 7 & 13)
12	Farm the Forest (Chapter 14)
13	Wonderful Woodland Wildlife; Other Income Sources; Start a New Forest (Chapters 6, 15, & 16)
14	Health and Wellness (Chapter 5)
15	A Burning Problem (Chapter 11)
16	Health and Wellness; Wonderful Woodland Wildlife (Chapters 5 & 6)
17	The Taxman Cometh; Keep Your Woods as Woods; Leave a Legacy (Chapters 9, 17, & 18)
18	Changing Climate, Changing Woodland; A Burning Problem (Chapters 8 & 11)
19	Chowing Down (Chapter 12)
20	Farm the Forest (Chapter 14)
21	Other Income Sources (Chapter 15)
22	Chowing Down (Chapter 12)
23	Health and Wellness (Chapter 5)
24	Get Out and Play!; Leave a Legacy (Chapter 4 & 18)

CHAPTER 3

Nature's Beauty

I think that I shall never see / A poem lovely as a tree.
—Joyce Kilmer, "Trees"

When foresters like me ask landowners what they enjoy most about their land, the answer we hear most, from almost 70 percent of landowners nationwide, is "beauty and scenery."[1]

I became a forester for the same reason. I love the country: the open spaces, the peace and quiet, the burbling of a stream far back in the hills.

It isn't shocking to me, then, that landowners often fear making changes to their properties because of the risk of damaging this beauty. But if you're careful and know the right techniques, you can take action on your land while maintaining its natural appearance. And if you know what to look for, you can make your land's beauty even more impressive.

OPPOSITE: *Indigo buntings rely on open, shrubby areas at the transition between grass and woods. They feed on seeds and insects in the low vegetation, then climb to a higher perch to sing.* Photo credit: Steve Maslowski, USFWS

Appreciating What's Already There: Reading Your Woods

Woodlands are hands-on. You can learn about them from maps, workshops, and books, but to really delve into them, you have to get outside and experience them.

When I was starting out in forestry, I would go on woods walks with more experienced foresters to learn their techniques. Every time I hiked with them, I was amazed by how much they noticed. To a beginner like me the forest was a green sea, all the same. But to the masters I was lucky enough to accompany, every step brought something new: an unusual species, a flicker of a bird through the treetops, an insight into the land's long history.

At the time I thought these foresters were just more observant than I was. That may be true, but as I've gained a little more experience, I realize there's more to it than that. Through their long years and innumerable hikes, these foresters had developed such knowledge of the woods that they could read the forest just as you are reading this book. They understood what the details meant, so they could pick them out from the background.

For someone who can read the woods, no two hikes are ever the same. Each one provides a vastly different experience. Even if you've owned your land for years, you can find new beauty on it by increasing your knowledge of what's there and what those things mean.

I can't begin to delve into all the details those older foresters saw. Frankly, I'm still learning them myself. It's the work of a lifetime. What I will share are three ways to help you get more out of every woods walk.

READ THE WOODS TECHNIQUE #1: LEARN COMMON TREES

There's a lot to forests besides trees, but trees are the biggest visual presence. One of the easiest ways to get more out of your time in the woods is to learn what kinds of trees you have.

The United States has more than 700 native tree species, but you don't need to know them all to figure out which ones you have. Unless you own a lot of land, you probably only need to learn a dozen or so trees to know the most common ones in your woods. Why? Because different trees like to grow in different places. Some need frequent rain; others survive in near desert conditions. Some need deep, nutritious soil; others grow on rocky, windswept mountainsides.

Thanks to these differences, you can eliminate most of the country's trees from the ones you need to know just based on which state your land is in. If you live in California, you won't be seeing black cherry. Alternately, good luck finding a Sitka spruce in Alabama.

You can use a general field guide to help you identify your trees, but that will give you a lot of irrelevant species along with it. A better option is a state-specific guide. I've included a link to one for each state in the "State Resources" appendix. I've focused on free downloads, but some guides are books you'll need to purchase.

If you'd rather not use a traditional guide, a more high-tech option is the free app Leafsnap. Developed by Columbia University, the University of Maryland, and the Smithsonian, Leafsnap identifies a tree based on a leaf picture you take with your smartphone. It was originally developed for the Northeast, but it's now expanding to include trees from across the continental United States. I've included a link to it in "Beyond the Book."

READ THE WOODS TECHNIQUE #2: LEARN COMMON BIRD CALLS

I need to start this section with a confession. Even though I'm a forester, it's only been in the past year or so that I've developed an interest in birds. It's not that I don't like them; I've just never been that excited to learn all the different kinds.

That changed for me after one spring hike in 2015. The songbirds had returned from their winter migration, and they were singing as they called to attract mates. I realized there were many species around me, yet I couldn't tell them apart. I knew each one had its own song, yet to me their treetop orchestra just sounded like cacophony. Had I known those calls, I would have had a much more interactive and rewarding walk.

Part of what kept me from learning about birds for so long was that I found it intimidating. North America has hundreds of bird species. How would I ever learn to tell them apart?

The single best resource I've found for learning bird calls is the Peterson Field Guides' *Birding by Ear* CD sets. Rather than a monotonous list, the CDs group birds by types of calls, like "whistlers" and "chippers and trillers." The narrator introduces each bird and then highlights key sounds to listen for. For instance, he describes the black-and-white warbler's song by saying it is "like a squeaky wheel turning round and round." The CDs even have a quiz at the end where they shuffle the birds and replay them without names, sorting them based on where they like to live, like "forest interior" and "wetlands."

I bought the *Birding by Ear* CDs for eastern North America in October 2015 and listened to them in the car during my commute. Within three months, I had learned nearly all 85 species on the set.

There's a *Birding by Ear* set for both eastern and western North America, and each set highlights the

TRY THIS: PAINT CHIP SCAVENGER HUNT

If learning species is overwhelming to you, here's an alternate way to improve your woodland observation. In a Paint Chip Scavenger Hunt, you don't need to know species names. All you need to do is spot colors.

Here's how it works. Go to your local hardware store and look through the free paint chip samples. Grab a few of whatever colors catch your eye. They can be obvious forest colors like green or brown, but don't be afraid to pick outlandish ones like hot pink or blaze orange.

Now head out to your woods. Your task is to find something on your land that matches each paint chip you collected. When you find it, write down what it is (if you know) or take a photo.

The Paint Chip Scavenger Hunt will force you to really observe your land's variety. It might seem impossible that you would find certain colors, but if you look hard, it's rare that you'll end up with no matches for any of the chips.

For more fun, do this activity with your family, especially if you have young kids or grandkids. Challenge each other to see who can find all their colors first. If there's a color someone can't find, everyone can work together at the end to look for it.

most common birds in those regions. I've included links to both of them in "Beyond the Book."

Speaking as someone who only recently started learning bird calls, I can say that the CD set is absolutely worth the effort if you spend time outdoors. Never again will I walk the spring woods and hear only noise. When you know common bird songs, your ears will instantly pick out those songs in the distance. Though you may never see the bird itself, you'll know it's there, adding its beauty to your land.

READ THE WOODS TECHNIQUE #3: YOUR WOODS' LONG STORY

What's the history of your land? What did it look like a hundred years ago? Was it farmed? Burned in a fire? Hit by a tornado?

If your land's been in the family a long time, family lore might answer these questions. Your parents or grandparents may have passed down the story of the time a windstorm knocked down all the trees on the hill, or the year forest tent caterpillars chewed the woods bare.

If you've only owned your land a short time, though, it's harder to know that history. You may not have anyone you can ask. If that's the case, you can still learn a lot about your land's long story. You won't talk to a person. The land itself will tell you.

Woods change over time, but they respond in generally predictable ways to certain events. When farmland is abandoned, for example, trees come back in a known way. They all establish themselves within a few years of each other, taking advantage of the bountiful light. They grow tall and straight as they fight with each other to keep from being shaded out. As they grow, they leave little undergrowth, because there's simply not enough light at ground level for shrubs, young trees, or grass to survive.

Even though your trees may be different widths, if they're all about the same height, you can be reasonably sure that they all started around the same time. When one of them falls or is cut for logging, count the rings: that will tell you how old the tree was. That age will give you an idea of when your woods got their start.

There are other signs of your woods' history if you know what to look for. Lilac bushes and apple trees often signal that a homestead was once nearby. Settlers would plant these trees and shrubs near their log cabin, and the plants often remain long after the cabin is gone. Look also for stone walls, which typically marked field edges. Walls with small stones indicate fields used for crops; the farmer would remove them while plowing. But if you see mostly large stones, it's more likely that livestock— probably cows or sheep—once grazed your land.

There's a lot more to reading your woods than these few tips. If you want to dig even further into your land's history, I recommend Tom Wessels' book *Reading the Forested Landscape*.

Enhancing Your Land's Beauty

It's one thing to recognize the beauty your land provides on its own. But can you go a step further and improve that beauty?

You can, though I'll caution you upfront that your woods aren't a garden. Your goal shouldn't be to tame them or make them more orderly. Rather, I believe enhancing a woodland's beauty means making it more diverse and helping it become a better spot for wildlife.

There's an art and a science to this woodland cosmetology, an approach called woodscaping. And the best place to start is right in your own backyard.

FEATHER YOUR LAWN

My home sits in a village on a small plot, less than a quarter acre. I mow my lawn because if I don't, I get a notice from the town that I'm a public nuisance. Welcome to suburbia.

Out in the country, we often apply that suburban logic to big fields. Instead of a quarter acre around your woodland home or cabin, you might have several acres. A lot of landowners mow that whole space right up to the woods, thinking they have to do it or that it's more orderly.

But straight lines and hard breaks are rare in nature. Instead, you'll typically find a transition area between two land types. If you have one area of old trees and another of young trees, it's not uncommon to find a few of each type in the border space between the two.

This gradual transition also happens between woods and grasslands. You start off with no grass on the forest floor. Then the trees start to thin. They get smaller. A little grass grows. As you keep walking, the trees spread farther and farther apart, and shrubs appear. A few more steps, and grass takes over more of the ground level. Eventually you're in an area of total grass, and there are few if any larger plants.

These transition areas have immense wildlife value. A lot of plant species, particularly shorter trees and shrubs, can only get enough light in these more open areas. In turn, animals that depend on those short woody plants for food or cover can only survive in these places.

Unfortunately, transition areas are disappearing. Farming and development often lead to hard edges between woods and other land types.

As transition areas vanish, so too do the wildlife who need them. Indiana, for instance, has lost 85 percent of its grassland birds and 65 percent of its shrubland ones.[2] The biggest cause? Loss of places for these birds to live.

You can help by feathering your lawn's edge rather than mowing right up to your woods. Feathering mimics a natural transition between field and forest. It involves five zones:

1. **Lawn**—This is the area closest to your home or cabin. You can go ahead and mow here.

2. **Forbs**—Forbs are non-woody plants other than grass. You can still mow in this area, but do it less frequently, perhaps once a year. Wait

Transition areas of forbs and shrubs between your lawn and woods create a more natural appearance and provide unique homes for wildlife.

until after August 1st to avoid disturbing ground-nesting birds.

3. **Shrubs**—Now you're getting into short, woody plants. Birds in particular love this dense vegetation to find food and safety from predators. You won't mow here, but every three to five years you can enter this zone with a brush hog to keep the plants from growing up into taller trees. As with the forb area, brush hog after August 1st.

4. **Small trees**—This area will contain trees, but they won't be trees like you'd find deep in the woods. Shorter species like dogwood and apple do well in these areas. You may need to plant some to get this area started if trees aren't already on your land.

5. **Woods**—You've completed your transition, and you're into full woods. Congratulations!

To be effective, you'll want at least 30 feet of transition distance between your lawn and the woods, with 10 feet each for zones 2–4. If possible, a wider area is better.

If creating these zones seems like a lot of work, don't worry. It's actually less work than mowing all that space. Nature wants to make these transitions. All you have to do is get out of its way by not mowing or by mowing less often.

REMOVE INVASIVE PLANTS AND PLANT NATIVE ONES

There are more than two thousand invasive species in North America alone[3], and many of the worst ones are plants. These human imports reproduce quickly and cover the ground, blocking out light and preventing native species from growing. Unchecked, they can turn your diverse woodland into a single-species tangle.

Invasive plants often start as plants you use for landscaping. Honeysuckle, Japanese barberry, and multiflora rose all came to this country as ornamentals, but they've long since escaped cultivation and now range throughout many woodlands. On your property, you can reduce the chance of an infestation by choosing only native plants for your landscaping.

If you already have invasive plants in your woods, removing them (if possible) and replanting with native species can help both your land's aesthetics and diversity. Getting rid of invasives is difficult work, though, so focus your effort initially on small patches. In some cases you may be able to remove the plants by hand, but in more severe situations your only option may be to use herbicide.

Removing invasive plants once isn't enough. To really control them, you'll need to retreat the area over a period of years, and it's vital to get native plants growing there so the invasives can't reestablish on the bare ground.

WATCH OUT!
THE PARK FOREST

Many landowners, perhaps because they've spent time in urban parks, want to recreate that manicured look for their woods. They want a neat and tidy woodlot with nothing on the ground and a clear line of sight. To accomplish that goal, they'll cut short trees and remove downed logs to make a clean, open forest floor.

But while this park-like appearance can work in an urban setting, it's not best for your woods. Leaves and upper branches hold a lot of a tree's nutrients. Leaving treetops on the ground lets them decay over time and return those nutrients to the soil.

Those fallen tops and shorter plants have other uses too. Seedlings often depend on dropped limbs to shelter them from hungry deer. And many small animals thrive in woody underbrush, using it to find food, build nests, and hide from predators.

Nature isn't neat and tidy. Doing right by your woods means accepting a little chaos.

An open, park-like appearance might be visually appealing, but creating it harms the woods by removing valuable nutrients and ground cover for seedlings and wildlife.

If you're trying to control invasive plants such as Japanese barberry (the red plant on the far side of this stone wall), it's best to act when the infestation is small. Left alone as they were here, the invasives will spread, replace native plants, and reduce your ability to get through your woods. Photo credit: Brendan Murphy, Watershed Agricultural Council

Protecting Your Land's Scenic Beauty during Timber Harvesting

If you've taken the time to learn more about your property's natural beauty and then to enhance it, it's understandable that you would want to keep that beauty safe. And what could be more destructive to that natural aesthetic than logging?

There's no getting around it. Even a well-done timber harvest by the most conscientious logger will change how your woods look. There will be openings where trees were cut. Treetops and limbs will lie on the ground. Especially right after a harvest, before remaining trees have time to grow into the gaps, your woods can look like a mess.

That ugliness, while temporary, keeps a lot of landowners from harvesting timber. But as we discussed in the last chapter, there may come a time when you need or want to have some trees cut. If that should happen, there are ways to protect the natural aesthetic you enjoy so much.

BUFFERS

Buffers are strips of woods separating timber harvesting and a common viewing spot, like your home, cabin, or driveway. Their purpose is to provide a visual screen between you and the tree cutting.

You have a lot of options when it comes to buffers. At the expensive end, you can prohibit any logging in them. This "no-cut zone" will provide the strongest aesthetic barrier of any of the techniques I'll discuss in this section.

But a no-cut zone comes at a high cost, because you'll be losing out on income from those areas. Fortunately, you can often maintain the visual shield just by changing how loggers operate inside the buffer. Only letting them remove smaller trees, for instance, will limit the number of big openings. Alternately, you can allow cutting but prohibit heavy machinery. Loggers can typically use winches to pull trees from a buffer without having to take equipment into the buffer itself.

In general, the wider your buffer, the less likely you are to see cutting deeper in the woods. Wider buffers cost more, though, so don't make the buffer wider than it has to be. For light harvests, 100 feet will usually be enough. In heavier cuts, you may want to widen the buffer to 200 feet or more.

Buffers don't all have to be the same width on your property. Consider wider buffers near high-visibility locations, such as your cabin, and narrower buffers in areas that aren't as commonly visited.

Your logger will need to know where you want the buffers, so you or your forester should clearly mark these places in the woods. You can do this by tying strips of biodegradable flagging to trees. You can also paint an eye-level mark on tree trunks. If painting, use tree-marking paint from a forestry supply outfit to ensure it remains visible throughout the harvest.

In addition to marking buffers in the woods,

Uncut tops left behind after logging are harmless to the forest (except in fire-prone areas), although they may create an aesthetic concern. Lopping, or cutting, tops as shown in this photo is one way to reduce a harvest's visual impact.

communicate your expectations in your "timber" sale contract (more on those in Chapter 13, "Timber!"). Here are two example clauses from actual contracts:

- "The logger will not cut trees in the designated 150' buffer area (flagged in orange flagging) next to the main road (see harvest map)."

- "The logger will avoid equipment operation in the red painted areas within 100' of the pond (see harvest map for location)."

LOPPING TOPS

In addition to creating buffers, you can reduce a harvest's visual effects by having your logger lop, or cut, fallen treetops so they don't stick up as high off the ground. Many loggers lop tops to around 4 feet high, but a lower height will make the tops less visible and break down more quickly. Keep in mind, though, that a lower height means more work for the logger, which in turn means it will cost you more. Limit low lopping heights to your most important high visibility areas.

Top lopping is especially valuable if your woods are in a fire-prone part of the country. Lower lopping heights hold moisture better, so if the tops were to catch fire, they'd be less likely to spread the flames to remaining trees than if they were unlopped.

As with buffers, make sure to explain your desires for lopping tops in your sale contract. Here's an example clause:

- "The logger will lop all tops to less than 3' in height throughout the 100' buffer area between the house and woods (see harvest map). The buffer area is flagged with fluorescent green flagging."

GUARD AGAINST TRAIL EROSION

For me, the most unsightly part of a timber harvest isn't the cutting itself. It's what happens to the roads and trails the loggers use to remove trees from the woods. If loggers aren't careful, they can leave big ruts in your trails. When it rains, those ruts channel water, and your trails wash away into unusable mud pits.

If you're like a lot of landowners, your trails are where you spend most of your time on your woodland. You can have a buffer between logging areas and your home, but you can't have one between logging areas and your trails.

Once erosion happens, it's difficult, expensive, and sometimes impossible to repair the damage. The best approach is to take preventive action to keep your trails from washing away in the first place. I have a whole chapter on ways to safeguard your trails coming up ("The World's Biggest Water Filter"). Check it out for tips to keep your trails stable and looking good whether you log your woods or not.

CHAPTER 4

Get Out and Play!

Not all those who wander are lost.
—J. R. R. Tolkien

If you pay attention to the news, you've probably heard a narrative that goes something like this: "Americans today are spending less and less time outdoors. As technology advances, we're ever more glued to our screens and removed from the natural world."

Makes sense, right? Except it's wrong. Outdoor recreation is booming. The numbers of hunters, anglers, and wildlife-watchers have all gone up in the past decade, according to the US Fish and Wildlife Service. Each year more than 90 million US citizens over the age of 16 participate in some form of wildlife-related recreation.[1] That's almost 40 percent of the adult US population.

As a landowner, you're part of this resurgence. You probably already use your property for outdoor recreation, from something active like mountain biking to something relaxing like an evening stroll around the pond.

There is one population, though, where the news narrative applies: kids. Participation in hunting or fishing by children aged 6-15 has dropped 22 percent since the mid-nineties. The number engaged in wildlife-viewing has fallen by even more: 27 percent.[2]

These children are our future, and the lands we own will one day depend on them just as they now depend on us. So while I could spend this chapter talking about any number of outdoor activities, I'm going to focus instead on fun, simple ways you can get the kids in your life more connected with the woods.

Have a Campfire (without Burning Down the Woods)

When I think about what inspired my love of the outdoors, two childhood experiences leap out at me. The first is the campfire. There's something magical about the way the flames dance and snap. Add to that the s'mores, late-night conversations, and boundless stars, and you have a recipe for outdoor perfection.

That assumes, of course, that you can get the darn fire started. My parents were not woodsy people, and it was always something of an adventure getting the fire built and lit. To help you avoid the same embarrassment, here are some tips on starting, maintaining, and putting out a campfire safely.

First, before setting a fire, check local weather conditions. Fire can spread rapidly in hot, dry, and windy weather. Find out if there are any burn bans, high fire dangers, or red flag warnings for your area. If any of these exist, build your campfire another time.

When siting your campfire, use an existing fire ring or pit. This ring will help keep your fire small and contained. If there are any gaps in the ring, fill them in with rocks.

Keep any flammable gear—including your tent if you're camping—at least 15 feet from the fire ring. Ideally, there should also be 15 feet between the fire ring and any shrubs or trees, to reduce the chance of a fire spreading.

Gather your firewood on site in advance, and store it upwind of the fire ring. Use only dead, fallen wood. Never cut or rip branches from live trees.

You'll need three sizes of wood to get a good fire going:

1. **Tinder**—dry leaves, grass, pine needles, or twigs

2. **Kindling**—sticks smaller than one inch around

3. **Fuel**—larger pieces of wood

There are a couple ways to build your fire, but the simplest may be the "tipi" method. To make this fire, first ball some tinder in your hand. You want enough so that some pokes through the gaps in your fist. Place that tinder in a loose pile in the fire ring's center. Next, stack kindling on top of the tinder so one end of each kindling stick touches the ground. The final shape should look like a cone or pyramid.

You can ignite the tinder with a match or lighter. I prefer the long-stemmed lighters with a trigger used for grills. I know they aren't as outdoorsy, but they keep your hand away from the fire and can sustain a light if your tinder doesn't ignite right away.

As your fire grows, add more tinder to keep it going. You may need to blow lightly on the fire's base to give it enough air to grow.

The bigger your fire gets, the more kindling and ultimately fuel you can add to it. Be careful not to add big fuel too soon, as it can snuff out your fire before it catches alight. Take care also to limit how much fuel you give the fire so that it remains under control.

At least one person should be near the fire at all times. Keep water on hand in case the flames start to spread.

When you're ready to put out your fire, stop adding fuel and let the fire burn down to ash. Then pour water over the whole fire to drown all embers. Keep adding water until any hissing stops. Stir the ashes with a shovel, and make sure everything is cold to the touch before you leave the site.

Oh, and don't forget the most important part of having a campfire: other people. Campfires are a social activity. Bring along your stories, sense of humor, and of course marshmallows, graham crackers, and chocolate.

Explore with Aerial Photos and Topographic Maps

Aside from campfires, the second—and probably bigger—reason I got into the outdoors is that I grew up on a farm, and exploring the woods and ponds around that farm was part of my daily childhood. I remember whole days where the few neighbor kids and I disappeared after breakfast, popped back in for lunch, and then were gone again until dinner. We spent entire days in nature, just wandering and playing.

To be sure, I look back on some of those experiences and say, "What were we *thinking*?" Unstructured play isn't risk-free, and it's important to know what's acceptable for your child or grandchild.

Despite that risk, my unstructured time in nature helped mold me into the person I am today. It taught me how to be creative, solve problems, and work in a team. More important, it gave me an unquenchable desire to explore and never stop learning.

As a woodland owner, you have a rare opportunity to help your kids and grandkids develop these same traits, to help them be the exceptions to the decline in outdoor experiences among today's youth. Encourage them to explore and play on your land.

If you aren't comfortable letting your kids completely roam free, one way to help them get out is to teach them to navigate using an aerial photograph and topographic map. Thanks to the Internet, you can get both for your property at no cost. For aerial photographs, use an online mapping service like Google or Bing Maps. For topographic maps, the US Geological Survey has an online mapper that lets you zoom in on a spot in the country and download current and historic topo maps as well as some aerial photos. I've included a link to this mapper in "Beyond the Book."

But what do all the images and funny lines mean on these photos and maps, and how are they useful for finding your way around your land?

To start, each map gives different kinds of information. An aerial photo is great for learning what the landscape looks like. At a glance you can spot roads (gray or white lines), rivers (brown lines), fields (light green patches, often with straight edges), villages (clusters of white dots), and woods (dark green).

A topo map is more complicated, but once you know what all those crazy lines mean, it's pretty straightforward. In fact, many of the features you can see on an aerial photo are marked on a topo map. Blue lines, for instance, represent streams. Red and black lines show roads, and dotted purple lines indicate power lines. Ponds show up as purple blobs.

But even though a topo can tell us all that, its real purpose is to show elevation. Topo maps take a 3D

TRY THIS:
STREAM STOMP

Streams are great places for kids to explore. They tend to be cool and shaded. The running water provides constant sound and activity. And of course, there are always opportunities for playing, splashing, and just working through that boundless childhood energy.

Streams are also great places for kids to learn. They're wonderful spots to introduce children to outdoor concepts without making it feel like a lecture.

A fun combination of learning and exploration is what I call a Stream Stomp. First, you and your kids should don shoes and clothes you don't mind getting wet and muddy. Then head out to a stream and hike along the bank.

As you walk, look for large rocks in the water. Pick them up, turn them over, and check out what you find with your child.

What you're looking for is a group of water-loving animals called macroinvertebrates. These critters form a key link in the stream's food chain. Many of them feed on submerged leaves and algae. In turn they become food for fish like trout, which then provide food for creatures like otters and eagles.

Macroinvertebrates are easy for kids to find in streams, which makes them a useful introduction to wildlife and the interactions between different kinds of animals. They also exist in a wide variety of shapes and sizes, which makes identification of each individual animal easier. I've included a basic, printable key in "Beyond the Book" to get you started.

Not only do macroinvertebrates provide a way to talk about animals, looking at them can also introduce kids to the impacts of pollution. Some macroinvertebrates, like stonefly nymphs, are extremely sensitive to water contamination. You'll only find them in the cleanest streams.

Stonefly nymphs like this one, found in the Niobrara River in Nebraska, are easily identified by their six legs, long antennae, and two tails. They can often be found clinging to the undersides of stream rocks, but only if the water quality is excellent. If you find these nymphs during your Stream Stomp, you know your stream is doing well. **Photo credit: National Park Service**

surface—the land—and squish it into a 2D form. They do that with a series of lines called contour lines.

Contour lines are the brown lines that fill the topo map. Each contour line represents all the points on the ground that are a specific elevation. A typical contour map separates its contour lines by 20 feet of elevation, and they will mark every fifth line with a number, say 2100, that indicates the elevation above sea level.

How does a topo map help you get around? Aside from letting you know whether you need to go up- or downhill, a topo map can help you pick easier travel routes. Because the lines indicate elevation, how close or far apart they are tells you how steep the terrain is. If you see a bunch of lines close together, that indicates a steep hill. If they're spread apart, that area is flatter and likely represents a gentler walk.

Aerial photos and topo maps individually tell us a lot, but together they reveal even more. Aerial photos don't show elevation well, but topo maps do. By contrast, topos do a poor job of showing what the ground cover looks like, something aerials excel at. By having them both, you and your family will get a much better feel for the terrain. That will go a long way toward keeping you from getting lost.

We can learn even more from aerial photos, in particular, by zooming in. Modern aerial photos, such as the ones you find on online mapping sites, can reveal not just whether an area is wooded, but what kind of woods it is. Often, aerial photos are taken in spring, after snowmelt but before the leaves come out. That makes it easy to spot conifers, because they'll be the only green in the image. Trees that lose their leaves will show up as brown.

That distinction can tell you a lot if you know what to look for. A tightly packed, perfectly rectangular patch of dark green may indicate a spruce plantation. Seeing a mix of brown and green would suggest that this area has a mix of conifers and trees that lose their leaves.

We can even get a sense of tree age from close-in aerial photos. Small, tightly packed tree crowns indicate a younger woods, while big, more spread out crowns suggest that the area of woods is older. If you have an aerial photo with you in the woods, a quick look around at your surroundings will often be enough for you to figure out approximately where you are on the map.

But once you figure out which way to go, how do you know you're going in that direction? For that you'll need a compass, and rather than try to explain how to use one, I've found it's much better if you see one in action. I've linked to a video in "Beyond the Book" that walks you through the basics.

Once you and your kids or grandkids are comfortable with aerial photos, topo maps, and compasses for your land, you can take the next step by getting maps for a local park or forest area. In these cases, you might no longer let your children go by themselves, but instead go exploring with them. That's all right. Actually, it can be as beneficial for you as it is for the kids. As we'll discuss in the next chapter, grownups can benefit from time in the woods too.

Blaze a Trail

In addition to using maps, you can help your family find their way around your property with a technique common at public parks: trail markers. There are lots of ways to do it; colored signs or paints are the most common of these. Whichever method you use, the goal is to make it easy for those using your trails to know where they are and how much farther they have to go to get home.

To mark your trails, first you'll need a decent idea of where they are. If you only own a few acres, you may already know the paths by heart, but on larger properties, it helps to build a trail map.

Creating a trail map sounds intimidating, but it can be easy if you have a handheld GPS unit with a tracking function. You simply turn it on with the tracking enabled, then hike all the trails on your land. The GPS will follow you wherever you go, and then you can transfer those lines to your computer. Depending on the software you have, you may be able to display those lines on a program like Google Earth.

If this techno-wizardry sounds out of your league, that's OK. You can get a professional forester to help. They'll be well-versed in the equipment and techniques you'll need to make an excellent map. You'll pay a little more than you might if you did one yourself, but a good understanding of where your trails are is a cornerstone for recreating more on them.

Once you know where your trails are, you can pick out the ones you'd like to mark. Look especially

Painted blue blazes make this trail easy to follow even when snow blankets the ground. Photo credit: Brendan Murphy, Watershed Agricultural Council

for loops; that way you won't have to double back as you hike. Indicate these trails on your map with different colors, such as blue, white, and pink.

Once your trails are marked on a map, it's time to mark them in the woods. As with marking buffers from the last chapter, use tree-marking paint when painting trail marks.

Alternately, you can use metal or plastic trail signs. Signs will last longer than paint, but they require you to put a nail or screw into every tree with a sign.

Whichever method you use, you'll probably need to order materials from a special forestry supply company. I've included links to a couple of possibilities in "Beyond the Book."

Supplies in hand, head out into the woods. Along your trails, mark a tree about once every 150 feet. If you're marking with paint, simple rectangles at eye height work well.

The goal in trail marking is to be able to see the next mark from the one you're standing beside. For long, straight sections, you can space marks farther apart. For denser, more twisting trails, marks will need to be closer.

Trail marks can do more than just point the way along a straight trail. They can also indicate when a trail splits or changes direction. Putting a marker above and to the left of another mark on the same tree, for example, indicates that the trail turns to the left. Putting one above and to the right means the trail turns to the right. This technique is standard for marking trails, and it will help keep your family from getting lost while exploring your property as well as many public lands.

A trail marker above and to the left of another marker, as shown here, indicates that the trail turns left. Photo credit: Brendan Murphy, Watershed Agricultural Council

CONTINUE STRAIGHT	START OF TRAIL	RIGHT TURN
SPUR LEADING TO A DIFFERENT TRAIL	END OF TRAIL	LEFT TURN

Knowing these standard trail-marking symbols is a big help in navigating not only your own trails but those on public lands as well.

TRY THIS:
MARK A TRAIL WITH CAIRNS

Cairns provide natural-looking trail markers, blending in with the landscape like this one at El Malpais National Monument in New Mexico. **Photo credit: National Park Service**

Trail marking with paint or signs can help your kids and grandkids find their way around your land, but it isn't a kid-friendly activity by itself. If you want to involve your kids in your trailblazing, I suggest a third method: cairns.

Cairns (pronounced "kerns") are human-made piles of stones. They can be almost any size or shape, and people have used them as navigational guides since prehistoric times.

Here's how you build them: Much like with tree painting, choose spots along the trail to place your cairns. Always make sure the last cairn is visible from the one you're standing by. Place a few starter stones to mark the site, then move on.

Now for the fun part. Each time someone hikes your trail, that person adds a stone to each cairn. The stone can be any size, as long as it comes from near the cairn. This hands-on construction makes cairns fun for kids, because even a pebble can count as adding to the cairn.

The more you and your family hike your trails, the bigger your cairns will grow. You'll literally be able to see how much use your trails get by observing the cairns.

One caveat for building cairns: avoid using rocks from streams. As you'll discover on your Stream Stomp, lots of animals use those rocks for their homes.

CHAPTER 5

Health and Wellness

It is not so much for its beauty that the forest makes its claim upon men's hearts, as for that subtle something, that quality of the air, that emanation from the old trees, that so wonderfully changes and renews a weary spirit.
—Robert Louis Stevenson

As *Treasure Island* author Robert Louis Stevenson observed, there's something about the woods that's therapeutic, something beyond the value of exercise from activities like hiking or horseback riding. The benefits are real, and you don't need to be an outdoor sports pro to gain them. All you need is a little time, a water bottle, and a comfortable pair of shoes.

This is no new-age medicine or celebrity fad. This is hard science with more than two decades of data to back it up. In one study, for instance, researchers from Chiba University had 280 people walk both in the woods and in a city area. After walking in the woods, the participants had reduced blood pressure, a slower heart rate, and lower levels of the hormone cortisol—all indicators of reduced stress—compared with the levels attained when they walked in the city.[1]

Being in the woods also boosts the immune system. In a pair of studies, researchers brought groups of men and women into the woods for a three-day, two-night trip. The trip involved some walking, but it wasn't intense exercise. Throughout the trip, the researchers measured the level of natural killer cells in the people's bodies, an indicator of immune function. By the second day of the trip, in both studies, the level of those cells had increased 56 percent. More impressive, even a month later, immune function remained significantly higher than before the people spent time in the woods.[2]

These decreases in stress and increases

TRY THIS:
TAKE A FIVE-SENSES WALK

One of the keys to forest bathing—and the reason it's called that in the first place—is that you're doing more than just passing through nature. You're actively experiencing it. One source recommends that if you spend a four-hour afternoon doing a forest bathing hike, you should travel no more than three miles, less than one mile per hour.[3] That's a really slow pace; the average human walking speed is about three miles per hour.

One way to achieve this relaxed pace is to engage multiple senses. In a Five-Senses Walk, you'll do just that. You'll walk your trails slowly, stopping often. You won't have a destination in mind. The point is the journey, not where you wind up.

As you wander, make a conscious effort to use all your senses. Pay attention not only to what you see, but what you hear, smell, feel, and even taste (though note my caveat below). Take time to smell the spring flowers. Rub your hand against the barks of different trees. If you've started learning your bird calls, apply that knowledge. Can you pick out a particular species from the background?

How long you spend on your Five-Senses Walk is up to you. If you only have fifteen minutes, that's fine. If you want to make an afternoon or day of it, even better.

Now for my promised caveat: be careful with taste and touch. There are edible plants in the woods, but there are poisonous ones too. Don't eat anything if you aren't sure what it is. Similarly, some plants like poison ivy can give you a rash if you touch them. Learn to spot them and leave them be.

That said, don't let this caveat keep you from getting outside. Even if you aren't eating or touching any plants, you can still engage those senses. How does the breeze feel on your skin? Is it different when the wind blows from the north as opposed to the south? Next try taking a few deep breaths. Can you taste anything? Is the air different under the deep cover of dense pines than it is in a meadow?

in immune function help fight many diseases. Researchers have linked spending time in the woods to reductions in heart disease, Type II diabetes, insomnia, depression, and even cancer.

There's also evidence that time in nature benefits childhood development. In his bestselling book *Last Child in the Woods*, journalist Richard Louv documents the positive health effects of time in nature for kids: lower levels of obesity, ADHD, and a variety of mental health disorders. As we discussed in the last chapter, time in nature also boosts kids' creativity, perception, and problem-solving skills.

With all these benefits, it's no wonder "nature therapy" is increasingly popular. In Japan, where much of the research into forests' effects on human health has occurred, spending time in the woods has become a national pastime. They call it *shinrin-yoku*, literally translated as "forest bathing."

Forest bathing doesn't mean stripping down and scrubbing with a pine cone. It simply means taking contemplative, relaxing walks in the woods.

Even if you're not as physically active as you used to be, you can still do some forest bathing and gain the health benefits of time in nature. Take a casual hike. Relax by a pond. Watch the sun set and the stars come out. The benefit comes not from the physical activity, but from slowing down and letting go.

Getting Out There: A Day-Hiking Primer

Whether you're forest bathing or just taking a normal hike, it helps to be prepared. Even if you're only going for a few hours, having the right gear can help ensure your trip is as safe as possible.

Regular hikers have developed a standard list of the "Ten Essentials" for safe, enjoyable hiking. How much of these items you'll need depends on how far you're going, how well you know the terrain, the weather you expect to encounter, and how much time you plan to spend outdoors.

1. **Navigation**: On any hike, bring a map. An aerial photo and a topo map like the ones I discussed in the last chapter are ideal. I also recommend bringing a compass. If you have a GPS unit, you can bring that too, but it's not a substitute for the trusty, no-batteries-required map and compass.

2. **Sun protection**: Make sure you wear sunscreen, lip balm, and sunglasses. I also wear a hat to keep the sun off my head (and for another, more disturbing reason we'll talk about in a future chapter).

3. **Insulation**: Dress for the weather, and consider bringing layers. If you start out in the morning, you may shed clothes as the day warms. On the other hand, the temperature will drop as the sun goes down. Regardless of the weather, you're better off wearing synthetic or wool clothing rather than cotton. When cotton gets wet, it takes a long time to dry and no longer insulates your body against the cold.

4. **Light**: Bring a flashlight in case you get delayed and wind up returning after dark.

5. **First aid**: You don't need anything fancy, but some basics will help if you get into a bad situation. A small kit with bandages, gauze, tape, and antibiotic cream is lightweight and can literally save your life.

6. **Fire**: If you end up stuck outdoors after dark, a fire is great to have. You can bring matches, but store them in a watertight container. They won't

work if they're wet. You can also use a lighter or manual fire-starter that makes sparks.

7. **Multi-tool**: A compact multi-tool comes in handy for all kinds of situations in the woods. Look for one that has a fold-out knife, flathead screwdriver, can opener, and scissors. I prefer the pliers style like those made by Leatherman over the traditional Swiss Army Knife setup. I find the pliers arrangement more robust and reliable in the field.

8. **Food**: Always bring more food than you'll need. You'll want a mix of carbs, fat, and protein to keep you going, especially if you plan to hike for extended periods. Nuts and dried fruit are excellent low-weight, high-nutrition options that will withstand jostling in a pack. Call me old-fashioned, but I also love a good peanut butter and jelly sandwich when I'm out in the woods.

9. **Water**: However much water you think you need, you probably need more. Plan on at least two quarts. I like to keep my hands free when I hike, so I prefer the water bladders like those made by CamelBak over traditional water bottles. When I go out in the woods, I use a daypack with one of these bladders built into it. It carries my water and all my other essentials in one easy package.

10. **Emergency shelter**: If there's even a chance you may unexpectedly spend the night outdoors, an emergency shelter will make that night much more comfortable. You don't need a huge tent or sleeping bag, but a lightweight option like a space blanket or bivy sack will help keep you warm, especially if it's windy or raining.

Beyond these ten standards, I keep a few other objects handy when I'm stomping around for field work. If you get cell reception on your woodlot, bring your phone. I know that's departing from the "get away from it all" mentality, but practically speaking, a phone is excellent for getting help in an emergency. Not only will you be able to call someone, but if your phone has GPS, first responders can use the signal from it to locate you quickly.

As a rule, I prefer waterproof hiking boots. Few things make a hike more miserable than wet feet. To reduce blisters, don't wear brand-new boots. Break them in first with some short walks.

Don't forget your camera. It's common for me to take dozens of photographs during an afternoon hike. I find having a camera also makes me more observant, as I subconsciously look for things to photograph.

Finally, in addition to what you bring, a little planning will make your hike more enjoyable. Eat a hearty breakfast before you set out so you have plenty of energy. I'm a fan of oatmeal with a little maple syrup. Also, check the weather. If there's even a chance of rain, bring a raincoat to keep you warm and dry. And most importantly, tell someone where

you're going and when you expect to be back. In a worst-case scenario, they'll know you're late and can point rescuers in the right direction.

Avoiding Common Woods Hazards

The day-hiking essentials are great, but at the end of the day, your best piece of gear is your brain. Knowing how to avoid bad situations in the woods— and what to do if one occurs—can make the difference between a satisfying hike and one that ends with a doct or visit.

Foliage for poison ivy (top left), oak (top right) and sumac (bottom). Note the three leaves for poison ivy and oak. For poison sumac, look for smooth, red stems on plants growing in wetlands. Photo credits: National Park Service (ivy), Erika Williams, NPS (oak) and Kevin Hansen (sumac)

POISONOUS PLANTS

Most plants you'll encounter in the woods won't cause you trouble, but there are a few to watch out for. Your best defense is knowing what they are and keeping your distance.

The most common dangerous plants you'll encounter are three you may have heard of, all related: poison ivy, poison oak, and poison sumac. All three plants produce an oil that causes skin rashes or, in severe allergic cases, swelling and trouble breathing.

For poison ivy and poison oak, remember the saying, "Leaves of three, let it be." Both these plants have leaves that cluster in threes. Don't rely on leaf shape; that varies between plants.

For poison sumac, the three-leaves trick doesn't apply. Look instead for dark green, glossy leaves clustered in groups of seven to thirteen. You'll also see a red stem leading to and connecting them. But the best identifier for poison sumac is where it grows; it's found almost exclusively in wetlands like swamps and bogs. If you're not in one of these areas, odds are you aren't looking at poison sumac.

If you rub against any of these plants, you may be able to prevent a rash if you wash the spot quickly with soap and water. If you do get a rash, you can usually treat it by soaking the area in cold water and applying calamine lotion to relieve the itching. Avoid scratching, as it can lead to infection. Also avoid topical antihistamines, anesthetics, and antibiotics. These creams can lead to allergic reactions of their own.

A brave man stands next to a giant hogweed to provide a sense of scale. Note his rubber gloves. The giant hogweed's large size, enormous leaves, and white flower clusters are key identifiers of this dangerous plant. Photo credit: Terry English, USDA APHIS PPQ

Severe cases with these three plants are rare unless you're highly allergic, in which case you should call your doctor on contact. Another poisonous plant, giant hogweed, is more dangerous. This non-native shrub looks inviting. It can grow up to 14 feet tall, has thick leaves that can be five feet wide, and has umbrella-shaped clusters of white flowers. As pleasant as it may appear, though, it's best to give this plant a wide berth. Touching the sap causes a severe reaction that can include blistering, permanent scarring, and even blindness. Breaking the stem or leaves, or even just brushing against the stem bristles, can be enough to trigger a response.

If you get exposed to giant hogweed, wash the area immediately with soap and water, and keep it dark for at least 48 hours. Exposure to light triggers the reaction to the sap.

WIDOWMAKERS

The final dangerous plants I'd like to mention don't have any poison. They aren't even alive. Yet they're deadlier than the four plants I've mentioned so far. In forestry, they've earned the dubious nickname "widowmakers."

Widowmakers are dead trees or limbs, especially those that have become detached from their roots or parent tree. They hang overhead, and in a breeze, they can come crashing down with lethal force.

It doesn't take much. Even a three-inch branch landing on your head is enough to kill you.

To defend against widowmakers, take three steps. First, look up. If you notice a hanging dead tree or limb, avoid it. Hike or camp someplace else. Second, be alert for trees with their bark falling off, a sign that the tree may be dead and decaying. Don't lean against these trees, as your weight alone may be enough to knock them over or break

Dead, broken, or suspended trees and limbs are known as widowmakers among foresters and loggers because they can fall in a breeze, or if you lean against a tree trunk. Keep alert for these on your woodlot and try not to walk under them.

limbs above you. Finally, keep the weather in mind. Widowmakers are more likely to fall during times of high wind. On breezy days, stay out of the woods.

WILDLIFE ATTACKS

Before I start this section, let me make something clear. You are extremely unlikely to be attacked by wildlife while spending time outdoors. The number of people killed by wildlife in the United States is exceptionally low. On average, only one person per year in the United States dies from a bear attack, and half a dozen die from venomous snakes. For comparison, domestic cows kill 20, and dogs kill 28.[4] Concern about bears, cougars, snakes, etc. is not a reason to stay out of the woods. You do far more dangerous things in your daily life (like drive) than going for a walk in the forest.

In most cases, wildlife attacks aren't caused by an animal. They usually occur when a human makes a poor choice. So in the interest of public safety, here are a few tips for avoiding unhealthy wildlife encounters:

- Keep your distance. Wild animals aren't pets. Don't try to touch them.
- Don't feed wild animals. In particular, don't hand-feed them. It teaches them that when they see humans, they will get food.
- Avoid surprising wild animals. It's one thing to walk quietly through the woods when you have plenty of visibility, but in dense brush, make plenty of noise when you walk.
- When camping, keep food out of your tent. Tie it between two trees at least 14 feet off the ground and four feet from the nearest tree trunk.
- With bears in particular, don't get between momma and cubs. Bears will typically leave you alone, but if you threaten their babies, momma bears will come to their defense. If you see a bear cub while hiking, leave the area.
- If a predator like a bear or cougar is sizing you up, make yourself look big and tough. Wave your arms and yell while backing away slowly. Whatever you do, don't turn and run. That can trigger a predator-prey response and cause the animal to chase you.

Ticks carry several diseases that can harm humans, the most well-known being Lyme disease. Photo credit: James Gathany, CDC

A MORE DANGEROUS ANIMAL

When I hike in my home woods in upstate New York, I'm not concerned about bears or any other large creature. No, the animal I worry about is much, much smaller: the deer tick.

Ticks are blood drinkers. They latch onto a host (that's you), drink your blood for a few days, and then drop off. They're tiny (and I do mean tiny; they can be as small as a poppy seed), and what makes them so dangerous are the illnesses they carry inside them. About ten of these illnesses impact people, and the most well-known of these is Lyme disease.

Lyme disease comes from a bacterium that lives inside the tick's gut. When the tick latches on to you, the bacterium travels up from the gut and into your body.

Fortunately, that travel takes a while. Even though ticks are small, the bacterium that causes Lyme is much smaller. A tick has to be attached to you for at least 36 hours for the Lyme bacterium to enter your body, according to the Centers for Disease Control and Prevention (CDC).[5]

Now you might think you'd have no trouble spotting a creepy-crawly on your body within 36 hours, but ticks are crafty. With their small size, they're easily missed, and they often hide in hard-to-check areas like your armpit or groin (are you itchy yet? I'm itchy writing this). There's also usually no pain associated with the tick bite itself, so you won't know the tick has latched onto you.

Lyme isn't fun. Early on, it triggers flulike symptoms: fatigue, chills, fever, and muscle and joint pain. Untreated, it can lead to loss of muscle control in the face, meningitis, arthritis, and severe pain. The disease can sit dormant inside the body for weeks, months, or even years, and then it can explode into full symptoms without warning.

About 30,000 cases of Lyme disease get reported in the United States every year. That number has tripled in the past twenty years. More distressing, only a small fraction of cases get reported. The CDC estimates that the actual incidence of Lyme in the United States is ten times higher than reported, or 300,000 cases annually. That means about one in every thousand Americans gets the disease every year.

Fortunately, Lyme disease doesn't occur all over the country. Ninety-five percent of reported US Lyme disease cases from just 14 states, all either in the Northeast or in the northern Lake States like Wisconsin and Minnesota.

How do you avoid Lyme disease while still getting out in nature? Here are some tips:

- Wear light-colored clothing, which will make ticks easier to spot.
- Wear boots, long pants, and a long-sleeved shirt. Tuck your pant legs into your socks, and tuck your shirt into your pants.
- Walk in the center of the trail and avoid dense, low brush. Ticks usually cling to tall grass and shrubs that grow no more than two feet off the ground.
- Avoid sitting or lying directly on the ground.
- If you have long hair, keep it tied back.
- Check yourself for ticks often while outdoors.
- Wash and dry clothes right away after wearing them outside. Run the dryer on high heat to kill ticks that may remain on clothing.
- When you get home, shower or bathe as soon as possible to locate and wash off ticks more easily.

- Do a full-body tick check, also at home. Get a family member to help check parts of your body that you may have a difficult time seeing.

If you find a tick on you, the best way to remove it is with a pair of pointed tweezers. Grasp the tick by the head and pull straight out from your body. Don't twist; that can cause the mouthparts to stay attached to you. Clean the bite area with warm water and soap as well as with a little rubbing alcohol. To dispose of the tick, either submerge it in alcohol or flush it down the toilet. Do not crush it with your fingers.

Even if you find a tick on you, remember that that doesn't mean you'll get Lyme. By checking for ticks and removing them promptly, you reduce your chance of getting Lyme to almost zero.

If you missed the tick but still got a bite, or if you aren't sure how long the tick was on you, you don't need to panic. Monitor the area of the tick bite for about a month. Look for a rash to develop, especially the characteristic "bulls-eye" rash with a distinct red ring around the bite area. If one appears, contact your doctor right away.

Should you develop Lyme symptoms, early treatment with antibiotics is usually highly effective. Even those who have had Lyme for a while often respond well to antibiotics.

There's no question that Lyme is a serious illness, and it's become more common over the past

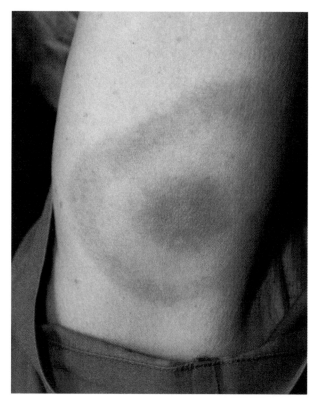

A bulls-eye rash around a tick bite is a symptom of Lyme disease. If you develop a rash like the one shown here, call your doctor. Photo credit: James Gathany, CDC

twenty years. Even so, you shouldn't let fear of ticks keep you from enjoying your woodland. With a few precautions, you can get out and enjoy the forest's health benefits without worry.

WATCH OUT!
TO DEET OR NOT TO DEET?

One way you can reduce your chances of getting ticks on you is with chemical insect repellent, the most common being N,N-diethyl-m-toluamide, better known as DEET. You'll find DEET in most commercial bug sprays, in varying concentrations.

DEET is a subject of debate among my fellow foresters. Some swear by it. Others refuse to go near the stuff.

The issue with DEET is that it can be harmful if not handled properly. It can react with damaged skin, for instance, so keep it off sunburns, rashes, and cuts. It irritates the eyes, causing pain. In extremely rare cases (about 1 in 100 million users), it has been linked to seizures.

Both the CDC and the Environmental Protection Agency consider DEET to present no risk to human health as long as it's used in accordance with product instructions. Both commend DEET's effectiveness in reducing the chances of tick bites and Lyme disease.[6] If you want to apply DEET, use it and don't worry about it.

There are a few precautions you should follow when using DEET:

- Any repellent with more than 50 percent DEET is unnecessary; you can get adequate protection from repellents with lower percentages.
- Don't let children apply DEET themselves. Put it on for them instead, and don't put it directly on their faces. You can spray a little on their hats to keep mosquitoes and other bugs out of their eyes.
- Wash any clothes you spray before wearing them again, and if you spray DEET on your skin, wash the area with soap and water as soon as possible after returning indoors.
- Most important, using DEET doesn't replace the other tick prevention tips I listed. Still perform a thorough tick check when you go inside.

CHAPTER 6

Wonderful Woodland Wildlife

The worst thing that will probably happen—in fact is already well underway— is not energy depletion, economic collapse, conventional war, or even the expansion of totalitarian governments. As terrible as these catastrophes would be for us, they can be repaired within a few generations. The one process now ongoing that will take millions of years to correct is the loss of genetic and species diversity by the destruction of natural habitats. This is the folly our descendants are least likely to forgive us.
—E. O. Wilson

In the last three chapters, I focused on ways you can benefit from interacting with your woods. Now I'd like to spend some time talking about how your woods can benefit from interactions with you.

The typical US woodlot supports dozens of animal species, and that's only counting the ones with backbones. Just by owning woodland and keeping it wooded, you are benefiting the natural world.

OPPOSITE: *Private woodlands can support a host of wildlife great and small, among them the beautiful bobcat.* Photo credit: Gary Kramer, USFWS

But not all woods are equal in the eyes of wildlife. The kinds of animals you'll spot on your property are determined by how well your land meets those animals' needs.

Generally speaking, animals need four things to live: food, water, oxygen, and shelter. A place that provides these needs is called a "habitat." If you want more wildlife in your woods, provide more habitat.

It's not that simple, though, because each wild species meets its basic life needs differently. As a result, the habitat that works for one animal may

The yellow warbler (left) and black-throated green warbler (right) share many similarities, yet they need very different habitats to survive. Photo credits: Donna Dewhurst, USFWS (yellow warbler) and S. Maslowski, USFWS (black-throated green warbler)

not satisfy another. Whatever you do—or don't do—on your woodlot, you'll have wildlife winners and losers.

To explain what I mean, let's take a look at two seemingly similar birds. The black-throated green warbler and the yellow warbler are both small songbirds that eat insects. They have overlapping ranges, both spending summers in the northern United States and southern Canada before migrating to Central and South America for the winter.

Yet despite their similarities, you'll almost never find these two birds close together in the woods. Why not? It comes down to where they like to live. The black-throated green warbler likes large, unbroken blocks of forest at least 250 acres in size. It will avoid breaks in the woods, staying at least 650 feet from roads or other openings. In particular, it favors thick, older forests, so it's commonly found among spruce and hemlock, which grow in tight groves. The yellow warbler is the opposite. It avoids old forests in favor of short, dense thickets, especially those near water and around field edges.

Unless you have a huge amount of acreage, it's unlikely your property will support both these birds. If you change something to help one of them, you'll harm the other at the same time.

So what should you do? Remember Rule #3 for doing right by your land: provide diversity. You can't have every species, but you can attract more species by giving your land more variety.

TRY THIS:
MAKE A FOOD PLOT

All creatures great and small need food to survive. Planting a food plot is one way to help them get it.

Food plots are quarter- to half-acre sections of the woods where you plant a mix of ground plants that supply extra nutrition for wildlife. The concept originated with hunters, and to this day a lot of food plot advice is geared toward providing bucks with food so they get bigger. But even if you don't hunt, food plots can help out the critters on your land.

The best places for food plots are those that get at least 50 percent sun. Old farm fields, powerline corridors, and past insect infestation or ice storm sites are all options. Once you've chosen your food plot location, take some soil samples and have them analyzed by your local Soil and Water Conservation District. Since you're planting a crop, you need to find out whether your soil is enough on its own to sustain what you plant. A soil test can help you identify what additions, like fertilizer or lime, you should make to help your food plot succeed.

As far as what to plant, a local extension office or hunting club might help you figure out what will work best in your area. Common food plot plants include clover, rape, cereal rye, and wheat. Some garden centers carry seed mixes designed for food plots.

Now that you have your seeds, you'll need to till your food plot's soil. A rototiller or cultivator pulled behind a 4-wheeler will make this job a lot easier, so try to locate your food plot close to a trail to provide vehicle access.

Seeding your food plot isn't like planting a garden. When you're ready to plant, get a hand-spreader and use that to distribute the seeds. Follow the directions on the seed package, and take care not to overplant.

After planting, there isn't much you need to do to keep your food plot going. If you really want to look after it, you can water it and add fertilizer to speed plant growth. You can also weed it to remove plants that compete with your wildlife food source. Finally, you can clear brush or trees that grow over the food plot to make sure it has enough sunlight.

You don't need a lot of food plots to make a difference for wildlife. Even a quarter-acre plot adds a lot of grazing food for plant-eaters.

Before we leave food plots, a point of clarification: food plots are not the same as baiting deer or other animals, say with a bucket of corn. Do not bait wildlife this way. In many places baiting is illegal because it leads to unnaturally high animal densities and can cause disease outbreak, particularly with deer. A food plot may be more work than a bucket of corn, but it's a better, healthier option for all involved.

Young woodlands like this eight-year-old pine stand in California may lack the majesty of older forests, but they're essential to many plants and animals. Photo credit: National Park Service

The Woodlot Time Machine

When it comes to boosting your land's variety, you're generally looking to do one of two things. The first is raising the number of plant species in your woods, and the second is increasing the age range of those plants. I'll talk about tree planting in a later chapter, so for now I won't focus on changing which plants you have. I'll focus instead on the second change: affecting the age of what's already on your land.

I understand if you're skeptical. A plant's age is its age, right? A person can't speed up or reverse time.

It turns out, though, that you can control time in your woods, at least to an extent. With that ability, you have the power to influence which and how many wildlife species are likely to visit your property.

REVERSING TIME: CREATING A YOUNG WOODLAND

We all know about old-growth forests, how important they are, and how rare they've become (more on them in a bit). But another kind of forest is disappearing too, and the species that live in this kind of forest are now some of the most at-risk animals in the United States.

Young forests, those dominated by shrubs and saplings, are currently at historic lows. This is particularly true of states east of the Mississippi River, but some western forest ecologists have called out the problem there too.[1]

Part of the issue stems from aesthetics. Younger woods aren't as pretty as older ones. They're dense, thick stands of small trees that are difficult to walk or even see through.

The other problem has to do with time. Young woods don't stay young. After about twenty years, they lose many of the traits that make them unique. The dense trees start to thin, less sunlight reaches the ground, and the woods go from being warm and dry to being cool and moist. If the young woods aren't maintained, or if new young woods aren't created, the habitat disappears.

But why would animals prefer young trees over old ones? Young woods offer wildlife two advantages. First, the warmer, drier conditions support more insects and other invertebrates that in turn provide food for bigger animals. A study in New Hampshire found that young woods had 1.5 times the variety and 3 times the abundance of inverte-

Found only in Florida, the threatened Florida scrub jay can only survive in young, dense, low vegetation that can shelter it from predators, such as hawks. Scrub jay survival plummets when the nearest tall tree is within 800 yards. Photo credit: Robert Owens, USFWS

brates as older ones.[2] More invertebrates means more food, and more food means more wildlife can visit and use that area.

Second, these wooded areas provide superb cover for smaller species. We might have trouble getting through all those shrubs and packed trees, but so do a lot of predators. That's why many songbirds prefer to nest in dense, young woods.

With these advantages, young forests can actually support more species than older ones. Audubon New York looked at more than 70 bird species in the state, examining their abundance in four different types of woods. Overall, they found both a higher

WATCH OUT!
INVASIVES INVADE

Patch cuts work by allowing a lot of sunlight to reach ground level and encourage new growth. Unfortunately, that sunlight also encourages invasive plants. If you do a patch cut and you have invasive plants like multiflora rose in or around the cut area, it's easy for those invasives to take over the opening and not allow the native plants preferred by wildlife to grow.

Before doing a patch cut on your land, get a forester to examine the area for invasive plants. Then do what you can to remove those plants from the patch area to give the native trees and shrubs a fighting chance.

quantity and a greater variety of birds in young forests than in woods that lacked that habitat. They also found that birds that needed young forests were the species most in decline in the state.[3]

These young forests are even valuable to birds that otherwise stick to older woods. In a four-year study, wildlife biologist Scott Stoleson found that, after nesting, many mature forest birds seek out young forests for food. Without access to younger forests, these birds were in poorer health when they began their southern migrations.[4]

All of this is more background than I've typically used in this book, but I'm supplying it for a reason. I'm sure many of you reading this are leery of intentionally replacing older forests with younger ones. Creating young forest on your land means sac-

rificing some areas for hiking and most other forms of recreation. But the payoff is that you attract a whole new set of animals to your woods.

Fortunately, you don't need a lot of young forest on your land to support the species that need it. A ratio of 15–20 percent young forest to 80–85 percent older forest is plenty.

Young forest areas also don't need to be huge. Don't clear-cut vast acreages in the name of wildlife habitat; it isn't necessary. Techniques like lawn feathering (see "Nature's Beauty") can incorporate young forest into your land without cutting trees.

Another way to create young forest is to mimic the conditions that naturally cause them: disturbances like tornadoes and fires. You do this through a special logging approach called patch cutting.

These are smaller cuts, usually less than 20 acres. Inside the patch you cut every tree, as though a storm had knocked them all down. The idea is to let lots of light into the patch so young trees and shrubs pop up and grow rapidly.

Depending on how much land you own, you can have one big patch of young woods or a few smaller ones. Once you have your patches, you can maintain them by brush hogging them about every ten years. Remember to wait until after August 1st so you don't disturb ground-nesting birds. For a more natural approach, you can also let your young patches grow older and then do a new patch cut somewhere else to replace them.

LEAPING FORWARD: SIMULATING OLD-GROWTH

While many species need young forests, others, like the black-throated green warbler, need older, unbroken ones. To protect wildlife, we need to think about these species too.

Turning back your woodland's clock is easy, since you're just mimicking a natural event. Going forward is trickier. There is no forestry technique for creating old-growth forests. Only time—a lot of time—can do that.

But while you can't create old-growth forest, there are ways to simulate old-growth's characteristics on your land. And as strange as it might sound, these methods involve cutting trees.

Before we get into how that can make any sense whatsoever, let's pause and answer these questions: what are the traits of an old-growth forest? We know wildlife like old-growth forests, but why? What is it about that these ancient woods that so many species love?

The answer is a word I've used a lot: diversity. Compared with other woodlands, old-growth forests have remarkable variety, and that variety allows lots of animals with different needs to find spots that work for them.

Old-growth forests' diversity takes several forms. First, old-growth forests have big trees. Old-growth trees have lived for centuries, and during that time they've achieved mammoth height and girth.

Not all the trees in an old-growth forest are huge, though. The second trait that makes old-growth forests so diverse is that they have trees of every size, from seedlings just starting out to shrubs a few feet off the ground to the ancient behemoths I just mentioned.

One of my forestry professors referred to old-growth forests as "green walls." No matter where you look, from ground to canopy, you see growing plants.

This height variation is crucial, because some animals like to hang out in treetops, while others live closer to the ground. If you're missing greenery in the middle, you'll also miss out on the animals that depend on it.

Living plants aren't the only things that give old-growth forests variety. Because they've been around a long time, some trees will have succumbed to disease, insects, or the effects of being shaded out by faster-growing trees. As a result, there's a lot of dead wood, both standing as deceased trees (called snags) or fallen as logs. These decaying trees provide homes for lots of animals, who take advantage of the softer wood to carve out nests and hunt for insects.

Finally, where trees have died, there will be openings in the forest that allow sunlight to reach the ground. These gaps provide places where plant species that need more sunlight can grow.

To summarize, old-growth forests have four traits that make them wonderful, diverse wildlife homes:

1. Some really big trees.

2. Greenery at every level.

3. Lots of dead, decaying trees, either standing or fallen.

4. Occasional gaps that allow more sunlight for young growth.

Knowing these traits, you can mimic old-growth conditions on your land. By using the following techniques, you will effectively speed up time and put your woods closer to old-growth status.

The most important part of making your

woods more like old-growth is finding the biggest, tallest, healthiest trees. Let's call these your legacy trees, because they'll never be removed from your woods. They will serve as your mammoth "old-growth" trees.

To get your legacy trees growing bigger and faster, cut the smaller trees around them, the ones whose branches touch the legacy trees' branches. This cutting will give your legacy trees room to expand their canopies, absorb more sunlight, and reach old-growth size sooner.

The trees you cut to free up your legacy trees likely won't go to a sawmill. Most of these smaller trees will have little lumber value. That's OK. Leave the wood on the ground, and it will become the fallen log habitat so valuable in old-growth environments.

Getting greenery at every level is more difficult than freeing legacy trees, but it's still doable. The best approach is to follow the patch cut recommendations for creating young forest, but on a smaller scale. In creating young forest, you simulated a big event like a tornado. Now you're replicating what happens when one of your legacy trees dies of old age, falls, and smashes a bunch of other trees on its way down. So instead of multi-acre patches, you might only clear an acre or even less. These smaller gaps will let in light and get some new growth started, but they won't disrupt the older overall nature of the woods.

Mimicking old-growth on your property is

TRY THIS:
BUILD A BRUSH PILE

Whether you're patch cutting for young forest or creating space for big trees to simulate old-growth, you're going to wind up with wood on the ground. While some of it might be sellable, other parts of it, especially the treetops, won't have much economic value. In addition to letting that wood decay on the ground to create a wildlife habitat, you can go a step further and turn it into an even better animal home: a brush pile.

A brush pile is pretty much what it sounds like: a pile of twigs, sticks, and logs of various sizes. The idea is to build something sturdy that also has enough space for animals to move through it. A good brush pile has lots of hiding spaces and interlocking branches that creatures can use for shelters. Done well, brush piles make excellent homes for a variety of woodland creatures such as butterflies, chipmunks, foxes, lizards, quail, rabbits, salamanders, skunks, snakes, songbirds, squirrels, toads, and woodpeckers.

To make a brush pile, start out with some larger logs to form the base. These logs should be about 6 to 10 feet long and 4 to 6 inches thick. These thicker logs will keep the brush pile off the ground and create space for animals to build dens and tunnels.

Position the logs so they make a lattice structure. Do this by putting four logs on the ground parallel to each other, then put four more logs on top of them going in the opposite direction. When viewed from above, the end result should look like a big wooden tic-tac-toe board.

Now that you have your base, it's time for the brush. Work from big to small branches, adding in the occasional large limb or log to keep the pile stable. You don't need to work at right angles. It's better if the branches point in lots of different directions, so they hold each other while leaving air space.

When the pile's done, it should be about 6 feet high, 6 feet wide, and igloo-shaped. It should last 10 to 15 years, though you may need to add new brush every 5 years to make up for whatever decays.

When your brush pile ultimately breaks down, you can build a new one next to it. Leave the old one in place rather than dismantling it. Odds are a few critters still make it their home!

tough. It requires a thorough understanding of which trees to leave, which ones to cut, and what to do with the wood after the trees are on the ground. If you want to simulate old-growth on your woodland, I recommend not going it alone. Instead, work with a professional forester to draft a plan for when, where, and how you'll create gaps. Then use the tips in the coming chapters on water quality and timber harvesting to ensure you get a good result.

Deciding What to Do

With a few chainsaw cuts, you have the power to affect what kinds of wildlife, and how many of each, visit your property. You can reset the forest clock, or you can speed up time to bring your woods closer to old-growth status.

That's a lot of responsibility. How do you know what's right for your woods?

We can answer that in a couple ways. First, there's the human approach. What kinds of wildlife do you want to see? Are there certain species you really enjoy? If so, creating more of the habitat they prefer can help make sure you see more of them. I worked with one landowner who absolutely loved American woodcock. She adored their nasally *peent* calls and the aerial acrobatics that make up their courtship ritual. American woodcock need younger forest, so we picked out some spots where she could open up her woods and get new growth going. Doing

that won't guarantee that more woodcocks will use her land, but she's far more likely to see them with their desired habitat present.

If you don't have a specific wildlife preference, another way to decide what to do is to look at your property in the context of the land around it. Is there some habitat missing from the broader landscape around your property? You might attract more wildlife by providing it.

Back in "Get Out and Play!," I talked about how you can use aerial photographs to pick out different types of woodlands. Colors and canopy shapes reveal if a woodland has old trees or young ones, conifers or broad-leafs.

You can use this same knowledge to figure out what habitat you may want to create. On an online mapping site like Bing or Google Maps, find your woodland. Then look beyond it to see the lands your neighbors and their neighbors own. What do you see a lot of? If you see all older broad-leaf trees, planting some young conifers would add diversity to the landscape. On the other hand, if you see a lot of open, abandoned farm fields, you might focus on making your woods simulate old-growth.

Caring for your woods is an activity in which it's OK to be different from everyone else. In fact, being different is a great way to bring more wildlife to your property. If your woods are like all your neighbors' woods, animals have no more incentive to come to your land than theirs. But if wildlife know your prop-

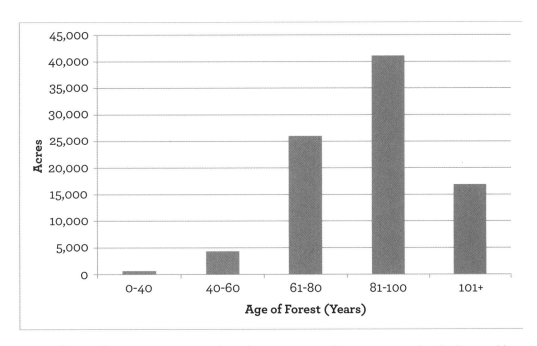

New York City's forests are concentrated in a forty-year range, from sixty to one-hundred years old. The city has almost no young forest, and the amount of old forest is well below what used to exist in upstate New York. As a result, the forest has little diversity and provides less wildlife habitat.[5]

erty is the only spot with a dense hemlock stand that makes a perfect winter bedding area, they'll come from far and wide to take advantage of it.

Should We Bother?

Beyond the question of how to shape your woods' habitat, perhaps a more important question is,

should you do anything? Is it right to manipulate the woods to alter the kinds of habitat it provides? Shouldn't we let nature handle that?

These are ethics questions, and like a lot of ethics questions, I'm sure different people would give different answers. There isn't a "scientific" response here. What I'd like to do to close out this chapter, then, is explain why I think it's OK for you to make the kinds of changes I've described.

I work in upstate New York in the region where New York City draws its water supply. In 2011, the city completed its first-ever plan for the almost 90,000 acres of forests it owns to protect that water supply. As part of that plan, the city estimated those forests' ages.

Predictably, there was little old forest. Less than 20 percent of the city's forests were more than one-hundred years old.

More surprising was the near total absence of young forest. Only 6 percent of the city's forests were less than sixty years old, and just one percent were younger than forty.

New York's forests simply don't provide what a lot of species need. They have neither old nor young forests. They've broken Rule #3: they haven't provided diversity.

A lot of US woods have the same problem as New York's woods. We have a lot of "middle-aged" woodlands, but we have few young or old ones. That lack of variety hurts wildlife.

But can't we rely on nature to provide those habitats? Not necessarily. Young forests happen naturally as a result of events like fires and floods, but especially east of the Mississippi River, we've suppressed fire well below what historically occurred. We've also built dams and other structures to control water and reduce flooding. Without these disturbances, nature can't create the young forest that so many species need.

On the opposite end of the time scale, allowing enough time would permit more woods to become old-growth. Unfortunately, we don't have centuries to wait for that to happen. The species that need older forests are declining right now. If we don't act, those species may not be around by the time nature makes more of the forest old-growth.

As a landowner, you have the power to help nature along and bring more variety to America's woods. While it's a power to use responsibly, it's not a power to fear. With careful planning and help from a professional forester or wildlife biologist, you can use your land to help protect our most vulnerable forest neighbors.

CHAPTER 7

The World's Biggest Water Filter

The Nation that destroys its soils destroys itself.
—Franklin D. Roosevelt

In the last chapter I mentioned that I work in New York City's water supply region, so I thought I should explain where that is. The New York City Watershed is about 2,000 square miles in rural upstate New York. At one point, it's more than a hundred miles from the city it supplies. Massive pipes, 15 feet across, transport a billion gallons a day of fresh, clean drinking water from reservoirs in the Catskill Mountains to more than 9 million people in and around the United State's largest city. And the whole system works entirely on gravity.

New York doesn't rely on manmade filtration systems to keep its water clean. Instead, it uses the natural water-cleaning power of the 1,500 square miles of forests that dominate the Watershed's land base. Thanks to those forests, the city saves $8 billion in water treatment construction costs and more than $300 million annually in maintenance.[1]

How can forests clean the water for a big city like New York? It all comes down to those amazing trees. Trees are natural filters. They protect the ground around them from erosion, the wearing or washing away of soil by wind or water. They provide this protection in three ways. First, their leaves block rain, reducing the speed with which it hits the ground. Once water reaches the forest floor, the thick layer of decaying plant matter built up from fallen leaves and wood traps it; the water then seeps into the ground rather than rushing away and eroding soil. Finally, roots anchor the soil, further helping to hold it in place.

New York isn't the only city that relies on forests to clean its water. Nationally, 53 percent of our water supply comes from forested lands, and that's a good thing.[2] Water supplies with more forest cover have less runoff, better groundwater recharge, and fewer pollutants than those with other land uses like farming or development.[3]

That improved water quality translates into big savings for water suppliers and customers. The Trust for Public Land has calculated that for every 10 percent of forest cover lost, water treatment costs jump by 20 percent.[4] In a city like New York, that's an average of almost $200 per family each year.

As a woodland owner, the actions you take affect the streams and rivers on and near your property. You have in your hands the power to impact, for better or worse, the drinking water quality for all those downstream of you.

Fortunately, there are ways you can protect water supplies from damage during activities like logging. Even better, there are ways you can improve the water coming off your land.

And at the same time that you're helping others, you'll also help yourself. Many of the practices that protect water quality will also make your property easier to access for recreation and make your woods more attractive to wildlife.

The Big Issue for Forests and Water: Soil Erosion

If you're like most landowners, you probably don't apply fertilizers or chemicals to your woods, or if you do (say for a food plot), you're doing so in tiny amounts. When it comes to woodlands, then, we typically don't worry about human pollutants harming the water. Instead, the biggest water quality issue for forests is soil loss due to erosion.

Erosion is a natural process, and it's been happening since the Earth began. You don't need to stop erosion on your land, but you should avoid making it worse than it would be naturally.

Erosion lowers water quality in two ways. First, by washing away soil, it pushes sediment (a fancy term for soil particles) into the stream and ultimately into drinking water supplies. There, the sediment clouds the water, incurring treatment costs downstream to remove it. Sediment also harms wildlife by smothering the habitat for stream invertebrates that fish depend on for food.

Besides adding sediment, erosion harms water by introducing more nutrients, especially nitrogen and phosphorus. We typically think of nutrients as good things, but in streams, lakes, and other water supplies, they can be a big problem. They lead to algae blooms, which can cause massive death of aquatic life, especially fish.

According to the US Geological Survey, damage from sediment pollution costs $16 billion every year.[5] While much of that damage comes from urban and agricultural runoff, poor forestry practices also contribute. Even if your land isn't part of a public drinking water supply like the New York City Watershed, the plants and animals that live on and downstream from your property depend on you to keep the water they need clean.

Trail destruction from erosion is, sadly enough, something I've seen too often here in the mountainous Catskills, where steep slopes and flashy rains wreak havoc on unprotected trails. Once a trail has eroded as much as this one has, there's little you can do to fix it, and it becomes all but unusable for most recreation. It's better to prevent this kind of damage by using simple techniques called Best Management Practices.

What You Can Do about Erosion, Part 1: Best Management Practices

The biggest human-caused erosion from woodlands takes place because of logging. When we talk about limiting erosion in forests, we're talking about how to make logging gentler on the land.

It isn't the cutting of trees itself, though, that leads to erosion from logging. Rather, the big problem spots are the roads and trails loggers use to access those trees. The US Environmental Protection Agency reports that up to 90 percent of sediment pollution from forestry comes from these road networks.[6]

For a landowner, this is great news. It means that if you harvest timber, controlling erosion on your roads and trails can eliminate the vast majority of the cut's water pollution potential.

This focus on roads and trails can have other benefits for you, as well. When erosion washes away your trails, it can make them unusable for recreation. Formerly nice walking trails break down into rutted mud pits, or worse, they cut deep into the ground, hit bedrock, and turn into gullies. Even if you never intend to cut trees, taking steps to protect your trails from erosion can keep them in better shape for hiking, biking, and any other outdoor activities you like to do. And it is best to protect your trails upfront rather than let them erode. Once a trail has washed away, it's expensive to fix—if it can be fixed.

But how do you keep your trails from washing

away, whether they're used for logging or not? In the forestry world, we rely on erosion-controlling techniques called "Best Management Practices," or BMPs.

TRAIL BMPS

BMPs are simple, low-cost approaches to trail design that reduce the chance that a trail will wash away. In general, BMPs are intended to do two things. First, they get water off easily eroded roads and trails and back into undisturbed ground cover that's less likely to wash away. Second, they steer water away in small amounts before it can build up enough strength to erode soil.

Every state has its own BMP guidelines unique to its woodlands and terrain. Most guidelines are developed around protecting trails during and after logging, but the same approaches work for recreational trails too.

A great example of BMPs is the waterbar, an earthen berm installed periodically across a trail using a small bulldozer or excavator. Waterbars divert water off the trail before it can flow to the point of causing erosion. Loggers will typically put in waterbars after logging finishes. They provide a cheap, fast, and effective way to keep trails stable.

The steeper a trail is, the more waterbars it should have. Steeper trails are more subject to erosion, because water can pick up more speed and energy on them. If you can, locate your trails on gentler slopes. If you already have an existing steep trail network, be prepared with more waterbars to protect them.

STREAM CROSSINGS

While it's important to think about erosion on all your trails, the most critical places to pay attention to are your stream crossings. Erosion far up on a hill might never make it to a stream, but at the points where roads meet streams, the potential for pollution is high, especially during timber harvesting. Make sure to plan out any and all logging stream crossings with your forester.

Stream crossings also require that you know your local and state laws. In many states you'll need a permit to cross a stream with heavy equipment. Do your homework, and make sure your forester or logger has all the needed permits before the harvest starts.

During timber harvesting, loggers typically use one of three methods to cross streams: temporary bridges, fords, and culverts. Of the three, temporary bridges are the best option. They're easily transported and easy to install, and most importantly, they leave the stream bed largely untouched (equipment may need to cross the stream once as part of the installation process). They come in a variety of sizes, from small arch culverts to 50-foot behemoths that will support fully loaded log trucks. You won't need to buy these bridges yourself; loggers or sawmills usually have their own or have access to them.

While temporary bridges work well for logging, they're less useful for a permanent crossing. If you

OPPOSITE: *Waterbars—berms of soil spaced periodically along trails—divert water in small amounts so it doesn't wash away soil.*

Cheap, easy, and effective, portable bridges (top left) and arch culverts (top right) make excellent temporary stream crossing structures for timber harvests. Fords (bottom left) can work if the stream has gentle banks and a firm bed. Culverts (bottom right) are not recommended, as they're prone to washing away without proper sizing and regular maintenance. Photo credits: Heather Hilson, Watershed Agricultural Council

want or need long-term access across a stream on your land, a bridge can be an expensive choice. Unlike temporary bridges, permanent bridges require extensive planning and engineering, which raises their cost.

Because of this expense, many landowners opt for culverts if they want a long-term crossing. A logger places the culvert in the stream and then builds up the crossing with rocks and soil to allow vehicles to drive over the water.

WATCH OUT!
WATERBARS AND RECREATION

Where BMPs like waterbars are voluntary, some landowners don't install them because they fear they'll lose access to their property. Waterbars in particular are a common concern, since right after installation they may be two feet or more above the level of the trail. That's a lot of dirt to climb over while hiking, biking, or riding an ATV.

But recreational use and BMPs don't have to be mutually exclusive. There are alternate approaches that allow you to divert water from your trails without having huge mounds of earth to crawl over. Also, keep in mind that if you do nothing, your trails could erode and become hard to use anyway.

Your first, best option is simply patience. Waterbars are big when first put in, but the soil in them settles over time. You should stay off waterbars for at least three months after they're installed to give them this settling time. Once that time passes, they won't be as tall, and they'll be firmer and easier to cross even with an ATV.

If berms are absolutely unacceptable to you, other techniques do exist, though they're more expensive. One moderate-cost option is for loggers to cut two small logs and place them in a groove that goes across the trail. The logs should be separated by a few inches to form an open channel. These channels let water flow off the trail, but they're narrow enough that vehicle tires can drive over them.

On the more expensive end, well casings with holes cut in the top or rubber belts sandwiched between wooden boards can be installed into the road or trail. Although these options cost more money, they allow easy, frequent vehicle access while protecting the road surface.

When deciding which BMPs to install, think about the kinds of traffic your roads and trails receive and how often they experience that traffic. Then discuss options with your forester and choose the one that will work best while accommodating your budget. And remember, laws in your state may require you to meet a certain minimum level of protection, regardless of your recreational desires.

Although culverts provide a permanent crossing, I don't recommend them. Since I work at a water quality organization, my coworkers and I look at a lot of stream crossings every year. From that experience, we've learned that as appealing as culverts are, they also come with a lot of headaches. The biggest one is that the culverts loggers and landowners install are almost always too small. They size their culvert based on the current water level, but that's not good enough. A permanent crossing has to withstand more than average streamflow. It needs to handle the maximum amount of water a stream experiences: a flood. Meeting that need demands a much bigger culvert. Otherwise, the culvert will plug up with debris during floods. Water then dams up, and the crossing—culvert and all—washes away.

If you must have a culvert, be sure to choose one big enough to handle a major flood. Your state's BMP guidelines probably recommend culvert sizes based on how large a stream is.

When it's first installed, an appropriately sized culvert will look ridiculously large. That's all right. In the long term, it will look a lot better than a smaller one that a flood has crushed and beached half a mile downstream.

Aside from sizing, the other reason I don't recommend culverts is the amount of maintenance they require. You should check them after any major rain event for debris and then remove that material from the culvert. Without this regular cleaning, even a large culvert can become clogged over time.

In rare cases, your logger may not need a bridge or culvert to cross a stream. Where streams have low banks and a firm rock bed, equipment may be able to ford the stream without damaging it. These fords are the exception, not the rule, though, and often even in these cases a bridge will still help protect your stream and its banks.

You may not always have a choice of which stream crossing structure you use or which BMPs wind up on your trails. Many states require BMPs during timber harvests, and loggers must install them to meet specifications. Other states have voluntary BMPs, while still more have a mix of required and optional practices. I've provided a link in "Beyond the Book" to an interactive map that lets you pick a state, find out whether BMPs are required there, and then access that state's BMP guidelines. When harvesting timber, check your state's guidelines and with your forester to confirm which measures you should adopt and which you need to follow by law.

OPPOSITE: *If your trails see frequent traffic, you have erosion-control options beyond waterbars. Open-topped culverts made with onsite logs (top) or recycled well casings (bottom-left) are more expensive but allow for vehicle traffic. Alternately, an old rubber machinery belt (bottom-right) will deflect water but bend when a tire drives over it.* Photo credits: Brendan Murphy (top) and Heather Hilson (bottom), Watershed Agricultural Council

What You Can Do about Erosion, Part 2: Plant Trees along Streams

BMPs protect trails and water quality from damage, but it's possible to go farther than that and make the water coming off your land even cleaner. Remember how trees are natural water filters? That power increases when they're close to streams. Trees near the water help remove excess nutrients, and their roots help keep stream banks in place during floods. They also provide shade, which keeps the water temperature cooler and more suitable for fish.

If you already have woods along your streams, all you really need to do is protect those areas. During timber harvests, keep equipment and logging roads away from streams except at crossings. A 100-foot buffer is a good minimum, though if your land is steep you may need a wider one. Check your state BMPs for specifics, and be aware that some states mandate minimum buffer widths.

If you don't have trees near your streams, planting some is a great way to protect water quality, improve fish and wildlife habitat, and make stream hikes more pleasant. It's also a good family activity, because tree planting goes much faster with a group.

You won't be able to plant just any tree near a stream. Especially within the first fifteen feet from the water, the ground may be wet and poorly drained. Not every tree species can handle those conditions. Which trees will work for your land will vary based on climate, but a few stalwarts are silver maple, sycamore, and willow. In northern woodlands, tamarack, white cedar, and red or black spruce are also options. Wherever your woods are, consider planting a mix of species to make your streamsides more natural and diverse.

Whichever trees you pick, get them from a local source, ideally one within 100 miles of your woodland. Even in the same species, trees that grow well in Kentucky may not survive in Wisconsin weather, and vice versa. Many states have official nurseries, so look into them before you buy your trees. It can also help to contact your county's Soil and Water Conservation District or your local extension office for advice, species suggestions, and nursery contacts.

Nursery trees come in a variety of ages, from seeds to multi-year-old saplings. In general, older trees require less maintenance, but they're more expensive. You'll need to weigh the amount of maintenance you're willing to do against the number of trees you want to plant and your budget.

We run a tree-planting program here in the New York City Watershed, and for our projects we use three-year-old nursery trees. We've found the three-year-olds offer a good balance of solid survival rates and low costs.

In addition to coming in different ages, nursery trees also come in a couple different packages. Some have their roots wrapped in soil and are inserted into a container, either a plastic pot or burlap wrapping. You'll also find "bare-root" seedlings, which have their roots exposed without soil around them. Bare-root seedlings are cheaper, but they must get in the ground quickly. If not, the roots will dry out and kill the tree.

For our tree planting, we favor trees in plastic pots. They're more resilient than bare-root seedlings, and they're lighter and easier to move than the bulky burlap-wrapped trees.

Once you have your trees, it's time to plant. Because potted trees are what I have the most experience with, I'll describe the process for planting them. The technique is similar if you use burlap, but not if you're planting bare-root seedlings. If you want to plant those, I've included a link in "Beyond the Book" to instructions from the Arbor Day Foundation.

In most parts of the country, it's best to plant trees either in the fall or early spring. These planting times give the tree roots a chance to grow into the soil before it freezes in winter or dries in the summer heat.

To plant your trees, you'll need a hole as deep as the pot the tree came in and 2–3 times as wide. Remove the tree from the container by grasping near the base of the trunk and pulling. If the tree doesn't come out easily, you can use a utility knife to cut the pot on two sides and peel it away.

Be careful not to cut into the root ball. Some people believe cutting into the roots loosens them, but actually it just injures the tree. If your roots are

tightly bound from being inside the pot, a better method is to break up the soil with your hands. This will give the roots freedom to grow without your having to cut or break them. You don't need to shake the soil off the roots after loosening them. Leaving the soil on will give the tree extra nutrients and make planting easier.

Next, put your tree in the hole. Check the hole's depth; the top of the root ball should be about an inch above the ground. The tree should sit in the hole so that the trunk stands up straight. If it leans, shift the tree to correct the problem.

With your tree in place, you can fill in the hole with soil. As you do, tamp down on the soil with your foot to push out air pockets and get good root-to-soil contact.

Congratulations! You just planted a tree. Stand back and admire your handiwork.

If you're planting multiple trees, space them about ten to twelve feet apart. You aren't creating a plantation, so there's no need to plant in defined rows. Scattering the seedlings will create a more natural look as the trees grow.

If a good, soaking rain isn't in the forecast for the next 24 hours, give your trees a thorough watering. The soil should be moist but not soggy when you're done.

In most cases, you don't need to fertilize your trees. Soils along streams tend to have plenty of nutrients, and it's easy to over-fertilize and kill your trees.

What a difference five years makes! My coworker, forester Brendan Murphy, planted trees at a farm in upstate New York in 2010 (left photo). By 2015 (right photo), many of the trees were out of their tree tubes, and the tallest ones were more than 20 feet high. Note the bark protector around the base of the front tree in the 2015 photo, which protects it from deer rubbing their antlers against it. Photo credits: Brendan Murphy, Watershed Agricultural Council

More important for protecting your baby trees than fertilizing is making sure hungry animals don't eat them. For our planting program, we guard our seedlings with 60-inch plastic tree tubes secured with wooden stakes. These keep animals—especially deer—off your trees until they grow above a point where critters can reach.

Depending on how much open space you have near your stream, you could wind up planting dozens or hundreds of trees if you want to fill in the area. You can spread planting out over multiple seasons, so only plant as many trees as you feel comfortable planting. Also, even a few trees are better for water quality than none, so if you can only plant five or ten, it's still worth going for it.

It's a huge achievement to plant a tree, but if you want your seedlings to survive, getting them in the ground is just the beginning. Check back on your trees at least once a year to make sure they're doing well. Take off the tree tubes and clear out any debris that's accumulated inside them. Mice sometimes make nests in the tubes, so remove those nests if you see them.

Once your trees grow taller than the tree tubes, remove the tubes so they don't prevent the trees from growing wider. In areas with heavy deer pressure, you can leave tubes on a little longer to protect the trees from having their bark stripped by bucks rubbing their antlers on them. Alternately, you can replace the tree tubes with plastic mesh bark protectors, which require less maintenance than tubes do.

Planting trees is one of my favorite projects to encourage landowners to do. Not only does it benefit your land and water, but you'll see results immediately. Better still, you can watch your work grow with time. You may not see the change on a day-to-day basis, but it's amazing how quickly a tree can grow if you give it a good start.

CHAPTER 8

Changing Climate, Changing Woodland

Although people's worries about global climate change most often focus on things like summer heat, drought, flooding, rising sea levels, and polar bears, there's another big worry that isn't so well publicized—the effects of all these changes on plants, particularly trees. People and animals can walk, run, swim, or fly to a more suitable habitat, but trees can't escape the heat.
—Dennis May

Why talk about climate change in a book about woodlands? Because woodlands and climate are intertwined. Trees gradually become accustomed to certain ranges of temperature and moisture. Mess with those ranges, and trees that used to grow well in one spot may not do well there anymore.

OPPOSITE: *One sign of a changing climate in the woods: by 2100, scientists predict that fall colors will occur on average 2 weeks later than they do now because of longer, hotter summers.*

Whatever you may think of the causes of climate change, most people generally accept that the climate is indeed changing in ways both large and small. As a landowner, it's worth being aware of this challenge and preparing for it.

In addition, woodlands are important for reducing climate change in whatever form it takes. Trees take in the greenhouse gas carbon dioxide and convert it to oxygen through the amazing process of photosynthesis. As they do, they store the carbon in two other amazing things: wood and soil.

As an owner of trees, you can help protect the planet from climate change. You may not reverse the warming trend by yourself, but small steps added together can make a major positive contribution.

Preparing for Climate Change: What Will Happen to My Woodland?

When I was deciding what quote to put at the start of this chapter, I almost went with the adage, "It's hard to make predictions, especially about the future." There are lots of climate change models that evaluate all sorts of potential scenarios and impacts. Not surprisingly, there's a lot of variation in those models, in their estimation of just how much things will change.

That's a problem for those of us who care about woods. Trees take a long time to grow. When we think about woodlands, we have no choice but to think far into the future.

When it comes to climate change impacts on US forests, the best resource I've found is the US Forest Service's Climate Change Tree Atlas. It looks at where different kinds of forests grow now, and then it applies various climate models to predict where those forests will grow in 2100. The atlas gives predictive ranges for more than 130 tree species throughout the eastern United States.

Under one Atlas model, there's little change; the landscapes look identical save for the northernmost

regions of Maine, Michigan, and Minnesota. But apply a different model, and the change becomes extreme. Common northern species like spruce, fir, maple, beech, and birch all disappear, replaced by southern species like oak and hickory.

So according to the best models available, climate change could completely change the trees that will grow in your woods, or it might have no effect on them whatsoever. Now you understand why I considered the prediction quote.

Even if we knew which model was right, it would still make decisions on the ground difficult. These models only look at suitable tree habitat based on factors like temperature and rainfall. That doesn't mean northern species will all keel over and die one day. They may just grow more slowly, or they may become heat-stressed and more vulnerable to disease or insect attacks.

More importantly, the models also don't guarantee that new species will just jump in and replace the old ones. Among foresters, oak in particular has a notorious reputation as a pain to get started. If northern states become better oak habitats, it could still be a long, difficult process to get oaks growing there.

With so much uncertainty, is there anything you can or should do in your woods to prepare? The answer depends on where your land is and how worried you are about climate change. Regardless of the model used, southeastern forests don't change much, even under high emissions. They'll continue to be dominated by the trees they have now, like loblolly and shortleaf pine. If your land is in a southern state, there's little risk that climate change will alter the kinds of trees that can grow on your property.

In northern states, the situation is different. There, the possibility that your woods will support different species a hundred years from now is real.

A few intrepid northerners are taking this possibility seriously, and they're experimenting with a concept called assisted migration. In northern Minnesota, a team from the environmental group The Nature Conservancy has planted 100,000 oak and pine tree seedlings. Some of those seedlings are local, but others come from hundreds of miles away, from southern Minnesota and Michigan.[1] The team is testing to see whether the historically more southern trees will fare better than northern Minnesota's traditional conifers.

Planting trees from hundreds of miles south is an extreme step. I stand by my planting advice in the last chapter: choose seedlings local to your area. While I'm curious how the Nature Conservancy's experiment will play out, you probably shouldn't copy it.

Rather than assisted migration, climate change and its potential impacts simply reinforce my rule about providing diversity. If you have many tree species on your land, then your woods will be better prepared to deal with whatever climate change throws at them. If the ho-hum model comes to pass, your woods will be fine. By the same token, if extreme change occurs, you'll likely have a few southern trees on your land that can produce seeds and replace the northern trees that disappear.

If you're particularly concerned about climate change's impacts on your woods and feel the need to do something beyond having a diverse species mix, there is an option besides assisted migration. Rather than plant trees from hundreds of miles away, simply favor trees already on your land that also grow farther south. If you do a timber harvest, for instance, you can cut trees around the biggest, healthiest warm-adapted ones. You might thin out around an oak, for instance, to give it more room to grow and a better chance to produce more acorns.

If you favor warm-adapted species over time, you'll gradually transition your woods to a more southern mix. Just be careful not to overdo it. Remember how hard predicting the future is. A diverse forest is still your best tool against the uncertainties to come.

Fighting Climate Change: Steps You Can Take on Your Woodland

Climate change's impacts on your land are difficult to predict, but your land's impacts on climate change are better understood. Woodlands are natural climate change fighters. Trees suck carbon dioxide from the atmosphere and store it as wood. Just by owning woodland, you're helping address climate change.

But what you do on your woodland influences how well it can battle climate change. Depending on your actions, you can go beyond what nature can

WATCH OUT!
IT'S MORE THAN TEMPERATURE

The Climate Change Tree Atlas focuses on the eastern United States. What about the other half of the country? How will climate change affect western forests?

Although we don't have maps to go off of like we do for the East, it's likely climate change will hit the West harder. It will do that for a simple reason: water. The historic drought we're seeing in California highlights a future where some western trees may not have the water they need to survive. Already there's evidence that in the aftermath of some southwestern forest fires, trees aren't coming back.[2] The area has become too dry to support a forest.

Even where trees can handle the drought, the added stress makes them more vulnerable to other problems. A tree suffering from drought is more likely to die when it gets attacked by insects such as the mountain pine beetle. In addition, a drier forest is a more apt site for a powerful wildfire.

It's these secondary effects of climate change—drought, infestation, and fire—that make climate change such a serious issue for western forests. Several western species, among them quaking aspen and lodgepole, whitebark, and piñon pines, are already decreasing in number and range.[3]

For western landowners, there are actions you can take to make your woods more resilient in the face of these secondary effects. There are two chapters devoted to these techniques coming up: "A Burning Problem" and "Chowing Down."

do to keep carbon out of the atmosphere, or you can release the carbon your woods have worked so hard to store.

Let's get the bad out of the way so we can focus on the good. Three of my six rules for doing right by the land apply to protecting your woodland's ability to fight climate change: protect the soil, leave something for the future, and keep the land intact.

Soil matters here because it's a long-term carbon storehouse. When trees die and decay, much of the carbon they absorbed as wood goes into the soil, not the atmosphere. As long as the soil remains undisturbed, it can hold increasing amounts of carbon almost indefinitely.[4] When that soil is churned up, though, the carbon may be released.

In the last chapter, I described Best Management Practices and how they can protect water quality by limiting soil disturbance and movement. Because they keep soil stable, these practices will also lower the amount of carbon released by logging. If you needed one more reason to use BMPs, there it is.

In regard to leaving something for the future and keeping the land intact, those two rules relate to changing land use and its impact on climate change. Forests are powerful climate change fighters, but lawns and homes aren't. Keeping your woods as woods rather than subdividing them and allowing them to be developed is critical to protecting your land's carbon-storing ability.

Just because you're keeping your woods as woods doesn't mean you have to leave them alone. Not only can you protect the carbon-storing power of your soil and trees, you can improve your land's ability to store carbon through careful tree cutting.

That probably sounds backwards. If trees are so good at pulling carbon from the atmosphere, why would we want to stop that by cutting them down?

There are two reasons. The first has to do with the way forests grow, and the second has to do with a beautiful material called wood.

CARBON STORAGE IN WOODLAND

Forests of all ages act as carbon sinks, meaning they take in more carbon than they release. But as woodlots age, their overall growth slows. University of Washington researchers studying Douglas fir forests in the western United States, for instance, found that these forests achieve their fastest carbon storage when they're thirty to seventy years old, which isn't that old for a tree.[5]

Keeping your woodlot healthy and in a state of fast growth will help it store carbon more quickly. You can do this through logging to remove trees that are slower-growing or diseased. Like weeding a garden, removing these trees gives the healthier ones more room. With that space, they'll grow even faster than their normal speed combined with that of the trees competing with them. And while the wood you remove won't make great lumber, it might have a chance as firewood, which can help you offset your fossil fuel emissions (see this section's Try This).

TRY THIS:
CUT YOUR OWN FIREWOOD

When you think of carbon emissions, two big sources come to mind. One is electricity: big coal plants spewing carbon dioxide into the air. Driving is another: all those cars burning all that gas.

But there's a third way we use energy, one that receives less attention. It's heat. The US Energy Information Administration reports that we use more energy to heat our homes than any other home energy use. In northern regions like the one where I live, home heating consumes more energy than all other home energy uses combined.[6]

Much of that heat comes from fossil fuels. Natural gas and electricity dominate, but fuel oil and propane are also common, especially in rural areas without natural gas infrastructure.

When we burn these fuels, we release carbon dioxide into the atmosphere that has been trapped for millions of years. That's not good for the climate. But if we burn wood, especially wood we've grown ourselves on our woodlots, the wood contains carbon that was in the atmosphere recently. That means we're not introducing new carbon from underground into the system. Plus, if we're careful about which trees we use, we can speed up the pace of carbon storage on our woodlands and draw even more carbon from the air. That's a climate win-win.

Of course, that climate benefit depends on harvesting the right trees. How do you know which ones to cut, and which to leave? Here are some tips on choosing your firewood trees so they both keep you warm and your woodlot growing well:

- It takes less land than you'd expect to grow your own firewood. If you own more than 12 wooded acres, your land will grow enough wood to heat your home year after year without depleting your timber. If you only use wood for secondary heat—as in a fireplace—you won't even need that much.
- Live broad-leaved trees make the best firewood. Maple, oak, cherry, hickory, ash, beech, and hophornbeam (also called ironwood) are all good firewood choices.
- Avoid conifers like pine, spruce, and hemlock (basically, anything with needles). These species burn quickly, so the heat doesn't last. They also have a lot of sap and creosote that, when burned, can lead to chimney fires. If you live in a part of the country that only has these species, you can use them, but they aren't preferred.
- Pick trees that are four to ten inches across

at about chest height. This is a good size for most fireplaces and wood stoves.

- Pick live trees, not dead ones. Why? Three reasons. First, dead trees often have rot, which prevents them from burning well. Second, as mentioned in an earlier chapter, dead trees make great wildlife habitats. Whether standing or fallen, they provide nesting spots for birds and mammals, and insects provide a ready food supply. Finally, dead trees don't compete with your live trees for growing space, so removing one won't help remaining trees grow faster.

- While you should cut live trees, choose those that show signs of disease or poor health. The goal in cutting your own firewood isn't just to get wood to burn. It's also to give your best trees room to expand. Leave the large, straight, healthy trees in the woods. Instead, cut ones that have cankers, dieback in the canopy, or a crooked trunk, especially when their leaves are touching the leaves of a large, healthy tree.

- If you're concerned about wildlife, cut trees around healthy oaks, cherries, and hickories. These trees grow fruit and nuts that wildlife love. Giving them more room will help them produce even more of these excellent food sources.

Before you head out with your chainsaw, I want to end this section with a note on safety. Most of my Try This activities are easy and safe. Cutting trees isn't. I've included it because many landowners want to harvest their own firewood, but keep in mind that felling trees is dangerous and requires skill to do safely. In the past few years, logging has surpassed commercial fishing to become America's deadliest job.[7] If you don't know what you're doing, a trip to get this year's firewood can end in disaster.

If you want to cut your own firewood, take the time to learn proper tree felling. I've included a link to a video about it in "Beyond the Book," but the only real way to learn tree cutting is to attend a chainsaw safety class. Programs like Game of Logging give hands-on instruction in proper chainsaw care, maintenance, and use.

Even if you've been cutting firewood for years, I encourage you to take one of these trainings. I know professional loggers with decades of experience who have taken these courses and come away with new information.

In addition to having knowledge, make sure you have the proper safety equipment before felling trees. Wear logging chaps to protect your legs, and get a full face shield with hardhat and hearing protection built in. Finally, bring a first aid kit whenever you go in the woods with a chainsaw.

WATCH OUT!
THE WAY YOU BURN WOOD MATTERS TOO

While heating with wood can improve your wood-lot's health and fight climate change, the way you burn that wood matters. Improper wood burning can offset all the good you're doing and end up causing both environmental and health problems.

If you've driven around a rural area in the winter, you've probably seen black smoke billowing out of somebody's outdoor wood boiler. Those boilers have given wood a reputation as a dirty fuel, but it doesn't have to be that way.

The biggest problems with wood heat are the old wood-burning appliances used for it and improper wood use. Correcting these two issues will let you enjoy the benefits of wood heat without upsetting your neighbors.

Improper wood use is the easier problem to correct. First of all, as obvious as it sounds, burn only wood in your wood-burning appliance. Never burn garbage or tires. Wood stoves and boilers are not trash incinerators.

Apart from only using wood, make sure all firewood has time to properly dry before burning it. Not only will dried wood burn cleaner, but because it has less moisture, it will burn more easily, give you more heat, and leave less creosote in your chimney. It's best to let firewood air dry for at least a year, and denser species like oak should dry for two years.

To help your wood dry, keep it off the ground. If you have the space, build a woodshed to store it. This shed doesn't have to be complicated. In fact, it's better if it's open on three or even all four sides, to allow air to circulate. All it really needs is a roof to block rain and a floor with some pallets to keep the wood elevated.

If you don't have the space or desire for a woodshed, you can stack your firewood on pallets and cover the top of your pile with a tarp. Be sure to leave the tarp's sides open so air can circulate through the pile.

Whether you use a shed or simple pile, give your wood stack plenty of sun. Wood stored in the shade will stay damp. If possible, locate your firewood so it gets at least six hours of sunlight daily.

It's also a good idea to split your firewood. Split wood will dry better and faster, and it will burn more easily. When stacking split firewood, place it with the bark facing up if you're not using a woodshed. If you have a roof over your wood, bark direction matters little.

That takes care of the wood. The other issue with wood heat—the appliance you use—is more difficult. Old wood stoves and boilers burn poorly and produce a lot of smoke. Newer units are much more efficient, and as a result, they produce more heat with less wood and fewer emissions. If your wood stove or boiler is more than twenty years old, you can probably cut your wood use by a third or more by replacing it with a modern unit. You'll give off a lot less smoke, too.

The tradeoff, of course, is that replacing an existing burner with a new one costs thousands of dollars. Don't let that cost be a turnoff, though. To encourage people to replace old wood stoves and boilers, more and more states are offering change-out programs. These programs give you a tax break if you exchange an old, dirty wood-burning appliance with a new, clean-burning one. Rules and specifics vary by state, so it's worth doing some research. Combined with your reduced wood use, the tax break from a change-out program could make upgrading to a new unit well worth the investment, air quality benefits aside.

When choosing a new wood-burning appliance, look for ones certified by the US Environmental Protection Agency. The EPA maintains a list of certified units on its Burn Wise website, which I've listed in "Beyond the Book."

Finally, be aware that there may be state or local laws that restrict which appliances you can buy and when, or even if, you can burn wood. Look into these rules and secure any necessary permits before installing or replacing a wood-heating system.

Even if you aren't able to use the wood and just leave it to decay, that's alright too. The fallen logs will provide wildlife habitat, and when they break down, their carbon will go into the soil rather than back into the atmosphere.

CARBON STORAGE IN WOOD

Trees and soil aren't the only places carbon can be stored. Long-lived wood products like lumber also keep carbon out of the atmosphere. The framing in your home, the cabinets in your kitchen, and your grandmother's antique rocking chair are all forms of stored carbon. If you purchased a paper copy of this book, congratulations! You're fighting climate change.

Because wood stores carbon, environmentally conscious architects are increasingly looking for ways to use it instead of steel or concrete. These other building materials have huge environmental impacts, including high carbon footprints. In one study, researchers from the Universities of Washington and Oregon compared the environmental performance of homes made from steel, concrete, and wood. Wood had lower air and water pollution emissions than either steel or concrete, and it required 15 percent less energy to build and maintain the home over its lifetime.[8]

Thanks to these benefits, increasing our use of wood could be one of our best chances to make a positive impact on climate change. In 2014, Yale University researchers reported that the world currently harvests just 20 percent of the annual growth from its forests. The researchers calculated that if we increased that percentage to 34 percent and used that wood in place of steel and concrete, we could cut fossil fuel consumption as much as 19 percent and avoid up to 31 percent of global carbon dioxide emissions.[9] More importantly, our global forests would still be gaining wood three times faster than the rate at which we harvested it.

Harvested responsibly, wood has tremendous potential to fight climate change. If you're worried about the climate, don't feel like you're doing the world a disservice by being active in your woodlot. On the contrary, you can be part of the solution to one of Earth's biggest environmental challenges.

CHAPTER 9

The Taxman Cometh

In this world nothing can be said to be certain, except death and taxes.
—Benjamin Franklin

Landowners nationwide report that financial pressure, particularly from taxes, is the most common reason they give up on landownership.[1] High taxes have been singled out as a key driver of the trend toward greater development in woodlands, with all the ensuing damage to nature that development brings.

Yet as problematic as taxes can be, many landowners have no idea that programs exist that can reduce their land's tax burden. Here in the New York City Watershed, a pair of Yale University researchers talked to landowners who had subdivided and sold land. They found that while financial pressure and taxes drove land sales (as opposed to high land values or great offers, which were not common causes), more than half the landowners had no idea that New York has a program that can reduce woodland property taxes by up to 80 percent.[2]

New York isn't the only state that offers a program like this. Every US state has some form of property tax incentive for woodland owners, though the requirements and tax reduction amounts vary. I've included links about each program in the "State Resources" appendix, so you can dig into your state's program and see if it's for you.

That research is worthwhile, because these programs typically aren't just free money for woodland owners. A few states do automatically give woods lower tax rates, but they're the exception. Most states have commitments landowners must make to receive the tax break. Here in New York, for instance, landowners agree not to develop or subdivide their land for ten years. They must also follow a management plan written by a professional forester in consultation with the landowner. Landowners who don't follow their plan or who develop their properties within the ten-year window pay a penalty, a multiple of the back taxes saved plus interest.

Some programs provide flexibility in the commitments required. In New Hampshire, you get a tax break for agreeing not to develop your land, just like with New York's program. But while New York requires you to follow a management plan, New Hampshire makes that plan optional. You get additional savings if you purchase a plan and follow it. You can get even more savings by opening your land to public recreation.

Most property tax programs require you to enroll a minimum number of acres. Alabama's program requires five acres to participate. You'll need 20 for Missouri's program, and California tops the list at 160. The national average is 16 acres, so in most states you don't need a lot of land to qualify.

If you're considering enrolling in a tax program, start with some online research to learn the basics. Also, try to find other landowners who are enrolled in the program and ask them what they think of it. Are the savings worth it? Would they get out if they could? What are the biggest hassles? Getting real answers from folks in the program will help you decide if it's something worth getting involved in.

If you don't know anyone who's signed up for your state's program, that's OK. Check with your state's woodland owner association. (I have links to them in the "State Resources" appendix, too.) They can usually put you in touch with someone.

More than Property Taxes

While property taxes are the tax of greatest concern to most landowners, other taxes arise as a result of your landownership, like estate and income taxes. We'll talk about estate taxes in the last chapter of this book, but we'll deal with income taxes now.

Your woods can earn income in lots of ways, but for the sake of simplicity, let's limit our discussion to the most common way landowners make money from their property: selling timber. Let's also look only at the federal income tax. Most states have an income tax, but because the rules vary so much, it's hard to provide useful advice about them in a book like this one. The federal rules apply no matter where your land is, and federal tax rates tend to be higher than state rates anyway. If you want to learn more about state income taxes, contact a tax professional who can give you specific guidance.

As for federal income taxes, there are three main ways to lower your income taxes from timber harvesting. All of them require planning before a sale, so if you're thinking about having some trees cut, look into these issues first.

CAPITAL GAINS OR ORDINARY INCOME?

Trees are a long-term investment. Unless you're stripping the land you just bought of its timber—something I advise against—odds are you'll have owned your land several years before your first cut. That's good, not only because it gives you time to think and plan out your harvest, but because it lets

WATCH OUT!
ARE THESE TAX PROGRAMS FAIR?

This might seem like an odd question. Who cares if the programs are fair? They exist, and they can save you money, right? But I've been surprised by the number of landowners who tell me they aren't interested in these programs. It isn't because of the requirements or concerns about being in a government program. It's that the program seems unfair, that by getting a tax break the landowner is unjustly burdening the rest of the community with higher taxes.

If you have this concern, let me try to ease your conscience. The reason many of these programs exist is because property taxes are inherently unfair to open space, whether that space be farmland or woods. Property taxes are based on a property's "highest and best use"—the use that would generate the most financial benefit. That use is typically development; housing plots and strip malls sell for a lot more per acre than open land.

The problem with property taxes, then, is that your land gets taxed on its development value, even if you have no intention of developing it. And because your land is taxed as if it were developed, the value your land provides by growing trees doesn't compete with the property taxes charged.[3]

Beyond the tax amount itself, property taxes hit woodland owners especially hard because you pay them every year. A typical woodlot, though, can only provide timber income every decade or so.

Simply because of the way they're structured, then, property taxes encourage landowners not to keep their land as land but rather to develop it. But as a society, we don't want just development. We derive a lot of value from open space, from wildlife to water quality to amazing views. We don't pay for these values. We get them just because folks like you keep your land undeveloped.

That's why states have property tax reduction programs for farms and woodlands. They aren't about giving landowners a handout. Rather, they help correct the inherent bias against open land in the property tax system, and they encourage landowners to keep providing the many environmental benefits you already give us.

If you need further evidence that these programs aren't simply handouts, consider the 150-plus "cost of community services" studies conducted in towns across the United States. These studies compare the amount of money different land uses contribute in local taxes to the cost of local government services they receive. These studies repeatedly find that owners of open land contribute almost $3 in property taxes for every $1 they receive in local public services. By contrast, residential owners routinely pay about $.86 in property taxes for every $1 they get in local services.[4]

TRY THIS:
HIRE A TAX PROFESSIONAL

For many landowners, a timber harvest is a once-in-a-lifetime event. With the tangled mess that is the US tax code, I highly recommend that you work with a tax professional whenever you sell timber. It's an additional cost, sure, but it will save you a lot of time and headaches, especially if you get audited.

The right professional can even end up earning money for you. A Virginia Tech study found that knowledge of timber-related tax provisions increased the return on investment from the same harvest by as much as 79 percent.[5] Those tax savings will more than make up for the accountant's fee.

As with any professional, do your homework before hiring an accountant. Make sure you get someone with credentials, like a CPA or Enrolled Agent. I've included links to national databases for both these categories of accountants in "Beyond the Book."

Don't just pick a name off a list, though. If possible, get suggestions from neighbors, your forester, or your state's woodland owner association. Once you get accountants on the phone, ask about their familiarity with timber tax laws. General accountants may never have worked with this specialized branch of the tax code. Ask them how many clients they have helped who had timber harvest income. Finally, see if you can get a reference for at least one of those clients.

you treat your income from the sale as long-term capital gains.

Why does that matter? Capital gains tax rates are lower than the rates you pay on ordinary income, like the money in your paycheck. Depending on how much money you earn and what your income tax bracket is, you could save 50 percent or more in taxes on your timber sale income by treating it as long-term capital gains rather than ordinary income.

REDUCE YOUR TAXABLE INCOME
WITH YOUR TIMBER BASIS

To get the full savings of capital gains treatment, you'll need an additional piece of information, something known in the tax world as "basis." It can be difficult to figure out, especially if you've owned land a long time, but it's worth the effort.

To explain basis, let's step away from trees for a moment and think about something simpler. Say you go to a yard sale and find this nifty old clock for $50. You love how it looks, so you buy it and bring it home.

A week later, some friends come over. One of them is nuts about old clocks, and she tells you your new clock is actually an antique worth $500. Not a bad day at the yard sale!

You decide that as much as you like the clock, you'd like $500 a lot more. You sell the clock online and get the full $500.

Here's the question: how much money do you owe tax on? And don't say zero; that's tax evasion. You sold the clock for $500, but you don't have to pay taxes on all of that. You can deduct the amount you paid for it: the $50 at the yard sale. You only have to pay taxes on $450.

OK, back to the woods. In the world of timber taxes, your basis is like that $50 you spent on the clock. It's the amount you originally paid for the timber on your property. Be careful! It's not how much you paid for the *land*; it's how much specifically the *trees* were worth at the time you purchased or inherited the property.

That's why basis can be a pain to determine. It's not good enough just to go back and look at how much you paid per acre. You need to know the value of the trees at that time.

If you've just purchased your land, the calculation is easy. Get a forester to visit your property, and he or she can give you an estimate of what your trees are worth.

If you've owned your land for decades, the work is a little harder. You'll still need a forester to estimate what your trees are worth now. Your forester will then use that number, combined with the rate at which trees grow in your area, to estimate what your trees were worth when you bought your property.

Why go through all this hassle? Because, as with the antique clock, you can deduct a certain amount of this original purchase price from the income you earn on a timber sale. That means you'll pay less in income tax.

The amount of your basis you can deduct from timber sale income depends on how much wood your logger removes. Rather than get into messy and ultimately unhelpful calculations, I'll once again encourage you to talk to a professional accountant, who can help you figure out what portion of your basis you can deduct from your sale income.

MORE DEDUCTIONS: KNOW YOUR WOODLAND'S TAX CLASS

Your basis isn't all you can deduct on your income taxes. Costs of caring for your land, like hiring a forester and planting trees, are potentially deductible too. But not all landowners can claim these costs on their taxes. Determining which expenses you can and can't deduct depends on another bit of tax jargon—your woodland's tax classification.

The IRS recognizes three tax classes for woodlands: personal property, investment, and business. You get to decide which class makes sense for your property based on why you own it, and your taxes and reporting requirements vary based on what you pick.

Here's how the classes break down:

1. **Personal property**—You own your land primarily for enjoyment, not its income potential.

2. **Business**—You own your land for its income potential, and you regularly and continuously engage in boosting that potential.

3. **Investment**—You own your land for its income potential, but your involvement with the land does not rise to the level of a business.

If you're like most landowners, your land falls into the personal property class. You may occasionally earn some money from a timber sale, but that isn't why you own your woods. You own them instead for the scenic values, privacy, and recreational opportunities they provide.

From a tax perspective, personal property is the most restricted in terms of which costs you can deduct. Aside from losses due to disasters like fires or theft, you won't be able to deduct costs you incur in caring for your property.

At the other end of the scale, business ownership gives you the maximum ability to deduct costs. Tools needed on the property, hired labor fees, and disease control costs are just three examples of deductible expenses for business owners.

It might seem obvious, then, that any woodland owner would just call their woods a business, but it isn't that simple. In the event of an audit, you'll have to prove to the IRS that your woodland's tax class is what you say it is, and proving business ownership is difficult. The IRS will look to see whether you have "material participation" in the management of your land for profit. You can meet that requirement several ways, but the most common is to show that you work at least 100 hours annually improving your woods' income potential, and nobody else works more hours than you do on your land.

For most landowners, proving material participation and therefore a business tax class is tough. The third tax class option, investment, offers a middle road. You don't need active involvement in making your land more profitable; you just need to demonstrate that you own the land for its income potential. As a tradeoff, though, you can only deduct expenses when they total more than 2 percent of your adjusted gross income for the year.

Whichever tax class you choose, you can report income from timber sales as long-term capital gains as long as you've owned the property for more than one year. You can also deduct property taxes and losses from disasters.

For most landowners, that's sufficient. You may not be spending enough in deductible expenses to make the investment class worthwhile, and the reporting requirements from the business class can be onerous. Still, if you own your property primarily for income purposes, it's worth considering these options as ways to lower your tax burden.

When you talk to most foresters, they will recommend that you get a management plan, sometimes called a stewardship plan. Whichever name you use, a management plan is a report written by a forester that outlines the actions you or a logger will do on your property for the next fifteen years or so. For decades, these plans have been a forestry cornerstone, the starting point in any landowner's responsible action on their property.

Recently, though, some foresters—myself included—have challenged the wisdom of the management plan. Life changes so quickly these days that figuring out now what you're going to do in fifteen years isn't realistic. Research into management plans has found that they make little on-the-ground difference in what landowners do on their land. They're expensive, time-consuming, and at the end of the day, no more effective than cheaper alternatives like reading this book, getting advice from your local extension office, or paying a forester to spend a day walking your property with you.[6]

That said, you may still want to pay the cost and get a management plan. Why? Because while it may be overkill for determining how to care for your woods, it's a necessary checkbox for taxes and some government programs.

Both investment and business tax classes require that you demonstrate that you own land primarily for its income potential. The IRS wants documentation, and a management plan is an ideal place to spell it out for them. If you want to classify your property as either investment or business, get a management plan.

A management plan is also required for many states' property tax reduction programs. What the plan must contain and how closely you need to follow it vary from state to state, but if you don't have one, you may not be able to save on your property taxes.

Finally, while I haven't dealt with them in this book, some government cost-share programs for landowners also require a plan in order to qualify. These programs offer funding to offset a portion of costs for certain projects like tree planting and improving wildlife habitat. Competition is high due to limited funding, which is why I haven't talked about them. Still, you won't even have a shot at many of these programs without a management plan that documents the eligible practices you want to do.

To get a management plan, you'll need a forester. State and federal agencies generally won't accept a plan you write yourself. Your state may have a list of qualified or licensed foresters who can write management plans that meet program requirements. I've included links to forester lists in the "State Resources" appendix.

POSTED
PRIVATE PROPERTY
HUNTING, FISHING, TRAPPING OR
TRESPASSING FOR ANY PURPOSE
IS STRICTLY FORBIDDEN
VIOLATORS WILL BE PROSECUTED

CHAPTER 10

POSTED

The influences that really make and mar human happiness are beyond the reach of the law. The law can keep neighbors from trespassing, but it cannot put neighborly courtesy and goodwill into their relations.
—Walter Rauschenbusch

To be sure, most loggers and foresters are honest, hardworking people trying to make a living. Deliberate thieves are the exception in the industry, and so you shouldn't avoid working with professionals out of concern that they might rob you of your trees.

That said, don't let that honesty lull you into a false sense of security. While little discussed, timber theft is a serious crime in the United States. The remote nature of the crime makes wood thieves hard to catch, as they often need only minutes to steal choice trees.

That's the typical scenario in a tree theft situa-

tion. You don't wake up one morning and find your hillside bare. Instead, thieves take several large, high-quality trees of valuable species like maple, walnut, and cherry. Small-timers may load up the bed of a pickup truck, while bigger operations use traditional logging equipment.

Timber theft is rarely random. It often occurs in conjunction with a legitimate harvest on a neighbor's property. A big tree a few feet on the other side of the line is a tempting target.

Once theft occurs, it's difficult, time-consuming, and expensive to prosecute. One figure cited in a New York news story was that of 156 timber theft complaints statewide in a year, just 15 percent ended in convictions or settlements with the violators.[1]

Don't let yourself be a victim. Timber theft is a case in which the saying "an ounce of prevention is

OPPOSITE: *Posting your boundaries, whether with paint or signs, is the best way to reduce your chance of both accidental trespass and timber theft.*

103

worth a pound of cure" applies. While you'll never be risk-free, a little planning and vigilance will go a long way toward keeping your trees where they belong.

Mark Your Boundaries

Although timber theft is a serious crime, a lot of the time it may be accidental. The same is true of casual trespass by hikers or recreationists. Deep in the woods, it can be all but impossible to tell if you've crossed an unmarked boundary. Even with modern GPS systems, the thick canopy and inherent error in GPS devices mean a logger may not know if a particular tree is over the line. Mistakes do happen, and a good logger will do their best to pay the landowner a fair amount for the cut tree.

The problem is that thieves prey on this uncertainty. To convict someone for theft, a prosecutor must prove criminal intent: in other words, that the thief knowingly crossed the line and took your trees. If your boundaries aren't marked, criminal intent is almost impossible to establish. The thief simply says, "I made a mistake" and claims either not to know where the boundary was or that it was unclear.

That's why there's no better way to reduce your odds of trespass, accidental cutting, and intentional theft than by clearly marking your boundaries. If you're really woods savvy, you can do this yourself, but if not, it's best to get help from a forester.

It might seem obvious, but before you mark your boundaries, it's important that you and your neighbors agree on where they are. If you or your forester mismark a boundary, you could be liable.

To avoid that situation, first mark the boundary using a temporary material, like biodegradable flagging, so your neighbors can confirm you've put the boundary in the right place. If everyone agrees, then the real markers can go up.

If you and your neighbors can't agree on where the boundary is, consider hiring a surveyor. A survey is an expensive step, but it can be worth it to establish definite boundaries.

You can mark your boundaries in two ways: with painted marks on trees or with posted signs. Each option has pluses and minuses. Paint is cheaper, difficult to vandalize, and won't injure your trees, but it fades with time. Posted signs are more expensive and can be ripped down, but they offer higher visibility, spell out who owns the property, and clearly identify what is and isn't allowed on the land.

Some states have rules governing how to mark your boundaries. You may have to place marks a certain distance apart, and the marks may need to be at a certain height. Look at your state's rules so your final boundary passes muster in the event of a theft or trespassing incident.

If you paint your boundaries, use a high-visibility, oil-based tree marking paint for maximum durability. Choose a bright color like orange or lime green, but avoid red. Red paint quickly becomes hard to see as it fades.

Both paint and posted signs need maintenance,

so check your boundary line annually for faded paint or fallen signs. If any markers are unclear or missing, replace them.

Know Your Neighbors

While any landowner is potentially a timber theft victim, thieves prey on two landowner groups in particular: the elderly and those who live somewhere other than their land. Thieves choose these targets because they know it's unlikely that someone will happen upon their crime scene. By the time the landowner learns of the theft, the thieves will be long gone.

If you can't get around your property on a regular basis, it's especially important to get to know your neighbors. A common timber theft practice is to take trees that are across the line while cutting legitimately on a neighboring woodlot. If you know when your neighbors are having logging done, you'll know to pay extra attention. If you can't get to your boundaries during your neighbor's cut, ask your neighbor, a family member, or a friend to check on them so you can catch theft and report it quickly if it occurs.

Be on the lookout, too, for warning signs that something may be amiss with a neighboring job. Log trucks showing up at odd hours, particularly at night, can indicate that something inappropriate is happening. Missing posted signs or cut boundary trees are also red flags.

Even when logging isn't scheduled on a neighbor's property, it's helpful to have someone regularly check your land. Like other thieves, timber thieves often case targets in advance of moving in. They're looking for signs that your property isn't in use. If they know someone often visits your land, they'll look for an easier target.

There are lots of ways to get this help, and most of them won't require that you spend money. For example, you might give a local hunter permission to use your property in exchange for keeping an eye on the place. Letting friends or neighbors you trust recreate on your land is another way to maintain a presence on it. The key is to have people use your property often, even if you aren't one of them.

Protect Yourself

Timber theft doesn't only occur when someone sneaks across boundary lines. Some thieves will set up shop right on your land, and they'll do it under a seemingly legitimate pretense: a timber sale.

Again, let me be clear that most loggers are not crooks. Don't avoid having a timber sale for fear you'll be robbed.

Be aware, though, that thieves can use a timber sale as a cover to steal valuable trees. They may cut trees you didn't want removed, ones that weren't discussed prior to starting the harvest. In other cases, they might under-report the amount of wood they cut or what the mill paid them for it.

WATCH OUT!
THE FISTFUL OF DOLLARS

Has this ever happened to you? A guy shows up at your property wearing flannel. He pulls out a wad of hundreds and offers you five thousand bucks for permission to cut your trees. Maybe he tells you the trees look like they're dying, or that there's a nasty insect in the area. You'd better get a logger in there fast, he says, or you're going to lose them. If you don't pick him, he'll move on, and you'll be out five grand.

Thieves play this trick all the time, and it's one of the most insidious forms of timber theft. In truth, it isn't technically theft at all, because you're getting paid. It is theft, though, in that you're getting pennies on the dollar for your trees. The thief is preying on your lack of knowledge about how much trees are worth. You take the cash, and the logger has free rein in your woods. With little if any written documentation, he takes your trees and leaves the woods and trails a mess. Then he disappears, and you have nothing to fall back on.

To avoid this potential disaster, never make snap judgments about your woods. Forests do change, but they rarely change overnight. There's almost always time to get a second opinion, even in the case of disease and insect outbreaks. If someone shows up at your door offering cash to cut your trees, say no. Take the person's card and tell him or her you'll think about it. That by itself should scare away many fly-by-nighters and thieves. If the would-be buyer sticks around and tries to bully you into making a decision right now, take that as a glaring sign the person isn't legit.

Once the potential buyer leaves, go out and do some research. Bring in a professional forester and get an appraisal. Show the buyer's card to the forester and to other landowners in your area. Often folks will know who the reputable and disreputable loggers are.

This form of timber theft is especially trouble-some, because you've generally agreed to let the thieves onto your land. They've probably even paid you some money for your trees, though it's likely a small fraction of what they're worth. Nevertheless, it makes proving criminal intent difficult, which in turn makes proper payment back to you unlikely.

The best solution for this form of theft is the timber sale process I'll outline in Chapter 13. You can avoid many of the hassles of a poor logging job by working with a forester, marking all trees to be cut, bidding out the sale, having a written contract, and checking up on the harvest's progress. I'll cover all these steps in detail later, so I'll skip over them for now.

THE WORST CASE SCENARIO

Following the prevention tips in this chapter will greatly reduce your chances of both accidental tres-pass and deliberate timber theft on your land. Even so, you'll never eliminate the risk. If the worst hap-pens, you're in for a potentially long and difficult legal fight.

If a theft occurs, don't panic. Report it right away to both your local police and your state's Department of Natural Resources (or equivalent agency). These agencies often have their own police focused on environmental crimes, so they can be great allies in getting an issue resolved.

If your boundaries are well marked and your land is patrolled, your odds of a positive outcome improve a lot. With marked boundaries, proving criminal intent becomes much easier. By patrolling your land, you or a friend likely caught the theft soon after it occurred, so you'll be able to report it quickly. And if your neighbors have kept you informed of logging happening on their property, you'll likely have an idea about who committed the crime.

For all that planning, though, be aware that convictions on timber theft are rare, and reimburse-ment to victims is even rarer. It's unlikely you'll ever recoup the lost value of your trees. As sad as it is to say, you could wind up losing more time and money fighting for justice than you lost with the stolen trees. Again, that's why it's so important to focus on preventing theft in the first place.

Even if you can't get justice, you can help keep others from becoming victims. Tell your neighbors and any other landowners you know what happened. Most loggers I've met do little marketing. Their busi-nesses live or die on referrals. A logger who gets a reputation as a thief won't be around long. But if no one's blowing the whistle, there will be more victims in the future.

CHAPTER 11

A Burning Problem

This year, we are experiencing yet another devastating wildfire season, particularly in the drought-ravaged West. Climate change, drought, fuel buildup, insects and disease are increasing the severity of unprecedented wildfire in America's forests and rangelands . . . with more than 46 million homes in the United States, or about 40 percent of our nation's housing, potentially at risk.
—Tom Vilsack

Picture your woods. Imagine the view from your cabin, or by the pond, or wherever you like to hike.

Now imagine the woods gone, the trees burned to ash and toppled like matchsticks, destroyed in one single, horrifying event.

It's amazing how quickly and without warning a disaster like a fire or tornado can strike. In 2002, Colorado's Hayman Fire destroyed 60,000 acres in a single day.[1] That's more than 40 acres per minute.

OPPOSITE: *Wildfire scorches trees at Tetlin National Wildlife Refuge in eastern Alaska.* Photo credit: Tetlin National Wildlife Refuge, USFWS

Natural disasters are no joke for woodlands. Millions of wooded acres succumb each year to fires, hurricanes, and other storms.

That number is on the rise, too. Since the 1980s, the acreage burned in the United States has gone up sharply. The top six fire seasons on record—each burning more than 8 million acres—have all occurred since 2004.[2]

Wildfires have also become more powerful. In 1984, about 20 percent of forest fires in California's Sierra Nevada burned at high intensity, meaning they consumed even hardy, fire-resistant trees. By 2010, the Sierra Nevada Conservancy calculated that the percentage had risen above 30 percent.[4]

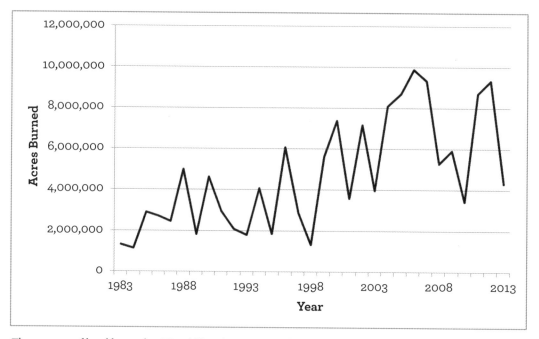

The amount of land burned in US wildfires has increased since the 1980s.[3]

Fires aren't the only disasters that can change a woodlot. Hurricane Irene and Tropical Storm Lee slammed into the Northeast in 2011, knocking down trees with powerful winds and flooding rains. An early snow on Halloween in my hometown of Hershey, Pennsylvania, a few years back brought down limbs and whole trees that hadn't yet lost their leaves.

To some extent, these disasters are unavoidable. In the face of nature's fury, your only option may be to evacuate and hope for the best.

Especially with fire, though, there are ways you can make your woods less likely to burn, or at least increase the chance that they burn less severely. In the process, you can make firefighters' jobs easier and safer in addition to potentially saving your home or cabin from the flames.

Should You Interfere?

Before we talk about how you can help your woods resist fire, let's deal with another ethics question: Should you?

I realize that's a strange question. Who wouldn't

want to prevent wildfire in their woods if they had the ability to do so?

But from a nature perspective, fire and other natural disasters aren't disasters at all. In fact, in the days before human life, they were essential to forests' survival.

Consider for a moment the problem trees create for themselves. Like other plants, trees need light to grow. To better compete for that light, they grow tall and make big, thick canopies of leaves. That works great for the trees themselves, but it doesn't work out so well for their children. Trees and forests effectively shade out their offspring from getting the light they need. The only way those baby trees get enough light is if the parents aren't around anymore.

That's why fires, tornadoes, ice storms, and other natural disasters are generally good for forests. They create openings that let in light and allow the next generation of trees to grow.

Some trees go so far as to require a natural disaster to release their seeds. Pitch and lodgepole pines have cones glued shut by resin. Only the heat from a fire will melt the resin and allow the seeds to spread. In this way, the pines' young can grow in the burned soil with little competition.

So if forests benefit from natural disasters, why would we want to keep such disasters from happening on our land? Putting the natural argument aside for a moment, there's the obvious: a burned landscape looks ugly. It's hard to walk through, because all the trees fall into a jumbled mess. Then there's the economic loss from trees that you might have wanted to harvest at some point.

Even considering just the natural impact, though, it's still worth protecting your woods against fire. That's because the fires experienced by western forests these days are no longer natural. They're fueled by climate change and a century-old policy of putting out all forest fires as quickly as possible.

Western forests have evolved so that they're made to burn. Trees grow far apart, and grasses and other low growth fill the space. The bigger trees, like ponderosa pines, have thick bark that can withstand most flames.

Frequent, small fires allow these forests to keep growing and maintain their open condition. In the past hundred years, though, we've fought these small fires with extreme prejudice. The result is that in many places in the West, we now have a century of unburned fuel: small, thin-barked trees that wouldn't naturally be growing in those woods.

These unnaturally dense forests create the conditions for the mega-fires we hear about on the news. Fire climbs rapidly from the ground up to the canopy, and because the trees are packed together, flames jump from crown to crown. That's what allows a fire like the Hayman Fire to spread so rapidly and cause so much damage.

Even though western forests have evolved to handle fire, they aren't prepared for these powerful blazes. In smaller, less intense fires, the environment responds positively. Seedling counts skyrocket, and the forest recovers. But in high-intensity burns,

Panoramic views from Looking Glass Overlook in Glacier National Park in Montana. The top photo was taken in 1937, the bottom one in 2008. Note the much more dense forest in 2008. While beautiful, this unnaturally packed forest—the creation of a century's worth of fire suppression—is also more vulnerable to extreme burns. Photo credits: Lester Moe, National Park Service (top) and Ian Grob, US Forest Service (bottom)

the fire cooks even the seeds, preventing or at least slowing regrowth. In the meantime, rainstorms wash away the bare soil, reducing the ability for plants to grow as well as polluting streams, rivers, and drinking water supplies. After the Hayman Fire, for instance, the city of Denver had to spend more than $26 million on water treatment and reservoir dredging to restore its water quality.[5]

If you own a western woodlot, your goal shouldn't be to exclude fire. That isn't possible. Fire is part of western forests and always will be. What you can do, though, is create conditions more like what the forest would naturally have, conditions that allow your woods to burn without exploding into an inferno.

Fight the Fire before the Fire Part 1: Fuel-Reduction Thinning

In May and June 2011, Arizona faced its largest fire in recorded history. By the time the Wallow Fire ended, it had consumed more than 500,000 acres in the White Mountains.[6]

Six days into the blaze, the Wallow Fire crested a ridge and charged downhill toward the town of Alpine. The community looked headed for a total loss.

Then something strange happened. As the fire neared Alpine, it slowed. The flames, which had risen into the canopy, returned to ground level. Firefighters who previously couldn't get close to the blaze could now safely combat it.

By the end of the day, firefighters contained the

The Wallow Fire charged downhill toward Alpine, but when it hit the half-mile-wide area loggers had thinned, it weakened, sparing the town. Similar thinning techniques on your land can make firefighting safer and help protect your home or cabin from wildfire. Photo credit: Tim Sexton, US Forest Service

flames around Alpine. Only one home burned; the town was spared.

Though ultimately firefighters saved Alpine, those firefighters wouldn't have succeeded had the fire not slowed before entering the town. What made it do that?

Starting in 2004, loggers had entered the forest that surrounded Alpine to do something called "fuel reduction cutting." They removed small, densely packed trees and left larger, more widely spaced ones. This open forest better replicated what would have grown near Alpine before people suppressed fires.

When the Wallow Fire came through, the extra space between trees meant the fire couldn't jump from crown to crown. With nowhere else to go, the fire dropped to the forest floor. This lower, slower burn created safer conditions in which firefighters could halt it.

Similar treatments have shown their effectiveness elsewhere. During Idaho's 2012 Mustang Fire, a prior fuel reduction project in the Hughes Creek drainage helped firefighters protect the community of Gibbonsville. And to go back to the Hayman Fire, a thinning project in Manitou Experimental Forest reduced the blaze's intensity enough to spare even small trees from destruction.

This method of fighting the fire before the fire is one you can practice on your land. If you live in a fire-prone part of the country, work with a forester and logger to thin out densely packed, small trees on your property.

Depending on your land's fire history, you may only need to remove a few trees, or you may need to take out a lot. In 2010 I toured the Santa Fe Watershed in New Mexico. At one thinning site, land managers had reduced the number of trees from more than 700 per acre to 100 per acre. They focused on keeping the big ponderosa pine while removing small, fire-prone trees like Douglas fir.

Removing six out of every seven trees sounds like a huge reduction, and it is. But it was needed to return that overgrown forest to a more natural condition. If a fire goes through that area now, it's likely to burn at ground level and at lower temperatures. Most of the big trees will survive, and the water quality impact on Santa Fe residents won't be as bad.

Fuel-reduction thinning doesn't always pay for itself. One of the drawbacks to removing smaller trees is that they usually have few, if any, profitable markets. Trees often need to be at least ten or twelve inches wide to have any use for lumber. Depending on where you are, you might have to pay the logger to remove trees from your woods. It's worth it, though, to make your property safer from extreme wildfire.

Note my use of the word "safer." Thinning projects aren't a guarantee against wildfire. Under extreme weather conditions of high wind, high temperature, and low humidity, a fire can become so powerful that it overwhelms even thinned areas. You're particularly vulnerable if your neighbors haven't thinned their woods, because a fire can grow on their land and then spread onto yours.

Fight the Fire before the Fire Part 2: Firewise Construction

Thinning can reduce fire's impact on your land, but by itself it won't protect your home or cabin. If you live in a fire-prone part of the country, it's also worth looking into a series of practices called Firewise construction. Developed by the National Fire Protection Association, Firewise construction includes both building and landscaping methods that reduce the chance of wildfire's spreading from the woods to your home.

Firewise includes a lot of recommendations, but

in general, it focuses on a concept called "defensible space." The idea is to create an area around your home or cabin made up of non-flammable materials. The more fire-prone the place where you live is, the wider this area should be.

I've included a link to more detailed Firewise resources in "Beyond the Book," but I'll hit a few basics as examples. In fire-prone areas, build with fire resistant materials, especially on your roof. In a wildfire, the roof is the most vulnerable part of a structure because burning embers traveling on the wind can settle on it and catch the house alight. Choose a roofing material that's less likely to burn, like asphalt shingles, slate, metal, or terra cotta.

Beyond fire-resistant building materials, landscaping is the other big component of a Firewise design. Here, Firewise divides your property into three zones that start at your home and fan outward:

1. **Within 30 feet of your home:** Keep plants widely spaced, and favor fire-resistant species. Mow the lawn regularly, and keep flammable materials like propane tanks and firewood stacks out of this area. Within this zone, the first five feet from the house should include only non-flammable landscaping.

2. **30 to 100 feet from your home:** Leave at least 20 feet between tree canopies, and prune any tree branches that are within six feet of the ground. Install driveways and gravel paths to provide fuel breaks.

3. **100 to 200 feet from your home:** This area can be wooded, but keep it thinned. In particular, remove smaller conifers growing between larger trees. Tree canopies should not touch one another.

After a Disaster: Should I Salvage?

Even with thinning and Firewise construction, a fire could still impact your land. In other parts of the country, your land could get hit by a tornado, straight-line winds, or a hurricane. When the worst happens, among the many decisions you'll have to make is whether to salvage the damaged or dead trees for whatever economic value they might have.

Your decision about whether or not to salvage comes down to answering three questions:

1. How important to you is earning a financial return from your land?

2. How much do you recreate on your property?

3. What was growing close to the ground when the disaster occurred, and how much of it was there?

We'll tackle these questions in order. First off, the decision to salvage is typically economic. Trees burned in a fire or knocked over by a hurricane may still have financial value, but only for a short time.

Within a year or two they start to decay, and their lumber value declines. If financial gain from your land matters to you, getting loggers in to salvage quickly is important for getting the most money from the damaged trees.

But even if you're financially motivated, salvage logging might not be the right option. If your woods didn't have a lot of trees larger than 16 inches across, there might not be much value to salvage. Larger, straighter trees of high-value species bring the most money, but these trees take time to grow. If your woods are younger, they may not have much wood that would be worth a logger's time to remove. In these cases, salvaging could earn you no income, or even cost you, as the logger may charge you to haul away material.

Before salvaging, then, it's worth it to have some idea of what's out there. Consider hiring a forester to do a site visit and give you an opinion on whether there's anything worth salvaging.

Financial value aside, your recreational use of the property could motivate you to salvage it. A natural disaster can make your woods unsightly, difficult, and even dangerous to travel through. Knocked over trees block trails. Multiple stacked logs can shift and roll, trapping anyone walking on them. Dead standing trees or broken limbs can fall and kill.

If hiking, biking, or otherwise getting out on your land is something you or your family enjoy, salvaging after a disaster can be helpful. Even if it costs you money rather than paying you, it can reduce hazardous conditions and make your woods easier to navigate.

Money and recreation are human motivations. What about the woodlot itself? Does the land need a salvage cut after a disaster?

In the 1990s, a group of researchers at Harvard University simulated a hurricane in a Massachusetts woodland. They pulled down trees but didn't remove them from the site, and then they waited to see what would happen.

Sure enough, the woods returned. Seedlings shot up. The woodland was diverse with a mix of trees of many species, shapes, and sizes. The evidence was clear: salvage harvesting wasn't necessary for the woods to recover from a hurricane.[7]

Two decades later, Hurricane Sandy slammed into the Northeast. In some areas around New York City's Kensico Reservoir in Westchester County, the hurricane wiped out 90 percent of the trees that were helping to protect the water supply.

Unlike in Harvard's experiment, though, this time seedlings didn't take off. Instead, invasive weeds started taking over the site. To protect water quality, New York City foresters salvaged the fallen trees and replanted.[8]

These two examples, less than 200 miles apart, illustrate the complexity of salvage cutting and its effects on the woods. In some cases it's unnecessary. In others it's essential.

But why did these woodlands have such different results? The answer boils down to what was growing—or not growing—near the ground when the storm hit. In the case of the Harvard experiment, lots of baby trees were already established. When their simulated hurricane let in sunlight, those baby trees responded and grew.

In the New York City Watershed, we didn't have those baby trees. The ground was bare. When the canopy opened, the invasive weeds saw their chance and took it.

When considering whether to salvage, think about your land's ground cover. Do you have baby trees? If not, you may need to salvage to get some money and prepare the woods for tree planting. If you already have a good group of baby trees going, though, intervening won't necessarily help. You might be better off letting the fallen trees decay while a young forest grows up around them.

TRY THIS:
TRACK YOUR WOODLAND'S RECOVERY WITH PHOTO POINTS

Among my most vivid memories as a forester is my first hike through a recent wildfire site. It was in central Pennsylvania in 2008. I can still recall the crisp sound my boots made as I crunched over the blackened ground. The place looked like a lunar landscape, and it seemed impossible that anything would ever grow there again.

I've never had the opportunity to revisit those woods, but if I did, I'm sure they would look nothing like the burned husk I saw in 2008. They would be alive with new greenery. Given time, the woods remind us that while nature is fragile, it's resilient, too.

Still, it's hard to see that recovery with your own eyes, because forests change slowly. It's like watching your child grow. You don't realize she's getting so big, but your sister who only sees your daughter at Thanksgiving always comments on how much your little girl has grown.

You can get a better sense of how your woods are recovering from a disaster by establishing photo points. Find a few spots of the disaster area that you can reach safely in any season. Then at least once a year, head out there with a camera and take a picture. Try to take it from the same position every time you go. Ideally, set the camera on a fence post or other constant object so every photo covers an identical area.

As the months and years tick by, put all those photos together in the order you took them. You'll have a slideshow of your land's amazing ability to bounce back from the worst nature has to throw at it.

WATCH OUT!
SAFETY FIRST AFTER A DISASTER

Immediately after a disaster, you might be tempted to go out and survey the damage. You might even want to start cleaning up or clearing trails. Take extra care if you do either of these activities. The days right after a fire or storm are the most dangerous times to be in the woods (apart from being out in the disaster itself). It may be better to keep out of the woods for a while until things settle down.

If you do head out, leave the chainsaw at home. Trees that have been knocked over in a storm or fire can create especially hazardous conditions when you cut them. A windblown tree with its root mass sticking in the air, for instance, can become a death-trap if cut. When the weight of the tree is removed, the root mass can tip back into the hole it created when it fell. Anyone standing nearby can be crushed beneath the weight.

Spring poles are another hazard after a storm. These are small trees whose tops have been pressed down by a fallen larger tree. That extra weight puts tension on the small tree, and if you cut it, the tension can release with explosive force, causing injury or death when the tree falls.

It's best to leave uprooted trees and spring poles alone rather than cutting them. If they absolutely must be removed, hire a professional logger to take them away rather than doing it yourself.

It's tempting to go out and check the damage right after a storm, but it's better to keep out of the woods. Downed logs, snapped trunks, and suspended limbs like those in this post-Hurricane Sandy woodlot all create safety hazards. Photo credit: Brendan Murphy, Watershed Agricultural Council

CHAPTER 12

Chowing Down

But Natural Selection, as we shall hereafter see, is a power incessantly ready for action, and is as immeasurably superior to man's feeble efforts, as the works of Nature are to those of Art.
—Charles Darwin, *The Origin of Species*

I mentioned in a previous chapter that whenever I go in the woods, I wear a hat to keep the sun out of my eyes. But there's another reason why I put one on, even on the cloudiest days.

My supervisor at my first forestry job wanted to teach me about the effects insects can have on woodlands. To do that, she took me to a forest in western Pennsylvania that was under attack by gypsy moths.

Introduced to the United States more than a hundred years ago, gypsy moths can devastate forests, especially oak-dominated ones like many in Pennsylvania. The gypsy moth caterpillars eat tree leaves, and in large enough numbers the insects strip the trees bare. Most trees can survive one or two years of this defoliation, but after that, they exhaust their stored nutrients and die.

On this particular day, we walked from the truck to the woodland my boss had chosen. It was a beautiful early summer morning: clear, cloudless, but not yet hazy, hot, or humid. All the same, I knew it would warm up quickly, so I dressed light: T-shirt, khakis, and (it still makes me shudder) no hat.

As we entered the forest, I heard a strange sound, a constant yet chaotic pattering that filled the woods.

"Don't look up," was my boss's advice, "and if you do, keep your mouth shut."

OPPOSITE: Though smaller than a penny, the emerald ash borer is North America's most destructive forest pest since chestnut blight, killing millions of trees and threatening multiple species with extinction. It spreads primarily through the transport of infested wood, especially firewood. Photo credit: Dr. James E. Zablotny, USDA APHIS

I didn't understand. When you're young, you never understand. I think my boss knew this was going to be an experience her wide-eyed intern would never forget.

The pattering grew louder. It sounded like rain, not a drizzle but a steady downpour. Another member of our group whistled. "I've never heard this many. That's disgusting."

Being the wide-eyed intern, of course I had to ask. "What's going on?"

"They eat leaves," the man explained. I'm sure he was enjoying himself. "What goes in one end comes out the other. The scientific term is frass, but you'd know it better as . . ."

That was the moment I decided I would always wear a hat in the woods.

That day in a western Pennsylvania forest sticks in my head for more than the insect feces in my hair. In addition to our up-close-and-personal view, our group also saw some of the gypsy moths' impact from a distance. As we drove both to and from the site, we saw hillsides denuded of leaves. It was June, yet every tree looked as bare as if it were January.

I had never truly appreciated the power of invasive species prior to that day. The idea that an animal population could become so overpowering that it would literally rain excrement never entered my mind. Ever since, I've understood why these non-native critters, whether they're plants or insects or wild boars, are considered one of our woodlands' greatest threats.

"Invasive" is an appropriate term for these aggressive creatures. They spread quickly, produce a lot of offspring, and, because they're new to the woods, they usually have few if any predators or diseases to keep them in check. As a result they take over, killing native species and preventing the species' regrowth.

Woodlots are usually poorly equipped to handle invasive species, and, all too often, so are we. The same rapid spread that allows invasive species to devastate forests makes them notoriously difficult to control. When was the last time you saw a large, healthy American chestnut? I count myself lucky to have seen a single 16-inch-diameter chestnut once on a landowner's property. A hundred and fifty years ago, chestnut trees dominated eastern US forests, but now they're almost gone. An invasive fungus, the chestnut blight, wiped them out. People did their best to stop the blight's spread, but they couldn't do it.

This story repeats itself with other invasive forest pests. Dutch elm disease all but exterminated the American elm. More recently, emerald ash borer has defied all efforts at containment, spreading across much of the United States and southern Canada within twenty years of arriving on our shores.

No matter where your woods are, invasives are a reality your land faces. The Center for Invasive Species and Ecosystem Health reports that North America has more than 2,900 invasive species.[1] Different states have different pests, but there is no place in the country that is free of them. Every US county has at least three invasive forest pests, and many counties—particularly in the Northeast and West Coast—have far more than that.[2]

So what do you do? In previous chapters I've been upbeat about your chances of handling challenges like taxes, timber theft, and even wildfire. There are things you can do to reduce all these problems.

It's much harder to maintain that optimism in the case of invasives. The dirty secret among environmental professionals is that we have no idea how to control, let alone stop, most invasive species. To be sure, some hardworking folks have come up with a few techniques, but rarely are these methods practical, affordable, and effective tools landowners like you can use.

As with timber theft, then, your best option is prevention: doing what you can to keep invasives off your property. Once they arrive, your options quickly dwindle even as they skyrocket in cost.

That said, having invasives on your property isn't necessarily a death sentence for your woods. Today the hillsides I saw denuded by gypsy moth have new growth on the forest floor. The gypsy moth population, like many other leaf-eating insects, cycles between boom and bust. Huge gatherings of moths eat all the available food in an area and then starve. That cycling gives the woods time to recover.

Your woodlot can be healthy even in the face of attack from pests and disease. In fact, some level of infestation can actually benefit your land.

What Is a "Healthy" Woodland Anyway?

What does the word "health" mean to you? Webster's dictionary defines it as "being well or free from disease." The World Health Organization goes a step further, saying that health "is a state of complete physical, mental, and social well-being and not merely the absence of disease or infirmity."[3]

In both these definitions, part of health is lacking disease. If you have a cold, you aren't healthy.

It's easy to apply these definitions to our woodlots. If we have insects or fungi killing our trees, then our woods aren't healthy.

But woods and people are different. Your woodlot can be healthy and still have pests and diseases. These infestations can even be beneficial. They help clear out poorer growing trees to give the better-adapted ones room to expand. They create standing dead trees and fallen logs that provide food and shelter for wildlife. And they make openings in the canopy that let the next generation of trees sprout and eventually renew the forest.

It's OK to have dead trees in your woods. The issue comes when insect or disease populations get out of control, or in the case of invasives, when they lack checks on their growth. Then the level of tree death can surpass what the woods would normally experience, and your woodlot's health suffers.

TRY THIS:
GIVE YOUR WOODS A CHECKUP

When you go for a checkup, your doctor takes measurements. From numbers like your blood pressure, weight, and cholesterol, your doctor gets a picture of your overall health.

Doctors train for years to learn how to interpret a person's health, but you can get a good idea of your woodlot's health with a simple walk. Like a doctor, you'll look for indicators that your woods are in good or poor health:

1. **Signs of disease or damage to trees**—Look for damage to different tree parts, like burls or wounds on the bark. Leaves that change color or fall out of season also indicate stress in your woods. Seeing a little of this damage is OK, but if you're seeing it all over the place, that indicates poor health.

2. **Different species and ages of trees**—Look for trees with different leaf shapes and bark patterns, and look for trees of various sizes, both in height and width. This diversity is a good sign of health.

3. **Lichen**—Lichen on tree trunks indicates good air quality and woodlot health. It won't damage the tree, so it's OK to leave it alone.

4. **Soil creatures**—This one requires you to get your hands dirty. Dig some holes in your woodlot's soil, or turn over some fallen logs. Seeing insects is good for your woodlot, as they help break down decaying plants and return nutrients to the soil.

5. **Baby trees**—Look for young trees ranging from a few inches to several feet tall. Having a lot of these small trees is good for woodlot health.

6. **Standing dead trees and fallen logs**—We've talked already about how valuable a few dead trees can be for your woods, so it's a mark in your land's favor if you have some.

7. **Many kinds of wildlife**—If your woods are doing well, they'll also support a wide variety of critters. Look and listen for birds, mammals, reptiles, amphibians, and insects.

If your land is missing most of the good health indicators, that suggests your woods are under stress and more vulnerable to pests, diseases, and natural disasters.

Slow the Spread: Don't Move Firewood

Of the many invasive species that threaten today's woodlands, the emerald ash borer has risen above the rest to become North America's most destructive forest pest since chestnut blight. It's a wood-boring insect, and it only attacks one kind of tree: ash. White ash is the most well-known; its light yet strong wood is favored for baseball bats. Other ash species, though, like green ash, are equally vulnerable.

The emerald ash borer doesn't kill trees by eating their leaves. Instead, it's a wood-boring insect, and its larvae grow inside the tree, under the bark. There they eat the tubes that transport nutrients throughout the tree. Eventually, the borers sever all these tubes and the tree starves to death.

Even healthy ash trees have no resistance to the emerald ash borer. In areas of high beetle concentration, more than 99 percent of infested trees have died.[4] Once attacked, an ash tree can die in as little as one to three years.

What makes the emerald ash borer so devastating, though, is how quickly it spreads. Introduced in the 1990s via shipping containers in Michigan, the borer needed just twenty years to spread to half the states in the country. As of 2015, it ranged from New Hampshire to Colorado and from the Canadian border to the Gulf of Mexico.

Emerald ash borer managed this remarkable spread thanks not to its own efforts, but to human carelessness. Individual borers only range a few miles in their lifetime. By itself, the borer would have needed centuries to cross the thousands of miles of territory it now affects. But it had a helping hand, thanks to the wood, particularly firewood, that we are always moving across the country.

Like other wood-boring insects, the emerald ash borer hides out inside the tree. When someone cuts down an infested tree and chops it up for firewood, the borers remain inside. Not realizing the wood is infested, the person moves the firewood to another location for future burning. Before the winter heating season, though, the beetles emerge into a new location, ripe for conquest.

The consequences of this movement have already proven extreme. Millions of ash trees have died, and millions more are on their way there. There is real concern that multiple ash species could go extinct in the coming decades due to this one insect.

By the time emerald ash borer arrives on your land, it's too late to do anything. You're better off limiting its ability to spread to your area, and the best way to do that is to simply not move firewood. If you cut firewood on your woodland, burn it there. Don't take it back with you to your home in the city or to another camp. Similarly, don't transport firewood from your home in the city to your land.

Some states have passed laws that either ban the movement of firewood outright or restrict the range in which you can transport it. In my state of New York, it's illegal to transport firewood more than 50 miles from where it was cut.

Densely packed trees like these have a hard time fighting back against insect and disease attacks. Each tree only has access to a little light, water, and nutrients, so they're more stressed than they need to be. Thinning a woodland like this one would help the remaining trees expand their canopies and become healthier. At the same time, it would help new growth sprout on the forest floor to encourage more wildlife to use the woods. Photo credit: Brendan Murphy, Watershed Agricultural Council

There are exceptions to these rules, but they require treating the firewood or other wood products to remove invasive pests. In general, you as a landowner won't be able to meet these requirements. They require specialized equipment, like kilns that can heat the wood to a hot enough temperature to kill any stowaways.

Protecting Your Woods from Pests through Thinning

Forest pests and diseases can kill trees, but with the exception of the emerald ash borer, most don't guarantee death. Often they'll slow a tree's growth or deform it in some way, but they're rarely lethal on their own.

That said, infestations are one more source of stress to your trees, and just like a person, trees can only handle so much. They might withstand the occasional gypsy moth defoliation or bark beetle attack, but when added on top of drought or poor access to sunlight, a pest's arrival can be enough to cause the tree to die.

To give your woods the best chance of surviving pests, make sure your trees are as healthy as possible. They should receive adequate light and moisture without having to compete too much with one another.

As with fire, thinning woodlots in advance of an infestation can reduce the odds of successful pest attack. By giving trees plenty of room to expand and develop large, full crowns, they'll be less stressed and in better shape to fight off threats.

Also, as with fire, this thinning isn't about getting the most money for your trees. Rather, it's about removing trees that are already stressed and in poor health. In effect, you're anticipating those trees' natural deaths and putting their wood to use while creating growing space for healthier trees better suited for your land.

Treatment Options

I include this section reluctantly because, as I've said, there's little you can do to stop invasive pests once they reach your land. It's too late to start thinning after they arrive. As for direct control methods, most are only practical for protecting a handful of trees. Applied to the scale of even a few acres, the cost becomes astronomical.

For most tree pests, insecticides are the only effective option. These are typically applied to the specific trees you want to protect rather than over large areas. Depending on the tree and the insect you want to control, the chemical might either be applied in a spray around the tree's base or injected into the trunk itself.

Individual insecticide applications can cost hundreds of dollars, though the price depends on the product used. Often they require professional assistance from an arborist to ensure the tree receives

WATCH OUT!
PREEMPTIVE CUTTING

As invasive species like the emerald ash borer approach your land, the decision about what to do with your trees becomes ever more complicated. Do you harvest ahead of a pest's arrival, capturing income while you can? Or do you wait, letting the trees grow while knowing an invader could swoop in and take them out?

The answer seems obvious. If the trees are going to die anyway, you might as well cut them and get what value you can from them.

Take care, though, in making that decision. Invasive pests spread erratically, and once they're in an area, it can take a while for their populations to build. Moreover, the interactions between an invasive creature and its host tree are often poorly understood. Even though it might seem like the native tree has little to no resistance to the invading pest, there's always a chance that a few trees could have the right mix of genetics to fight back. If you cut preemptively, you could wind up removing trees that might have survived the threat.

This urge towards logging doomed the American chestnut. As chestnut blight spread in the early 1900s, landowners across the country raced to cut their trees before the blight took them. It made them some short-term money, but it also caused chestnuts that could have resisted the blight to get cut down. Had those resistant trees been left alone, they would have survived and spread seeds that probably also would have had blight resistance. In time, the chestnut might have recovered and rendered the blight a non-issue, but our hasty actions ensured that we would have almost no large chestnuts in America even a century later.

Unless your only objective in owning land is to earn as much money as possible, it's best not to preemptively cut in the face of an approaching invasive. Rather, continue caring for your woodlot following the six rules in Chapter 2, focusing on diversity and keeping your trees as healthy and unstressed as possible. The healthier individual trees are, the better their chances at resisting a new threat.

enough insecticide to kill the pest but not so much that it harms the broader environment.

Insecticide treatments won't last forever. Depending on the species you want to control, some insecticides will only work for two or three years. The emerald ash borer falls into this category. Against other species, a treatment may last longer, but eventually you will need to reapply the chemical.

Because of the many costs and complications involved, the first step in treating your trees is to identify the ones you absolutely want to save. Focus on large, healthy trees that either enhance your view or that would be dangerous if they died. These will likely be yard or street trees rather than trees deeper in your woods.

There's a lot of debate among professionals about whether to treat trees with chemicals like this. Some argue that despite the costs, treating trees is cheaper than removing them, particularly when they're close to obstacles like power lines. Once ash trees die, for example, they're expensive to remove because they quickly become unsafe for an arborist to climb. If you elect to remove trees rather than treat them, it's best to remove them after they show signs of infestation but before they die.

I believe the insecticide option just isn't practical for most landowners. Environmental impact aside, it's a temporary fix to an ongoing problem. At best, I see treatment as a way of spreading out when your trees become infested. Instead of them all dying at once, only a few will die at a time, which means you won't have to bear the cost of removing them all in one year.

That said, if you have a few ash trees of great sentimental value, limited chemical treatment is probably the only way to save them. In these cases, I recommend that you hire an arborist to check out your specific situation and determine what will work best for you and your trees.

CHAPTER 13

Timber!

Then he'd yell "Timber!" and down she'd fall . . . for Paul.
—Shel Silverstein, "Paul Bunyan"

While there are lots of ways to earn some money from your land, the most common is through timber harvesting. A landowner receives money from a logger or sawmill in exchange for the right to cut and remove certain trees.

It's a popular misconception that "logging" is equal to "clear-cutting," but from reading other chapters in this book, I hope you've come to see that there are ways you can log your woods and keep them wooded too. More important, as we've discussed in chapters like those on wildlife and fire control, a well-planned, well-executed timber harvest can benefit not only your wallet but the land as well.

Even so, unless you own a lot of land, a timber harvest is something you'll rarely do. Here in New York, I usually recommend waiting ten to fif-

teen years between logging the same area to give the woodlot time to grow. With a decade or more between cuts, logging may well be a once-in-a-lifetime experience for you. It's worth taking your time and getting it right.

Whether you want to manage intensively for profit, do a single light cut to create some wildlife habitat, or anything in between, the same harvesting process applies. There's always the possibility something could go wrong, but by following the six steps in this chapter, you'll avoid the worst problems and be prepared to deal with unexpected situations.

Step 0: Planning

While a good timber harvest has six steps, there's a seventh step that needs to happen before you even start on the cut itself. You need a plan.

OPPOSITE: *Long before this guy arrives in your woods, plan ahead so you get the best job possible.*

TRY THIS:
GET ON-THE-GROUND ADVICE

It's great to say that you should take your time and do a timber harvest right, but how do you know if your land can even support a harvest in the first place? How do you find out if the wood out there has any value in it? Differences in tree species, size, and quality as well as operational issues like distance to a road and the number of stream crossings all impact how much—if anything—your timber is worth.

Before jumping into a timber harvest, consider bringing in someone to look at your woods and advise you on next steps. A private consulting forester, for instance, will know the most about local timber markets and be able to give you a good idea of whether your woods are ready for a harvest or not.

For an initial assessment, though, a private forester may not be the best choice (and I'm saying this as a forester). While many foresters will give you unbiased advice, most of them also make their living off the commissions on timber sales. Some may look for a way to make a timber sale "work," even if the actual best course would be to wait another five or ten years.

Rather than a private forester, choose either a government service forester or a knowledgeable landowner for your initial assessment. You won't get the detailed estimates that a private forester could provide, but you can at least get a basic yes/no on whether to proceed. If they indicate a timber sale could make sense, then you can bring in a private forester.

If you want advice from a service forester, start at the county or state level. Many counties have a forester on staff who will visit landowners. In other cases, your state's Department of Natural Resources or similar agency will have service foresters on staff. Unfortunately, there aren't a lot of these folks to go around, so you may find that you have to wait a while before one of them can visit your property.

Another way to get advice is to talk to a longtime landowner. There are some excellent training programs out there to help landowners teach other landowners. Cornell Cooperative Extension runs a program in New York called Master Forest Owner. The program provides educational classes for landowners, who then go out and do free site visits on other owners' land. Getting a visit from one of these owners is a wonderful, low-pressure way to find out more about your woods without involving a forester.

To find out if your state has a program such as Master Forest Owner, check with your local cooperative extension office or state woodland owner association. Even if your state doesn't have a formal program, these offices may know of knowledgeable landowners who would be willing to visit your property and give you their assessment.

I'm not talking about a formal management plan like the kind you would use to apply for a tax reduction program. Something like that can work, but it's often overkill if harvesting timber is something you only do once a decade.

The plan I'm referring to is more immediate. It considers the current harvest, what you want to get out of it—both for your wallet and your woods—and how it will be carried out. Here are some basic questions to answer:

1. Why are you harvesting timber? What do you hope to gain by doing so?

2. How much money are you hoping to raise? If you're doing a cut for wildlife or fire control, are you OK with earning no money or even paying a logger to do the work?

3. What parts of your land will be harvested?

4. How will loggers access the trees that will be removed?

5. Where will loggers load their trucks with logs?

6. What major obstacles, such as cliffs, wetlands, and streams, will the loggers need to work around?

7. What state or local permits will you or your logger need in order for work to take place?

8. What do you want your woods to look like after the loggers leave? How about fifteen years from now?

It's all right if you can't answer these questions by yourself. In fact, you shouldn't expect yourself to. They make the first step in the six-step process all the more necessary.

Step 1: Hire a Forester

Few of us would build a home without an architect, sell a house without a real estate agent, or go to court without a lawyer. These professionals have detailed knowledge of their fields, and that experience allows them to advise us on how to navigate otherwise complex processes.

Timber harvesting is the same way. In many states you don't have to work with a forester when you log. Many landowners choose not to because they don't want to pay someone they view as a middleman. But while I'm admittedly biased as a forester myself, I firmly believe that the best timber harvests require a forester.

A forester is more than your guide to the complicated world of timber harvesting. Good foresters have contacts with loggers and will be able to point you to a reputable person. They have similar knowledge of sawmills and other log buyers, which can help get your timber sale out to as many potential customers as possible. They have insight into how woodlands work and can help you identify which trees to cut to achieve your goals, whether those goals are financial, environmental, or aesthetic. Finally, a forester is your boots-on-the-ground advocate, overseeing the harvest and ensuring the loggers are completing the work in a way that protects the woods.

Foresters charge a fee to help clients with a timber sale. The ways they calculate their fees differ, with some charging an hourly rate while others charge per acre. The most common method, though, is a percentage of the final sale price of the timber, with 15 percent standard. That might sound like a lot of money, but good foresters will more than pay for themselves with more and better bids for your timber, not to mention all the other benefits in the last paragraph.

When you hire a forester, shop around. Different foresters focus on different things. Some are great for maximizing profit, but they're less concerned about the land itself. I tend to avoid foresters like that. Others focus on the woods and ignore the financial value. These foresters are great if you aren't concerned about money, but they may have trouble attracting loggers to do your job if there are more lucrative opportunities elsewhere. Still more foresters strike a balance between these extremes, sacrificing some valuable trees in exchange for getting the work you want accomplished done. Who the right fit is for you depends on your personality and your goals for your woods.

Some states require foresters to have a license, but most don't. That means it's on you to separate the pros from the fly-by-nighters. Here, your best weapons are credentials and references. Check with local or state landowner groups to see which foresters they recommend. Talk to your neighbors and see who they used and how they felt about the job afterward. Finally, look for foresters who are members of a professional society such as the Society of American Foresters, the Association of Consulting Foresters, or the Forest Guild.

Once you've chosen your forester, talk to them about the questions I posed in Step 0. If there were any you couldn't answer on your own, now's the time to figure them out with the professional's help.

Step 2: Mark Your Timber

Your discussions with your forester will help you figure out which trees to cut to meet your goals. The next step is to indicate those trees in the woods. Your forester will likely do this step as part of their duties.

Having your timber marked gives both you and your eventual buyer several advantages. The biggest one is that everyone knows which trees will be cut. When you walk the property, you'll know your forester is carrying out the plan the two of you discussed. In turn, potential buyers will know how much wood is available and can use that knowledge to offer a fair price.

Marking your timber also guards against timber theft. A forester will typically mark the trees with paint at both eye level and at the base. This way, either you or your forester can walk the job and quickly see if any unmarked trees have been cut. Insist on this double-marking from your forester.

Step 3: Bid Out the Sale

With your timber marked, it's time for the exciting part: finding a buyer. There are lots of ways to get one, but the most profitable for landowners is the bid sale. In a bid sale, multiple loggers and sawmills submit sealed bids for the amount they'll pay for the timber. The winning buyer then pays you in one lump sum before any cutting starts.

The bid sale gets you more money than other methods because it forces buyers to compete with one another and offer higher bids. How much higher? In one Massachusetts study, researchers examined the bids from more than 160 timber sales. They found that high bids averaged more than double low bids for the same timber.[4] If you don't shop around, you won't get the best deal.

Aside from the higher payments, bid sales also guarantee that you get paid for your trees, because you get your money up front. Rather than being based on a lump sum bid, some timber sales are paid based on a tally of logs as they come to the sawmill. That means you get money in several smaller amounts as the job progresses. This approach can lead to problems, because you may not get paid quickly even though your trees have been cut. In a worst-case scenario, unscrupulous loggers or mills will misreport the volume of wood coming off your land and pay you less than your trees are worth.

You should also avoid "percentage" sales, where you split the mill proceeds with a logger. As with the tally system, it's too easy for loggers to misrepresent what volume they're removing and how much the mill is paying them. It's better to have the lump sum payment up front and then let the mill figure out what it will pay the logger to do the work.

When your forester bids out your sale, part of the process includes a tour of the site. Potential buyers will visit your property, walk through the sale, and examine the marked trees. This step is

WATCH OUT!
HIGH-GRADING AND
DIAMETER-LIMIT CUTTING

Another advantage to having your timber marked is that it helps you to avoid two of the worst timber-cutting practices: high-grading and diameter-limit cutting. These unfortunately common logging techniques provide short-term income, but they can have disastrous long-term consequences for both your finances and your woodland.

Both high-grading and diameter-limit cutting remove the largest, straightest, most economically valuable trees from a woodlot. In diameter-limit cutting, loggers remove all trees above a certain width. With high-grading, no diameter is specified, but loggers focus on species and trees that yield the most money.

That might sound great at first, especially compared with the thinning techniques I mentioned in previous chapters that can require you to pay the logger. In the long term, though, both high-grading and diameter-limit cutting degrade your woodlot. By removing the biggest trees from your woods, these practices take away the trees that have the best potential for future growth and additional value. One forester I know grimly describes high-grading as "shooting the horse that wins the race."

Some loggers (and unscrupulous foresters) will try to fool you with the logic that "cutting the big trees will give the smaller ones room to grow." Don't fall for it. Smaller trees are smaller for a reason, and usually it isn't because of age. They may have a disease or a weak genetic makeup, or they may simply be of a species poorly suited to your property. As a result, even though they're just as old as your bigger trees, they can't grow as quickly. Cutting the bigger trees will speed up the growth of these smaller ones, but they'll never match the pace of the larger trees you removed.

By contrast, the larger trees will respond to thinning, and to a much greater extent. Even though it's an initial investment to remove the poorer-growing trees, in the long run you'll actually make more money.

Science has demonstrated this fact. A researcher at the State University of New York compared how much wood came off woodlots that were high-graded versus those that focused on promoting growth in the best trees. Over multiple sales, the high-graded forests gradually produced less and less timber, while those that were cut with an eye toward the long term produced more. Eventually, the high-graded woodlots couldn't sustain more cutting, while those focused on promoting the best trees continued to produce quality harvestable timber on a regular basis.[2]

It isn't just the amount of wood produced that suffers. By removing the best-adapted trees, high-grading leaves you with an inferior seed source, which means your next generation of trees won't grow as well. And because high-grading removes the most valuable species, your land will gradually become dominated by trees of poor commercial value.

Put together, the long-term financial drain from diameter-limit cutting and high-grading adds up to thousands of dollars per acre. The same State University of New York researcher found that, starting with identical woodlots, harvesting for the long term yielded $9,200 per acre more than high-grading after forty-five years. Even after only fifteen years, the difference was more than $2,000 per acre.[3]

High-grading and diameter-limit cutting aren't just poor financial decisions. They're poor environmental ones too. Because they selectively remove certain species, they make your land less diverse. In addition, some of the highest-value species like oak and cherry are also important wildlife food sources, meaning your woods will support fewer animals if your logger preferentially cuts these species.

Rather than removing your best trees right away, focus your early cuttings on poorer quality trees so your better ones can grow bigger and faster. Even though it means an initial sale with little income or even a cost, it's worth investing in your trees for the long term. By the time future cuts come around, you'll earn far more money and still be protecting your land.

crucial, as buyers will determine how much they're willing to pay you based on what they see during this visit.

As part of this step, you and your forester should develop a written prospectus to give potential buyers. The prospectus outlines your expectations for the sale, such as which trees will be sold, any requirements you have for the harvest, and how payment will occur. The prospectus will also prove useful in the next step, when you finally sign on the dotted line.

Step 4: Get a Written Timber Sale Contract

Buyers have visited your woods. They've read your prospectus. Bids have arrived, and the highest one is attractive. That's great! You're well on your way to a good harvest.

Before you rush off and let the buyer start cutting, though, hold on. Remember that a harvest is a big change in your woods, and you want to get the best job possible. To get that, it's important for

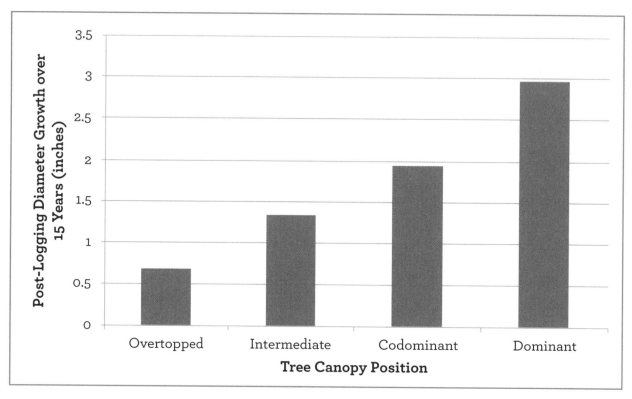

If a forester or logger tries to sell you on high-grading by telling you you're leaving room for small trees to grow, don't believe him or her. Smaller trees won't respond to more light and space nearly as well as bigger ones. Researchers at the State University of New York and the Forest Service studied how sugar maples of various canopy positions responded to thinning over fifteen years. They found that the biggest trees (those in the "dominant" canopy position) grew almost 3 inches wider over fifteen years with more room to grow, while smaller ones (those in "overtopped" or "intermediate" positions) added less than half that much.[1]

everyone to know each other's expectations for what should happen. The way to do that is to make a contract.

I can hear many of you groan at the mere mention of that word. But while contracts bring up images of lawyers and legalese, the fact remains that they are the best way to make sure everyone knows what's going on with a harvest and what to do if something goes wrong.

You don't have to be a legal expert to have a decent timber sale contract. Many foresters have template contracts they've developed over the years, and there are others online: I've linked to one in "Beyond the Book." If you followed my advice and created a prospectus when you bid out your sale, you can easily adapt it into a contract.

Depending on your situation, your contract may call for special wording or clauses to address unique circumstances. In general, though, any good timber sale contract will include the following:

- **Who's involved**: Information about the buyer, seller, and anyone else connected with the sale, like your forester.
- **Property description**: Where the cut will take place, how trees are marked, and how property boundaries are indicated. This section also usually includes a map showing the harvest area, access system, and any buffers.
- **Timber description**: Tables of species, sizes, and volumes that will be removed. Your forester can calculate this information based on the trees marked for sale.
- **Proof of ownership/Seller's declaration**: The sale of timber that isn't yours happens more often than you'd think. The most common instance is where a landowner sells his or her timber to one mill and then tries to sell it to another. The seller's declaration confirms that you have ownership of the timber and can sell it to the buyer.
- **Price and method of payment**: How much money the buyer is giving you and under what terms.
- **Easement clause**: Not to be confused with a conservation easement (which we'll talk about in a future chapter), the easement clause gives the buyer temporary permission to access your property to remove the timber.
- **A time limit**: You don't want a harvest dragging on for years and years. A typical maximum is one year with an option to extend for a second year. After that time, any uncut trees revert to your ownership.
- **Indemnification**: This is a legal term for waiving your liability due to the actions of others. For example, if a logger gets hurt on the land in your sale, the indemnification clause reduces the chance that the logger could sue you. Indemnification clauses are sometimes called "hold harmless" clauses because they read something like "The seller will be held harmless in the event of . . ."
- **Insurance requirements**: Loggers working on your property should have liability and workers' compensation insurance. If they don't, and there's an accident, the liability could fall back on you, regardless of whether there's an indemnification clause.
- **Regulation clause**: A line stating that the buyer agrees to obey all applicable federal, state, and local laws during the harvest. This clause also commonly states that it's the buyer's responsibility to obtain any necessary permits for the cut. Having this line is essential because you, as the landowner, are liable for environmental damage that occurs on your property, even if it's caused by a logger.

- **Arbitration clause**: If the worst happens, the arbitration clause explains the process for resolving disputes. It's usually the last clause in a sale contract.

In addition to these must-haves, there are some nice-to-haves you can negotiate with your timber buyer. Keep in mind that the more conditions you put in your contract, the more expensive the harvest will be for the buyer. They may offer you a lower price or even abandon the sale altogether if your demands are too severe. Discuss your needs with your forester to decide which of these extras are worth the cost.

- **Notification**: A requirement that the buyer has to notify you whenever they send someone to your property.
- **Performance bond**: This isn't required, but I strongly recommend it. A performance bond is like a security deposit on an apartment. The buyer gives you an amount of money that you hold in reserve to ensure a good job. If the buyer upholds the contract requirements, they get the bond back when logging finishes. Otherwise, you keep it as a way to help pay for damage done to your property. The size of this bond depends on how sensitive your site is to disturbance and how large the sale is. Discuss an appropriate amount with your forester.
- **Aesthetic clauses**: Stipulations about buffers, lopping tops, and other aesthetic concerns should be made clear in the contract.

- **Release clause**: Gives either the buyer or the seller the ability to withdraw from the contract given certain circumstances. Most commonly, a release clause lets you withdraw from the contract if the buyer isn't fulfilling his or her obligations.
- **Reservation clause**: Gives you access to the property while the harvest is going on. This is important if you want to periodically check on the job.
- **No subcontracting**: Stipulates that the buyer can't subcontract out parts of the harvest without your permission.
- **Fire clause**: The buyer assumes the risk that a natural disaster might occur during the timber sale, along with potential damage costs, and they aren't repaid by the landowner if the timber is destroyed.
- **Environmental needs**: I struggled with how to classify these. Your contract absolutely should include stipulations to protect the environment, such as requirements that loggers install Best Management Practices; avoid seasons when the ground is especially wet (like early spring); and restore roads, driveways, and log loading areas. But there's a lot of leeway to how general or specific you want your environmental stipulations to be, so I put them here under the optional items. As with aesthetics, it's important to be upfront with the logger about your expectations for protecting the land during and after logging.

I realize this is a lot to throw at you, but remember that your forester will have worked with most of these contract terms before. They can counsel you on which ones you need and which are overkill for your situation.

Step 5: Supervise the Harvest

Finally, after all that work, it's time to start cutting. When the crew arrives, arrange for a pre-harvest meeting between them and your forester (and you, if you're available). Often loggers are subcontractors rather than sawmill employees, so they may not know all the details that went into your sale contract. A pre-harvest meeting can ensure that everyone is on the same page.

Once logging starts, your forester should visit the site at least once a week at random times to check that the harvest is going according to the contract. If possible, you should check in now and then, too. It might seem like you're being a pain, but it shows the logger you care about the job and will motivate better work. More important, it gives you the chance to spot problems like timber theft quickly. If you see something that concerns you, bring it to your forester's attention right away.

As a safety precaution, always wear a hardhat when visiting an active timber harvest. Trees and limbs may be falling, and loggers likely won't hear you over chainsaws and other machinery. Make sure the loggers know where you are at all times, and keep your distance from loggers felling trees or pulling logs out of the woods.

Step 6: Clean Up Afterward

Once tree cutting finishes, your loggers aren't done. The time right after logging is also the time your land is most at risk of erosion, because places like your dirt roads and trails are exposed and unprotected. Before loggers leave the site, make sure they fulfill the clean-up responsibilities in your contract and install Best Management Practices.

As soon as possible after BMPs go in, do a final walkthrough of the harvest with your forester. Between the two of you, identify any problems that need addressing. Once the land is restored according to your contract, you can return the performance bond to whoever paid it.

A note of caution on inspecting your land after a harvest: as I mentioned in the chapter on water quality, many BMPs need time to firm up before they can handle vehicle traffic. Make your initial post logging visit on foot rather than on an ATV, and keep any vehicles off your trails for at least three months after logging finishes.

WATCH OUT!
LOGGING EQUIPMENT TYPES

Loggers come in all shapes and sizes, and so does the equipment they use. Some loggers will cut trees with a chainsaw; others have half-million-dollar machines called harvesters that cut, delimb, stack, and sort logs all in one go. Some loggers still use traditional animal power, particularly horses, to drag logs from the woods a few at a time. Others rely on bulldozer-sized machines called skidders. Still more loggers load the logs onto a mini-log truck called a forwarder that can carry out logs without dragging them along the ground.

The type of equipment that will work best on your property depends on your land's size and steepness. Steeper terrain may limit which machines can operate safely. Top-heavy forwarders, for instance, are limited to flatter slopes.

Some landowners, wanting a more natural approach, will favor horse loggers over those with machinery. While that sounds great in theory, in practice it doesn't always work out well. Horse logging is a lot slower than using machines, so loggers frequently can only make money removing the most valuable trees. That leads to high-grading. A slow harvest also leaves your trails exposed longer, meaning there's a greater chance for erosion to wash sediment into streams.

Besides speeding up the harvest, modern equipment gives loggers greater control in the woods. Loggers felling trees with a harvester rather than a chainsaw have a lot more influence over where the tree lands. That reduces damage to other trees that will remain standing. In addition, that control—and the reinforced cabin—provide greater safety for the logger, contrasted with cutting with a chainsaw, which leaves the logger more exposed.

Offering greater speed, control, and safety than chainsaw-felling, harvesting equipment like this feller-buncher works well in harvests that take some trees while leaving others. It can guide trees as they fall to limit damage to those left standing.

CHAPTER 14

Farm the Forest

Far better it is to dare mighty things, to win glorious triumphs, even though checkered by failure, than to rank with those timid spirits who neither enjoy nor suffer much because they live in the gray twilight that knows neither victory nor defeat.
—Theodore Roosevelt

We're getting far into this book, and you may have noticed that the further we go, the more complicated the topics I'm discussing are. It's one thing to go on a hike and enjoy the scenery, but it's quite another to make big changes like a timber harvest.

That's why I chose President Roosevelt's quotation to start this chapter. As we move into these last few chapters, we'll be hitting increasingly complex projects that will require a good bit of time, effort, and sometimes money on your part. Often they'll require specialized knowledge, and failure will always be a possibility.

It's easy to run from these projects because of their difficulty, but I encourage you to approach them with an open mind and a willingness, as Roosevelt put it, "to dare mighty things." Because while these topics are complicated, the rewards of success are great. Not only do they offer future benefits for you and your land, but they connect you and your family with your property in deep and powerful ways.

OPPOSITE: *American ginseng rarely grows more than a few inches tall, but its complex roots with traditional medicinal properties yield high prices and have an almost unlimited market in Asia.* Photo credit: Dan Pittillo, USFWS

FOODS	MEDICINAL HERBS	DECORATIVES	CRAFTS
Berries (blackberries, raspberries, elderberries, serviceberries, and huckleberries)	Ginseng	Rhododendron	Fallen pine needles
Mushrooms	Mayapple	Highbush cranberry	Willow twigs
Pawpaw	Saw palmetto	Flowering dogwood	Vines
Currants	Goldenseal	Ferns	Pine cones
Leeks	Bloodroot	Moss	Bark
Nuts (black walnuts, hazelnuts, hickory nuts)	Pacific yew		

Examples of native US woodland plants with established local or regional markets, according to the USDA's National Agroforestry Center.[1]

Blending Farm and Forest

We usually think of farms and forests as separate places, but the reality isn't so black and white. While woodlands' steeper slopes and thinner soils won't support conventional farming, they might handle a lighter touch that grows a more limited amount. And while shade will prevent most common farm crops from surviving, certain specialty crops can flourish beneath a wooded canopy. With proper site selection and care, the woods can provide food, medicine, and even art supplies, all without damaging the forest.

If that sounds impossible, just look to America's past. Many Native Americans sustained themselves with food grown, foraged, and hunted among the trees.

Today, there are dozens of farmable forest crops. The US Department of Agriculture's National Agroforestry Center lists more than 30 native woodland plants across the country that have local or regional markets. Your options for which ones you might grow, harvest, and sell are limited only by your property's location and your willingness to invest time and energy into it.

WATCH OUT!
FORAGING

More and more outdoor enthusiasts are getting into foraging—seeking out edible plants and fungi in the woods. When I hike the woods here in upstate New York during summer, I'm always on the look-out for wild raspberry and blackberry bushes. I can't get enough of their sweet fruits, and not even the blackberry's notorious thorns will slow me down for long.

To be sure, US woodlands harbor many species that are safe to eat. On the other hand, there are also many species that can be harmful or even fatal if consumed. Mushrooms in particular fall into this category. The line I've often heard from mushroom experts is that when it comes to eating wild mushrooms, "If you're wrong, you're dead."

Wild foraging isn't for the uninitiated land-owner. In general, I recommend against the practice.

If you're committed to dining from the woods, be safe about it. Before you ever eat anything wild, make sure you've identified it correctly. Check with local experts to confirm your find, and don't rely solely on field guides or online videos. There are a lot of look-alike plants and fungi out there, so it's easy to get mixed up.

Also respect the woods when foraging. If you harvest all the edible plants in an area, nothing will be left to reproduce, which means you won't be able to get more in future years. A good rule of thumb is to remove no more than a quarter of what's growing to ensure the plant's long-term survival.

With so many options to choose from, there's no way to hit them all in one chapter. Instead I'll talk about three. Then, in "Beyond the Book," I've provided links to resources that will give you more detail about other options.

If the idea of farming on your woodland seems intimidating, or if you feel like you would never have the time to do it, that's understandable. Even so, don't let that deter you from trying some of the techniques we'll talk about. You don't have to go big to start woods farming. Many landowners only grow and harvest enough for their own use. In other cases they might have a small surplus that they give away or sell to friends. Going big is your best bet if you want to earn a profit, but there are ways to test out different crops with little investment and decide what works for you.

Accept No Substitutes: Maple Syrup

When I was living in my first apartment and scraping by from paycheck to paycheck, I allowed myself one indulgence: I always used real, 100 percent pure maple syrup. There's a big difference in cost with that choice. While the artificial stuff sells for $2 or $3 a quart, the same amount of real maple syrup will run you closer to $15 or $20.

But for me, the phonies (often made from high fructose corn syrup) just don't cut it. For all the chemical knowledge the food industry has, no one has ever replicated the flavor of real maple syrup.

There's something magical about it too. The idea that you can take sap from a tree, boil it down, and turn it into something delicious frankly amazes me. Even more incredibly, people have been doing it for centuries, long before Columbus arrived in the Western Hemisphere.

If you live in the northeastern United States, you too can produce maple syrup. You don't need a lot of equipment, and you don't even need much land. In fact, a single yard tree can be enough to meet your personal syrup needs.

The two hardest parts of maple syrup production are having the right trees and the right climate. While multiple maple species can produce syrup, sugar maple is the traditional powerhouse because of its sap's higher sugar content. Fortunately, the sugar maple has a big range, growing from southeastern Canada down through the northeastern United States and Lake States to as far south as Tennessee.

Climate is the limiting factor when it comes to syrup. Sap only runs in late winter, and only under specific weather conditions. Good sap flow requires cold, sub-freezing nights paired with warm, upper-30s to lower-40s days. You'll only find those conditions in the northern parts of the sugar maple's range, and that's why maple syrup is a regional crop. In the US, only ten states produce any significant amount of maple syrup, and they're all in the Northeast or northern Lake States.[72] If your wood-

Maple tap holes (left) will heal over within a year (right), so you can tap healthy maple trees more than 10 inches across every year. To give the tree maximum time to heal, position new tap holes at least six inches away from those you drilled the previous year.

land is in the South or West, sorry, but this isn't the forest farming approach for you.

Apart from having the right climate, there isn't a lot you need to get started with maple syrup. As a first attempt, you'll need a tree to tap, a galvanized steel bucket with a cover, a good drill, a spout, 1–2 gallons of storage, a pan with high sides, a turkey fryer, a candy thermometer, a food-approved filter, and some jars to store the final product. You can get all these products through a maple supply store. Yes, they exist. You can even find starter kits online. I've linked to two sites as examples at the end of the book.

For your first tapping, choose a large, open-grown sugar maple close to your home. Open-grown trees with big canopies produce more sap, and they have a higher sugar content. Make sure the tree is at least 10 inches across at about chest height.

To tap your tree, use a 7/16" drill bit to drill about 2" into the tree at a slight upward angle. Do this on a day when it's above freezing at the start of the sap season. That's usually sometime in February, though that will vary, depending on where you live. Pick a tap spot free of scars, wounds, and rot. You'll know you have a good spot if the shavings coming off the drill are light in color. If they're dark, abandon that hole and try a different spot. The hole's height isn't crucial, but you should position it so that your bucket is off the ground and accessible for collection.

Once you've drilled into the tree, gently tap the spout into it. When seated properly, the spout will support the bucket all by itself. Hang the bucket on the spout and cover the top.

You should check the bucket daily during sap season, which can run through the end of March. A single tap hole can produce about 10 gallons of sap, and a yard-grown tree may produce more. It's important to collect and process the sap quickly, because bacteria grow quickly in its blend of sugar and water.

Dump any sap from the bucket into a clean container. To preserve the sap, keep it cool and in the shade. If there's any debris in the bucket, use a paper filter when pouring sap into your storage container.

Now that you have some sap, it's time to start boiling. Maple sap is about 2 percent sugar, but final maple syrup is 66–67 percent sugar. That percent-age is critical. Any lower and the syrup will grow moldy. Any higher and it will crystallize.

The way you get to that magic percentage is by boiling off some of the water. If you're making syrup for your own use, you can boil using a turkey fryer and stovetop. Use the turkey fryer for most of the boiling. Making syrup throws off a lot of steam, and you don't want all that moisture in your house. When the sap thickens, transfer it to a stovetop pan with high sides for greater control. When boiling, always keep at least 1½ inches of liquid in the pot or pan to keep the syrup from scorching.

Speed matters in boiling. The faster you boil, the lighter your final syrup will be in both color and flavor. Slow boiling makes darker syrup with a stronger maple flavor. Technically, the lighter syrup earns a higher grade when it comes to sales, but I prefer the darker stuff.

To know when your syrup is done, you'll need a candy thermometer that can read more than 200 degrees Fahrenheit. You're looking for the final temperature to be 219 degrees.

Once the syrup gets to temperature, put it in containers. Bottles or jars can work as long as they can stand the high temperature. Pass the hot syrup through a cloth filter before putting it in containers, and refrigerate it right after bottling to let it cool.

If you've bottled properly, you won't have to refrigerate unopened containers, and the syrup will keep for more than a year. Once you open a bottle, though, keep it refrigerated. Opened, refrigerated syrup will last up to six months.

Most commercial syrup makers use tubing systems that rely on gravity or vacuums to gather sap from multiple trees and funnel it to a central facility. Photo credit: Karl VonBerg, Watershed Agricultural Council

At the end of the sap season, remove your bucket and tap from the tree. The tree will regrow over the tap wound on its own. In future years, make your new tap hole at least six inches away from your previous one to give the tree space to heal. You can tap healthy maple trees larger than 10 inches across every year without harming them.

Even by tapping a single tree, you can get enough syrup for the whole year. It takes about 40 gallons of sap to make 1 gallon of syrup, so your big yard tree will net you about a quarter to half gallon of syrup.

Once you have the process down, you can increase the number of trees you tap. Tapping even a few trees will give you more syrup than you'll know what to do with, so you'll be able to start giving it away or selling it.

To truly make a profit with maple syrup, you'll need to go big. Modern commercial syrup operations tap thousands of trees. Rather than buckets, they use plastic tubing and vacuum pumps to draw sap from the trees and collect it in a central location. Instead of boiling over a turkey fryer, they use large stainless steel vats in a dedicated building, called a sugar house in the trade.

If you try out syrup making and decide you like it, the best way to learn how to expand your operation is to take some courses and get hands-on training. Cornell University's periodic multi-day Maple Camp is a great starting point for the serious beginner. If you don't want to travel all the way to upstate New York, check with your local extension offices to see if your state offers something similar. It can also be helpful to visit established commercial operations and examine their setups. Many syrup makers are proud of their work and will happily show you their processes.

When going commercial, research not only how to make syrup but the regulations around selling it, too. States often have specific rules about food safety, including restrictions on where and how food for sale can be produced. Make sure you know and follow these rules to avoid big fines down the road.

TRY THIS: DRINK THE SAP INSTEAD

You don't have to make syrup to enjoy maple flavor. Under the right conditions, you can drink the sap too.

Maple sap is 98 percent water and 2 percent sugar, so it has a slight sweetness. Though too thin to pour over pancakes, it's light enough that you can drink it like you would lemonade or any other beverage.

Maple sap is even coming into vogue as a health food. It's packed with minerals, antioxidants, and nutrients from the tree.

The important thing to remember about drinking sap, though, is that you have to treat it properly for it to be safe. Syrup has been boiled and bottled to prevent bacteria growth, but natural sap is a haven for sugar-loving microbes. Fortunately, the sap is sterile when it first comes out of the tree, so the risk of illness comes from poor or excessive storage, not the sap itself.

When producing sap to drink, make sure any containers you use to store the sap are sanitized. Store the sap in the fridge, and don't keep it longer than a week. Only drink sap from the early or middle parts of the sap season, because later sap will have an odd flavor.

For extra security in sap drinking, boil the sap a little before drinking it. You won't get it all the way down to maple syrup, but that brief boiling will kill harmful bacteria.

BOOSTING MEMORY—AND MONEY— WITH AMERICAN GINSENG

Maple syrup production is confined to northern climates, but another woodland crop, American ginseng, has a wider range. Except for Florida, it will grow throughout the eastern United States and as far west as the Great Plains. If you're willing to be patient, farming ginseng can be lucrative even if you don't have much land.

Ginseng's appeal comes from its traditional use as a medicinal in many Asian countries, particularly China. Though classified as a dietary supplement, ginseng has numerous purported health benefits, from memory improvement to stress reduction to male sexual enhancement.

These days, China dominates American ginseng demand. If you're growing ginseng commercially, your buyer will most likely be a licensed exporter who will sell it overseas.

That market is almost unlimited, and the prices paid for high-quality ginseng can be astronomical. The root is the desired part of the plant, and exceptional single roots have sold for thousands of dollars. Odds are you won't earn nearly that much for the ones you grow, but growing ginseng can still be profitable.

And you will have to grow it. American ginseng occurs naturally in US forests, but in much of its natural range, it's illegal to remove wild plants. Wild American ginseng has fallen victim to its own high demand, as collectors have harvested far more than the environment can support.

While you can't gather wild ginseng, it's perfectly legal for you to cultivate the plant in a wooded setting and sell it. In fact, growing it in a way that simulates its natural environment yields more profit than a traditional, controlled farm setup. That's because it's not so much the weight but the shape and complexity of the ginseng root that determines its value. The more the root resembles a person (I'm not making this up), the more valuable it is. These unusual growth forms are only possible in a wild setting.

This works out well for you if you're interested in forest farming, because you can command high prices for ginseng with little work on your part. Essentially all that "farming" ginseng involves is sowing seeds and waiting eight to ten years for the roots to grow large enough to sell.

Ginseng won't grow just anywhere. It's a short plant, rarely getting even knee high, and unlike a lot of plants, it loves shade. The best condition for it is about 70 percent shade. Good wooded sites for ginseng have large broad-leafed trees, especially maple, ash, and basswood at least 20 inches wide. Areas with conifers—even shaded ones like those under hemlock—make poor ginseng sites and should be avoided.

Which way the land faces also matters. Sites should face north, east, or northeast to provide the cooler, moister conditions ginseng prefers. Sites that face south or west are hotter and drier, making them poor choices.

Other site factors that make a difference include slope (a moderate steepness of 10–25 percent is pre-

Maidenhair fern (left) indicates a good potential ginseng site, but woody shrubs like mountain laurel (right) suggest poor locations. Photo credits: Brendan Murphy, Watershed Agricultural Council (maidenhair fern), National Park Service (mountain laurel)

ferred) and soil condition (you want a large plantable area with few surface rocks). You can determine if you've found a good site by looking for indicator plants like maidenhair fern, rattlesnake fern, and baneberry. Woody shrubs like mountain laurel and blueberry indicate poor ginseng sites.

Aside from these biological constraints, the other limitation for growing ginseng is security. Because of its high value, ginseng theft occurs often. If you don't live on your land, ginseng isn't a good crop for you. It's best if your ginseng site is within easy view of your home, or if not, located close to a place you travel through regularly.

Once you've chosen a site and sown your seed, monitor the area and remove diseased ginseng plants to keep the infection from spreading. If you have high deer pressure in your woods—something

we'll talk more about in a later chapter—you may need to install a fence to keep them from eating your crop.

After eight to ten years, you'll be ready to harvest. Be careful not to damage the root, as a large, intact root will bring you the most money.

When you harvest, you'll likely have some young ginseng plants that have come up naturally. Leave them in the ground. They'll continue growing and provide a future crop.

Once you have your ginseng roots, it will be time to sell them. But you can't hand them over to just anyone. Because of the plant's rare status, ginseng can only be sold to state-certified dealers. You can typically find a list of these dealers on the website for your state's Department of Natural Resources or a similar agency.

Livestock in the Woods: Profit or Peril?

Plants aren't all you can farm in the woods. Under the right conditions, livestock can have a place in the forest as well.

Let me start off by emphasizing the phrase "under the right conditions." Turning a bunch of cows loose in your woods is a recipe for disaster. Their hooves will churn up the soil and damage tree roots. They can also quickly eat all the ground cover, leaving your woods barren and ripe for invasive plants to take over.

When done well, though, livestock grazing doesn't have to destroy your woods. It requires frequent moving of animals, and fencing is critical. Grazing is not a set-it-and-forget-it type of forest farming. Only pursue raising livestock in the woods if you're willing to devote significant time to observing your animals and the impact they're having on your land.

As with maple syrup, you can graze livestock in the woods with differing levels of investment. At the low end, a few chickens or turkeys can be a good way to aerate and mix organic matter into your woodland soils. These birds originally come from forests, and they're well adapted to foraging in them.

Fencing for chickens and turkeys in the woods is optional, though predation may be a problem if the birds aren't contained. If you do put up fences, rotate where your birds are in the woods often so they don't rip up vegetation.

Fencing or not, give your chickens or turkeys access to open pasture for additional food options and a roost for safety at night. Portable coops exist and work well for woodland-grazing poultry.

At the next level of difficulty, you could raise goats. Goats require more maintenance than chickens or turkeys, as they will eat just about anything. Left to their own devices, goats will wipe out your undergrowth in a matter of days.

That voracious and flexible appetite, though, makes goats perfect for controlling invasive plants. Woodlots overrun by multiflora rose and kudzu have been brought back to life using goats.

You don't necessarily have to own goats to get the benefits of them. There are goat farmers who will, at your invitation, bring their goats to your land and let them graze. While you won't earn income from it, goat grazing is a low-cost, natural way to clear undesirable plants from your woodlot.

Goats and poultry have lighter touches in the woods, but if you're serious about livestock, you can go one step further and practice a technique known as silvopasture. Most commonly associated with cattle, this approach blends pasture and woodlot into one mixed environment.

Silvopasture doesn't just mean letting cows roam in your woods. To make it work, you have to make major changes to your woodland.

In typical silvopasture, you greatly reduce the number of trees in your woods, down to about a hundred per acre. You leave the largest, most valuable trees and remove the rest. The idea is to open up the ground enough that grass can grow. The cattle then eat the grass, and you get annual income from their milk and meat. In the longer term, you also make money by harvesting the bigger trees left behind.

Silvopasture can work in lots of forest types, but it has a particularly long history in the West. The naturally wider-spaced western forests are easily adapted to suit cattle grazing.

For farmers, silvopasture offers a way to get more production and income out of the same amount of land. It gives options for forest-based income, and in turn, it benefits livestock production by providing shade and reducing animal stress. Dr. Larry Godsey of the Center for Agroforestry at the University of Missouri reports that cows with access to shade produce 10-19 percent more milk than unshaded ones, and they're almost twice as likely to conceive a calf.[2]

Experiment, Experiment, Experiment

I've provided three examples of forest farming here, but as I said earlier, there are far more options for woodlands from coast to coast. Which one makes sense for you depends on how much work you want to put into your land as well as which markets are in your area.

More important than all that, though, you should have fun with whatever crop you grow. The experience of producing something from the land should bring you closer to your woods, not turn them into a place of sweat and toil.

The best way to find out if any of these forest farming techniques are for you is to try them out at a small scale. Tap one maple tree. Sow a few ginseng seeds. You'll get to see the rewards of your efforts, and you'll gain insight into how much effort it will take to ramp up your investment. You'll also get hands-on knowledge of what works and what doesn't, so that if you do scale up, you'll have the best chance, as Teddy Roosevelt would say, to win glorious triumphs.

Silvopasture works where trees are spaced far enough apart to allow grass to grow between them, like in this open pine stand in Alabama. Photo credit: USDA NRCS

CHAPTER 15

Other Income Sources

Think left and think right and think low and think high.
Oh, the Thinks you can think up if only you try!
—Dr. Seuss

Making money off the land has never been easy, and doing it in a way that can last, that allows the land to renew itself, is even tougher. It's one thing to pillage your woods for their short-term financial value, but that isn't what this book is about. It's about doing right by the land. Even when we profit from it, we should treat it well.

I've discussed how you can do that in the past two chapters, but those chapters focused on ways we've made money off the land for centuries: food and timber. In the 21st century, those traditional products aren't always enough. For the enterprising landowner who wants to earn more income from the land while still respecting it, what other options exist? We'll touch on a few of these in the next several pages, but my broader point in writing this chapter is to encourage you to think outside the box when it comes to land-based businesses. It's easy to jump to the traditional, but there are so many unexplored possibilities out there. What's your passion? What gets you excited? Is there a way you can link your passion to your land? Combining these two loves you have can be the spark that creates a new business.

Carbon Credits

To be frank, I'm hesitant to write about carbon credits. By the time this book comes out, whatever I write will almost surely be out of date. The carbon market varies a lot, and it's highly dependent on legislation and public attitudes toward climate change.

The basic approach to carbon credits is straightforward. A state or federal government institutes a cap, or limit, on carbon dioxide emissions. Emitters—think big factories and power plants—can meet the cap either by reducing their emissions or by purchasing offset credits.

As we've talked about, forests provide some of the best opportunities to reduce carbon dioxide. Trees store carbon in their trunks, and with their long lives, they keep that carbon out of the atmosphere a long time. With carbon credits, you as a landowner sell the carbon-storing power of your woods as an offset to a polluting company. The polluter pays you based on the tons of carbon your woodland stores, and in exchange you agree to keep your land wooded rather than converting to a field or housing development.

If you had asked me about carbon credits in 2007, I would have told you they were a guaranteed way landowners could make money. The Chicago Climate Exchange was booming. There was bipartisan support for climate change action. Democrat Nancy Pelosi and Republican Newt Gingrich did a joint ad, talking about how they both believed in climate change and the need to do something about it. It seemed only a matter of time before national climate change legislation became reality.

Then the housing crisis hit. In just three years the carbon credit model fell apart. National climate change legislation fizzled and died. The Chicago Climate Exchange tanked: its carbon price fell from more than $8.00 per ton to a nickel. The exchange closed at the end of 2010.[1]

Even as that market ended, though, California was working on one of its own. In 2012, armed with a state law mandating emission reductions, the United States's most populous state opened its carbon-trading market. As of this writing, carbon is trading in that market for around $13.00 a ton, more than the Chicago Climate Exchange's peak price.[2]

California's market has revived the carbon credit idea. Even though the state's emissions law only applies to polluters in that state, those polluters can purchase offsets from anywhere in the country. That means whether your land is in California, Maine, or anywhere in between, you can potentially earn income off California's carbon market.

I say "potentially" because as of this writing, most carbon credit buyers are only interested in dealing with big properties, typically a thousand acres or more. If you own less than that, carbon markets are still out of your reach.

Cost drives this focus on large ownerships. A lot of accounting and ground-truthing goes into forest carbon offsets. The polluter must verify that landowners are doing what they promised, and that verification requires periodic audits. Those costs are similar regardless of whether the property is ten acres or ten thousand.

This situation could change, though, if interest in climate change legislation improves in other states or in the federal government. If the demand for carbon offsets increased, there might not be enough large properties to support the market. In that case, polluters would start looking at smaller woodlots.

Do I expect that change any time soon? No. Still, it's worth keeping an eye on for future developments, particularly if you own several hundred wooded acres.

If you do own a larger property and want to find out more about carbon credit possibilities, your best bet is to seek out a broker. Polluters rarely work directly with landowners, connecting instead with middlemen who handle the contract negotiations and auditing requirements for a fee. A possible starting point is Finite Carbon, a national company focused on carbon credits for woodland owners.

Hunting Leases

Back in the chapter on outdoor recreation, I mentioned that hunting—among other outdoor activities—is increasing in popularity. The US Fish and Wildlife Service reports that the United States has more hunters now than at any time since 1996. Almost 14 million Americans over the age of 16 hunt.[3]

Those hunters depend on private lands. More than 80 percent hunt on private lands, and 60 percent use them exclusively.[4]

I understand why hunters prefer private land. Around here, I avoid public land during deer season. There are way too many people with way too many bows, shotguns, and rifles wandering around.

But even as our public lands become more crowded, private lands are becoming less accessible to hunters. In 1985, 25 percent of private landowners allowed public access on their properties, according to the Forest Service. Today that number is less than 15 percent.[5]

This trend is worrisome for the pressure it puts on public lands, but for private landowners like you, it's also an opportunity. More hunters are looking for private land now than at any time in the past twenty years, and those hunters are having a harder time finding it than ever before. If your property is large enough to support hunting, you may be able to earn income by leasing hunting rights.

In a hunting lease, a hunter or group of hunters pays you money in exchange for exclusive hunting access to your property. The lease's duration varies from as short a period as one season to multiple years. The rate you'll receive depends on how good your land is for hunting, but the rates can be attractive. The University of Georgia reports that in their state, hunting leases average $15 per acre per year, and the best properties can earn twice that.[6]

These hunting leases are different from the informal arrangements I discussed earlier as a way to deter trespassing. In those situations, money usually doesn't change hands, and there may not even be a written agreement. By contrast, trying to sell hunting leases for income warrants a more formal process, including a contract. As with a timber sale contract, a good hunting lease makes clear all privileges, conditions, and requirements for both you and the hunter.

Also like a timber sale contract, there's a lot of flexibility in what you put in a hunting lease. To protect you and your land, though, make sure that at a minimum you include the following:

- **A limitation on the number of hunters**: Only so many people can hunt the same area safely. If you're leasing to a sportsmen's club or other group, a maximum number of hunters permitted is essential.
- **Anti-subleasing clause**: You want to know who's hunting on your land. Don't allow the hunter to sublease the hunting rights to someone you've never met.
- **Specific permitted uses**: In addition to hunting, you might allow the hunters to camp on your land. Alternately, you might limit their use of your property to daylight hours. Specify these rules so hunters know what they are and aren't allowed to do.
- **Agreement to follow relevant laws**: Make it clear that hunters are expected to follow game laws while on your property. If they break them, they're off the land and will forfeit their lease payment.
- **Liability removal**: Liability is a big reason many landowners avoid hunting leases. What if a hunter gets hurt or killed? You don't want that coming back to haunt you. Include a hold harmless clause that acknowledges the inherent hazards of hunting and that the hunter understands them.
- **Cancellation**: Reserve the right to revoke the lease immediately if the hunter doesn't comply with its terms. This is crucial in the event you get an irresponsible lessee.

When leasing land on your own, it's best to lease to someone you know and trust, perhaps a friend, relative, or neighbor. By doing that, you can feel comfortable making the lease for a longer time. That's beneficial to both you and the hunter, as it builds the hunter's desire to take care of the property. If you're leasing to a stranger, start out with a one-season lease to get to know him or her before committing to anything longer.

While many landowners develop and manage their own hunting leases, you don't have to go it alone. Intermediaries exist that help to link landowners and hunters. Hunting Lease Network, for instance, acts almost like a real estate agency for leases. Hunters browse listings posted by landowners as if they were shopping for a house. The company then helps set the terms of the lease to ensure both buyer and seller have a positive experience. They even feature a liability insurance option in case something goes wrong. You'll have to pay them a commission, but having the support of a larger company might help if you aren't confident in your ability to manage a hunting lease yourself.

As with carbon markets, hunting leases aren't for everyone. Larger properties offer more hunting opportunities, so they're more likely to attract hunters and higher payments. There's also the simple reality that if someone leases hunting rights from you, you can't hunt on your own land. And even if you don't hunt, a lease may limit your property access during hunting season. If you mainly own land for outdoor recreation or hunting, hunting leases may not be for you. If you don't mind someone else using your land to hunt, though, leases can be an attractive way to get annual income while having the peace of mind brought by knowing who is recreating on your property.

Ecotourism

We're now leaving behind the world of established business concepts and venturing into the truly creative. "Ecotourism," broadly, is tourism focused on nature. You might see the term used to describe exotic locations like tropical rainforests, but this growing trend can also generate income closer to home.

Among those who use and study America's public lands, it's long been known that those lands aren't nearly enough to meet the outdoor recreation wants of the country's population. Particularly in eastern states, public lands are the minority of ownerships, and they're often crowded. That damages the experience for people, and it also puts pressure on wildlife.

As with hunting leases, though, this problem can be an opportunity for the enterprising landowner. There are millions of urban and suburban dwellers willing to pay for a slice of the country experience.

Now I can see a few furrowed eyebrows in the crowd. If you own your land to get away from peo-ple, opening it to the public likely isn't high on your desired activities list. But ecotourism doesn't have to mean turnstiles, lines, and public access. You can set your own limits on how open you want your land to be. If you only want a few close friends to use your property, that's OK. If you want lots of visitors, that's OK, too.

I realize I'm being vague, but it's only because ecotourism covers a lot of business models. To help make it more specific and get your entrepreneurial juices flowing, let's discuss a few quick examples.

FISHING LEASES

In 2011 (the most recent year information is available), more than 27 million anglers together took more than 369 million freshwater fishing trips. Combined, they spent more than $25 billion, and they spent over $3 billion just on land leases and ownership.[7] If you own a stocked pond or have access to a lake or stream, you may be able to get some of that money for yourself.

Fishing leases aren't as lucrative as hunting ones, primarily because so many lakes and major fishing streams already have public access. Unless you have private access to a major sport fishery or live in an area with little public water, a fishing lease alone may be a hard sell. In combination with a hunting lease, though, it can attract more hunters—many of whom also fish—potentially increasing the amount they're willing to pay.

The same cautions you might observe with hunting leases apply to fishing leases too. Make sure you

Fishing leases are rarely profitable on their own, but they can add value to a hunting lease. Photo credit: Jeff Vanuga, USDA NRCS

have a written contract with similar limitations to what I described for hunting.

FARM TOURS

Speaking as a kid who grew up on a dairy farm, one of the strangest sights I've ever seen happened shortly after I moved to the Catskills. A local dairy farm held a weekend event where families could come and pay the farmer to let them do chores.

I'm not making this up.

It sounds crazy, yet it was big business for this small farm. Their customers were mostly tourists from New York City or the surrounding suburbs who wanted to experience "country life." What I and this farmer considered everyday chores were rugged, rustic fun for these city folks.

I still don't completely understand why this business model works, but here's my best guess. Ecotourism attracts visitors by focusing on rare or threatened environments. In the United States, few environments are more threatened than the family farm. According to the US Census, more than 80 percent of the US population now lives in urban areas, and less than 2 percent of us are farmers.[8]

The rarity of the family farm attracts people. There's a nostalgia to it, a longing for days gone by when people worked with their hands for a living. For an accountant and her family who spend their weekdays staring at screens, the chance to milk a cow or pet a sheep is a wonder worth paying for.

Here in the Catskills, I'm seeing that more small farms are adding tourism to their business models. Some offer farm chores or a petting zoo. Others have set up B&B's to give urban dwellers the complete rural experience, rooster wake-up call included.

Admittedly, farm tours are a pretty extreme form of income generation. Doing them requires moving outside the farm or forestry business and into the tourism business. You'll have to manage people as well as the land, with all the associated headaches. If you own your land for privacy, steer clear of this option.

RECREATION OPPORTUNITIES

Your land likely already has a well-developed trail system. Maybe you put it in for your own recreation, or maybe a logger installed it to access timber. On many eastern properties, trails have existed for decades, reflecting the region's long history of land use.

These trails are potential income sources. Similar to the farm tour concept, urban and suburban dwellers might be willing to pay to use your property for outdoor recreation.

I'm not talking here about hunting or fishing, but rather activities that don't require taking something from the woods: birdwatching, horseback riding, and camping, among others.

Each year more than 5 million Americans engage in some form of wildlife watching on private land.[9] If you own woods near developed areas with little public land, your property may have value as an outdoor recreation site.

Will people really pay to recreate on your land? Yes they will, and you are the proof. After all, you pay something yourself for the chance to recreate: property taxes and other costs of owning your land.

That said, if you want to explore outdoor recreation for income, marketing is crucial. You have to distinguish your property from public lands and other private lands around yours. Demand isn't as high for recreational areas as it is for hunting areas, so you'll need to be creative when trying to attract paying customers.

If you embrace that creativity, the possibilities for both income and positive social impact are enormous. Remember when I said in an earlier chapter that being in nature has been shown to reduce illness? One landowner I know used that knowledge to turn his property into a nature therapy center for New York City kids with cancer. Another landowner in Maine built a leadership training camp on his land to teach people outdoor survival and team-building skills.

If you own land with financial gain in mind, traditional income sources are unlikely to cut it in the 21st century. Embrace your inner entrepreneur. Find that niche market, and then go out and capture it with all the spirit of the American Dream.

CHAPTER 16

Start a New Forest

I have watched the face of many a newly wolfless mountain, and seen the south-facing slopes wrinkle with a maze of new deer trails. I have seen every edible bush and seedling browsed, first to anaemic desuetude, and then to death. . . . I now suspect that just as a deer herd lives in mortal fear of its wolves, so does a mountain live in mortal fear of its deer. And perhaps with better cause, for while a buck pulled down by wolves can be replaced in two or three years, a range pulled down by too many deer may fail of replacement in as many decades.
—Aldo Leopold

Woodlands are long term. Trees need decades to grow from tiny seeds to some of the largest living things on this planet. The trees on your land are the result of events, both natural and human, that happened many years ago.

The actions you take now will shape what your woods look like fifty and one-hundred years from now. In some cases, they may even determine whether your land has woods on it at all.

For millions of years forests have renewed themselves. As older trees died, younger trees grew up and filled in the spaces left by their parents.

In the modern era, though, that cycle is no longer a given. We've made two changes to the woods that make it hard for young trees to survive. First, we've imported plants from other parts of the world,

OPPOSITE: *As a landowner, few tasks are more important than ensuring that the next generation of trees gets a healthy start in your woods.*

which have become invasive and have outcompeted native trees. Second, and perhaps more profoundly, we've all but wiped out top natural woodland predators like wolves and cougars. In losing them, as Aldo Leopold observed, plant-eating species, especially deer, have flourished beyond levels the land can support. According to Dr. Kurt VerCauteren, a wildlife researcher with the US Animal and Plant Health Inspection Service, we have more deer in the United States today than there were before Columbus arrived in the New World.[1]

With so many deer, baby trees struggle to grow beyond the reach of hungry mouths. As seedlings get continually chewed back, the invasive plants that deer don't eat grow and fill the void. Rather than diverse woodlands with many kinds of trees, we get tangles of multiflora rose, Japanese barberry, and other non-native plants.

The effect this change has on the environment is severe, though we rarely notice it until we take some extreme measures. Consider Yellowstone National Park, which reintroduced wolves in 1995. That act had a huge ripple effect on the park. The wolves killed some of the deer, but they also forced the deer to stay on the move. In the process, areas that had been barren from overbrowsing resprouted. Within a few years, the forest started coming back. It brought with it new habitat for birds, beavers, bears, otters, and a host of other species. Even more stunningly, as plant life increased near the streams, the streams themselves became more stable and less likely to wash away. All these positive changes occurred because reintroducing wolves kept deer populations at levels the landscape could support.[2]

Of course, the flipside to this astonishing recovery is that it reveals the damage an overpopulation of deer is causing on our woodlands. Our woods are much like Yellowstone before 1995, browsed beyond what they can handle. Most parts of the country haven't reintroduced wolves or cougars, and it's doubtful they ever will.

Yet our task as landowners and foresters remains: we have to get the next generation of woodlands started so our woods remain woods in the future. We can't rely on nature to do it for us anymore. Nature needs our help.

To give nature a helping hand, we have to do two things. First, we need to get more baby trees growing in our woods. Then, once we have those trees, we need to keep them alive in the face of heavy competition.

Renewing the Forest Step 1: Making Babies

If you want to bring some baby trees into the world, your woodland will need a few basics. It needs good parents: large, healthy, big-crowned trees that can produce a lot of seeds. It also needs the right mix of soil, temperature, and rainfall for those seeds to sprout. Finally, it needs enough light at ground level to give seedlings the energy to grow.

There isn't much you can do about soil, temperature, or rainfall, but you can do a lot to influence your parent trees and the amount of light. The simplest way to help both is through careful tree cutting.

Most of the harvesting techniques I've described in this book will create better parent trees and put more light on the ground. Consider the patch cuts I talked about for helping wildlife. They let in lots of sun by removing most if not all of the trees. At the same time, the trees along the patch's edge—the ones that will supply seeds for the future woods—get additional light that will help them grow faster and make more seeds.

But you don't have to remove all the trees to get a new generation started. In fact, it's often best to cut only some trees, mimicking natural processes like insect attacks to create limited openings. Many tree seedlings will thrive in partial shade, while opening the canopy raises the risk of an invasive plant taking over.

One of my favorite approaches for getting new trees is called a shelterwood. In this kind of harvest, loggers remove most of the smaller, less healthy trees and leave only the biggest, best-growing ones. It's similar to the fuel reduction cutting we talked about for fire control, though it usually removes even more trees. A shelterwood cut opens up space in the canopy for the biggest trees to grow larger crowns and produce more seeds. In addition, that same space brings ample sunlight to the ground so those seeds can sprout and grow.

As a method of getting young trees, a shelterwood cut provides a good balance of ground-level sunlight while keeping some older trees. The photographs here are of the same shelterwood in 2008 shortly after cutting (top) and in 2015 (bottom). You can see how much the next generation of woods has grown in less than a decade. You can also see the bigger canopies on the remaining trees, which made them healthier and able to produce more seeds to start all that young growth. Photo credits: Heather Hilson, Watershed Agricultural Council (top), author (bottom)

WATCH OUT!
CAN'T WE RELY ON NATURE
TO OPEN THE CANOPY?

The techniques for starting a new generation of trees mimic natural disasters that have historically caused woodlands to renew themselves. A patch cut mimics a tornado or wind storm knocking down all the trees in a small area. A shelterwood removes poorer-growing trees, imitating an insect or disease that would kill weak trees but not the healthiest ones.

But if these cuts mimic natural disturbances, why do them at all? Why not allow those natural disasters to do what they've always done and start forests over?

The answer to this question is twofold. First, as we talked about in connection with wildlife,

we've blunted the effects of fires and floods on eastern United States forests. Out west, today's high-intensity megafires cook the soil and the seeds in it, limiting regrowth. From coast to coast, young forests are now at historic lows.[3]

More important than the decline in natural disturbances, though, is that a deliberate intervention like a shelterwood gives you the opportunity to plan ahead. If you know where, when, and how you're going to open the canopy and start a new forest, you'll also know where, when, and how you should go about protecting that area from threats like deer and invasive plants. You don't have that advantage with a natural disaster.

Renewing the Forest Step 2: Keeping Young Trees Alive

Patch cuts and shelterwoods are well established in both forest research and in-woods practice. They do a good job of mimicking natural disasters that forests have evolved to respond to positively and are reliable for starting a new generation of trees.

But getting new trees is the easy part. The hard part is protecting those fragile seedlings long enough so they can grow into adults.

In many US woodlots, the biggest threats to young trees are plant-eating animals—specifically deer—and invasive plants that cover the ground and prevent seedlings from getting enough light, water, and nutrients. When it comes time to renew your woods, you'll need to plan for these threats if you hope to succeed.

PROTECTION TOOL 1: TREE TUBES

When I talked about planting trees along streams, I suggested the use of tree tubes—plastic protective barriers that wrap around individual trees—for protection against deer. You can use these same tubes to protect naturally growing seedlings.

As with planted trees, you'll need the tube itself, a wooden stake to support the tube, and some zip ties to hold the tube onto the stake. Position the seedling so it stands up inside the tube. Drive the wooden stake into the ground next to the seedling, then use the air holes in the tree tube to tie a couple of zip ties around the tube and stake.

Tree tubes work well in small areas of regrowth, as when you're mimicking old-growth structure with openings under an acre in size. In these cases, you'll have few seedlings you need to protect, so you won't need a lot of tubes.

At larger scales, such as in shelterwoods, tree tubes become problematic. In these cuts you aren't talking about a few seedlings, but hundreds or even thousands. For example, in 2009 I measured seedlings in the shelterwood cut pictured a few pages back. They numbered more than 20,000 per acre (not a fun summer, by the way).

That cut was 9 acres. With 180,000 seedlings, there's no way tree tubes can work. Cost aside, each one takes too long to install, and the work of maintaining them year after year is more than anyone could hope to do.

Once you get above a few dozen seedlings, it's better to protect them all through a single tool. The most common and effective way to do that is a deer fence.

PROTECTION TOOL 2: DEER FENCING

Deer fences are temporary. They're typically designed to last about ten years, long enough for seedlings to grow above a height where deer can still munch on them. Either you or a professional installs the fence around the entire cut area, blocking deer from entering it.

Tree tubes work well for protecting a few seedlings, as in this reverting field edge in Connecticut. Photo credit: Paul Fusco, USDA NRCS

For your fence to work, you'll want it to be at least seven feet high and for its base to be tight to the ground. This setup prevents deer from crawling under or jumping over it.

Fencing materials and costs vary, and cheaper materials often have a tradeoff in that they require more maintenance. The shelterwood cut photographed earlier in the chapter had a fence made from metal boxwire, which is strong and durable but costly. The one to protect those 9 acres cost almost $20,000.

Cheaper options do exist, such as plastic

WATCH OUT!
NATURAL VS. PLANTED TREES

Shelterwoods and patch cuts depend on getting baby trees naturally, by having parent trees produce seeds that fall where they may and then grow. But that isn't the only way to start a new forest. Like in the chapter on water quality, you can also plant trees.

Recognize, though, that planting trees isn't the same as letting nature make them. When most people plant trees, they only plant a few species, and they plant them in rows to make the work easier. That kind of planting doesn't make a natural forest; it makes a plantation.

Even if you spread out your plantings and use different species, it still won't match what nature can produce. Take a look at how dense the young trees are in the 2015 shelterwood photo. A person couldn't plant nearly that many. All those natural seedlings give a woodlot far higher diversity, increasing the chances that a few of those trees will have the good genes needed to survive and grow into healthy adults.

That's why whenever possible, I and other foresters prefer to depend on natural growth of young trees rather than planting. It might seem irresponsible to cut a tree and not plant a replacement, but in the long run, the forest is a lot better off if we let nature set up the next generation.

There are instances when planting is a preferred option. In woodlots decimated by poor logging in the past, there may not be any good parent trees left. Elsewhere, severe fire may have removed all the adult trees and seeds from the area. In these cases, the only option to get a new forest going quickly is to plant.

Planting can also help when you want to increase the variety of species on your land. If you only have broad-leafed trees, for instance, you'll need to plant conifers if you want some in your woods.

My point in this sidebar isn't to discourage you from planting trees. Tree planting is still one of the best things you can do for your land, especially along streams. Where you can, though, let your woodland start its own new trees. It will save you a lot of effort, and the result will be a healthier, more diverse young forest.

Temporary fencing keeps out deer and allows seedlings time to grow. In this picture, young trees have come up inside the fence (left), while hay-scented fern, which deer don't eat, dominates the area outside it (right).

fencing. The plastic is harder to hold against the ground, and fallen limbs can flatten it. It works best in smaller projects, but on a bigger site like the shelterwood, a metal fence will make up for its higher initial cost in reduced maintenance.

But is that cost worth it? $20,000 is a lot to invest in your property, and even though the price of that fence was on the high side, fencing is expensive regardless.

On the property where the photographed shel-

Unlike the shelterwood cut, this 2006 patch cut (top) wasn't fenced. Almost a decade later in 2015 (bottom), deer browse has kept the area from returning to woods. Photo credits: Heather Hilson, Watershed Agricultural Council (top), author (bottom)

terwood occurred, though, the fence was essential. In another section of that same ownership, a patch cut logged around the same time still has no baby trees. Instead grasses and shrubs the deer don't like have taken it over.

In that patch cut, rather than spend money on a fence, the forester assumed he could overwhelm the deer with more new growth than they could eat. In reality, more deer simply came to take advantage of the feast. How they knew the buffet was there I can't say, but they figured it out and mowed down the place.

Beyond keeping out deer, fencing also helps counter invasive plants. In the northern Lake States, for example, University of Wisconsin researchers found that invasive plants were twice as numerous outside deer fences as they were inside them.[4]

There's even evidence that some invasive plants aren't all that invasive—as long as deer are kept away. Deer prefer to eat native plants, which gives invasive ones the room they need to take over. Protect native species from deer, and they outgrow the invasives.

That's what UC-Berkeley researchers discovered in a study of hemlock forests in Pennsylvania and New Jersey. Across ten sites, tree seedlings inside deer fences grew faster and outcompeted highly invasive species like Japanese stiltgrass and barberry. Outside the fences, those invasive plants dominated the opened-up forest.[5]

A six-year University of Pittsburgh project went further, finding that reducing deer pressure on native trees could eliminate certain invasive plants altogether. Garlic mustard is invasive, but it's so common that most foresters don't bother trying to control it. The Pennsylvania-based research, though, found that inside deer fences, garlic mustard's "explosive growth in the presence of deer [declined] toward extinction."[6]

Installing a deer fence is one of the most expensive investments you can make in your property, but as a way to overcome two of the greatest challenges young woodlands confront, it's also among the most worthwhile. If you have a lot of deer, a fence may be your only chance at keeping your next generation of trees alive.

PROTECTION TOOL 3: HUNTING

Add this section to the list of the topics I begin with "I'm hesitant to write about this." Hunting is one of those subjects that sharply divides people, and it understandably brings out strong emotions, whether you support or oppose it. My purpose in writing this section isn't to present a moral case for hunting, but rather to describe the role it plays in protecting the next generation of trees. If you have moral objections to harming animals, please feel free to skip this section.

That said, the experiences from Yellowstone National Park show clearly the positive impact natural hunting from top predators has on the environment. Having some check on deer populations is crucial to a woodland's renewal.

That leaves us in a tough position. Most places in the country don't have natural top predators anymore. Fencing and tree tubes can protect small sites at distinct points in time, but they're costly, time-consuming, and ultimately don't address the underlying problem: more deer than our woodlands can support.

Hence, much as I would prefer to sidestep this emotional topic, we need to have a candid conversation about hunting. To keep America's woodlands going for the long term, deer hunting is a necessity.

And it's more than trophy hunting big bucks. Buck hunting does nothing to control deer populations, because one buck can impregnate many females. If you want to reduce deer pressure on your land, you have to be willing to shoot does.

Can you see why I'm reluctant to write about hunting? Who wants to be the guy encouraging people to shoot Bambi's mom? Yet that's the situation we're in. Without apex predators to do the job naturally, it falls to hunters to fill that role.

If you're a hunter, I encourage you to try to fill at least one doe tag on your land annually. The effect won't be instant, and success relies on others' adopting this approach too. But over time, deer surveys indicate that concerted efforts to fill doe tags have resulted in more stable deer populations, better forest regrowth, and, odd as it sounds, better trophy bucks.[7] That's because with less pressure for food sources, deer are healthier, put on more weight, and can grow larger antlers. If your bucks are young and starved for food, odds are their antlers won't be anything to write to *Field and Stream* about.

Now at this point, it's time for a confession. I'm not a hunter. I've never fired a gun in my life. Even if I ever go target shooting, I don't expect to become a hunter. It's just not something I'm personally comfortable doing.

If you're like me, but you still want to control deer populations on your land, consider letting a neighbor hunt your property, or look into the hunting lease option I talked about in the last chapter. Encourage hunters on your land to fill a doe tag before they shoot a buck. Communicate that your goal is to help your woods recover and ultimately support a stable, healthy deer population.

Figure Out Your Deer Impact

I've painted the deer issue with a broad brush, largely because overbrowsing by deer is an issue on many US woodlands. That said, it isn't a universal problem. Just in the different woodlots I visit around upstate New York, I see a mix of both empty and vibrant forest floors.

If your property has few deer, it would be a waste of money to invest in fencing or tree tubes. Before you put in all that expense, a good starting point is to assess how many deer your property has and whether your land can support them.

Deer move around a lot, so you can't just count them. You can't rely on your hunting success—or lack thereof—either. Instead, use these two methods: pellet counts and indicator species.

The first of these techniques is a little gross, but it works. In a pellet count, you use the amount of deer droppings in an area to estimate how many deer use your property.

Don't worry; you don't have to touch the poo. You just have to look for it. Deer droppings are small, round pellets about an inch across, and they occur in groups. Wildlife biologists have figured out that the typical deer produces 25 of these groups each day (doesn't your job sound better now?). Once you know that number, you can calculate deer density on your land.

Unfortunately (or fortunately, depending on how you look at it), this technique only works in areas that get snow in the winter. If your land is in a southern state, the indicator species method we'll discuss shortly is a better technique.

For those of you in northern climates, here's what you do. In the fall, write down what day most of the leaves have fallen off your trees. This is your property's "leaf off" date, and it's the starting point for your survey. Wait for winter to pass, and then in early spring—after the snow melts but before new leaves sprout—it's time to look for poo.

The idea is that any poo dropped when last year's leaves were still on the trees will be covered up by fallen leaves, so you won't see it. Therefore, any poo piles you see will have been dropped between the leaf off date and the date of your survey. And because of the cold winter temperatures and snowpack, the piles won't have had a chance to decay yet.

To do your survey, you'll sample points along a

line through your property. Which way the line goes is up to you, but ideally it should go through all the different wooded habitats on your land.

For your sample points, you'll need two people and a length of rope 11 feet 9 inches long. One person stands still while the other traces a circle the length of the rope. That circle is your plot, and you'll count all the deer poo piles you find in that area. Keep track on a piece of paper.

Now 11 feet 9 inches might sound random, but when used to make your circular plot, it works out to an area of 1/100 of an acre. That will make the math easier when you finish.

Do as many samples as you feel comfortable doing, the more the better. Do them at regular intervals along the line through your property, and try to get at least 20. The first time you do the survey it might take a while, but eventually it's possible to do 20 points in less than 2 hours.

After doing all your samples, you'll have a count of deer poo piles from each one. Calculate the average number of piles by adding up all your numbers and dividing by the number of sample points.

You're now ready to figure out how many deer you have. Take your average and multiply it by 100 to get the average number of deer poo piles per acre. Next, divide that number by the number of days between last fall's leaf drop date and the date of your survey. Divide that number by 25 to get the number of deer per acre on your property. Finally, multiply that number by 640 to figure out how many deer you have per square mile.

Written out, that looks like a lot of math, but I'll make it simpler. Take your average number of poo piles and divide it by the number of days since leaf drop. Multiply that by 2560, and that's your number of deer per square mile.

$$\frac{\text{Average Number of Poo Piles per Plot}}{\text{Number of Days Since Leaf Drop}} \times 2560 = \text{deer per square mile}$$

The number of deer a woodlot can support depends on the quality of food available, but for general woods, more than 20 per square mile can harm young trees and sensitive undergrowth. If your calculation comes back greater than 20, you may have a deer problem. If it comes back more than 50, you and your baby trees are in big trouble.

What if you don't want to do all that math? Or what if you're one of the unlucky ones who can't go out and count pellet groups because your woodland doesn't get snow? Can you still estimate how many deer you have?

It might be hard to get a number, but if you know your plants, you can get an idea of whether deer are a problem on your land. The key lies in knowing what deer like to eat.

Deer have favorite foods, just like we do, and they'll eat those plants before they eat others. You can use that knowledge to your advantage, because as you get more deer on your woodland, plants will disappear in a predictable order.

The easiest indicator plants are your seedlings

Wild lily-of-the-valley (top left) and white trillium (left) are preferred deer foods and thus good indicators of deer impacts. Wild lily-of-the-valley grows throughout much of the United States, while trillium is found in eastern states. Look for these plants in your woods, and if you see them, it's a sign that deer aren't an issue for you. By contrast, if you see browsed, broom-like shrubs and seedlings (above), you probably have some deer problems. Photo credits: National Park Service (wild lily-of-the-valley), Ryan Hagerty, USFWS (trillium), Brendan Murphy, Watershed Agricultural Council (browsed shrub)

themselves. If you don't see any at all, that's a clear sign that you have too many deer. At the other end, if you see many seedlings more than six inches tall without any sign that they've been chewed, you have few deer and your woods should be able to renew themselves.

You can also dig deeper between these extremes. If, in wandering your property, you find that at least half your seedlings are chewed on, that means you have a moderate level of deer. That level isn't ideal for getting a new woods going, but you're not headed for total failure either. If possible, do a few years' worth of pellet counts to discover whether your local deer herd is stable, increasing, or getting smaller. If it's increasing, you might have a problem in the future.

Beyond the seedlings themselves, other plants on the forest floor give clues to deer presence. Dominance by ferns is a bad sign, as deer tend not to eat them. If your woods have a fern carpet, you likely have a big deer problem and are going to have challenges getting a new woods going. By contrast, if you see plants sensitive to deer, that suggests you have few deer and are in good shape. Look especially for wild lily-of-the-valley and white trillium, two flowers that deer love to eat. They're among the first plants to disappear when deer numbers get too high.

CHAPTER 17

Keep Your Woods as Woods

The great use of a life is to spend it for something that outlasts it.
—William James

In one of the homes I lived in growing up, we lived across the street from a hundred-acre farm field in central Pennsylvania. To my childhood eyes, that field seemed to stretch on forever.

On the other side of that field was the local hospital. It's also a medical college, and they're always adding on one new building or another.

One day my father and I were sitting on our front porch and looking out over the field. He said to me, "The way they keep building, someday that hospital is going to stretch all the way across this field."

I scoffed. The field was massive. How could a hospital ever take up that much space?

On a recent visit home, I was stunned to see buildings across the road from where I grew up. They were part of an outpatient facility.

I won't go so far as to call my father a prophet, but in this case at least, his prediction came true.

Sadly, it's coming true across the United States. Between 1982 and 2010, the Natural Resources Conservation Service reports that we lost 41 million acres of open land to development.[1] That's about 1.4 million acres each year, an area larger than the state of Delaware. The problem is so bad that in 2014 the Family Forest Research Center—a collaboration between the Forest Service and the University of Massachusetts—ranked development as the single greatest threat to family forests nationwide. No other threat—not fire, not insects, not even climate change—posed as much risk to the values we all get from private woodlands, like clean water and wildlife.[2]

I often think about the farmers who worked the field from my childhood decades ago. I wonder what they thought the future of their land would be, or if they knew it would someday be transformed into parking lots. My guess is that they didn't.

Central Pennsylvania isn't the only place losing land to construction. These two aerial photos show the woods around Alsea Bay in Oregon. The one on the left is from 1954; the one on the right is from 2000. The lighter colors in the 2000 image indicate development, much of which replaced forest cover. Photo credits: US Geological Survey

I realize the world changes, that we grow as a society and need places to live and work. But our fellow creatures on this planet need space too, and the space is running out. Loss of habitat is the single greatest cause of species loss.[3] You can protect wildlife on your property in the short term through techniques like the ones discussed earlier in this book, but what about in the future? Is there a way to ensure your land never falls victim to development?

There is. The approach isn't for everyone, but it's among the most powerful tools available for keeping your land as land far into the future while retaining it in private ownership. It's a called a conservation easement.

What's a Conservation Easement?

Think for a moment about all the things you can do on your property, all the rights you have as a landowner. You can hike. You can cut trees. You can hunt. You can build a house. You can sit and simply enjoy the view.

A key part of easements is that you can also give away or sell these individual rights exclusive of one another. Consider hunting leases. In those, you give up your ability to hunt in exchange for money from a hunter. You still own the land, but someone else—for the duration of the lease—owns the right to hunt on it.

Conservation easements work the same way. Instead of giving up the ability to hunt, you're donating or selling the right to develop your property. The group that receives this right—typically a government agency or a private non-profit called a land trust—then agrees not to use it.

Confused? In simpler terms, a conservation easement is a voluntary, permanent agreement to keep your land undeveloped. You retain ownership of the property. You can still use it for hiking, birdwatching, hunting, timber harvesting, and all the other uses you enjoy. Only the ability to develop it goes away. Even if you sell the land to someone else, or pass it on to your heirs, the property can never be developed. It will remain forever as open land.

Why Would Anyone Give Up the Right to Develop Their Land?

I want to begin this section by saying that I don't intend to "sell you" on easements. Easements aren't for every landowner, and you should think carefully before entering into one.

That said, why would a landowner voluntarily abandon one of the most lucrative rights of owning land? Especially in places experiencing a lot of population or economic growth, the financial value of developing a property far exceeds what an owner could reap by growing crops or trees. Also, an easement isn't temporary like a hunting lease. It's a permanent restriction that attaches to your land's deed and will stay with the property forever. That's a big sacrifice for you to make.

The reason many landowners make that sacrifice is that they care about their land's long-term future. They don't want their property to wind up like the field across the street from my childhood home someday. They want to do whatever they can to ensure their land always remains open space.

Having this desire is critical in choosing to ease your property. If you don't have it, don't pursue a conservation easement. Although there are other tangible benefits, none of them are as important as your wish to keep your land undeveloped in the future.

While a desire to protect your land is essential, there are some financial benefits to easements that help make up for the loss of your development rights:

- **Charitable donation**: If you donate your easement (the most common approach), you can deduct the lost value of your development rights from your income taxes. Tax rules as of this writing let you make this deduction over several

TRY THIS:
MEET WITH A LOCAL LAND TRUST

Like a lot of big decisions about your property, getting an easement is one you should take your time to make. Get a lot of input. Talk to your family and hear their opinions. Meet some landowners who have easements and ask them why they made the decision and whether they would do it again.

One way to learn more about easements and decide if one is right for your property is to meet with your local land trust. While a few land trusts are national or even global, most are small, grassroots non-profits that focus on a particular town, county, or region. They're often run by volunteers or at best a handful of staff, so they're usually approachable and willing to talk with you. If you eventually pursue an easement, they're also the folks you'll be working with, so it's helpful to find out who they are and whether you can see yourself forming a long-term relationship with them.

You can do an initial greeting over the phone or at the land trust's office, but a better way to get to know them is to attend an event they sponsor. In addition to handling conservation easements, many land trusts also serve as nature educators, leading hikes and workshops. Attend some of these events and meet the land trust volunteers and staff. You'll see them in a more informal setting, away from the office, and that will give you a better sense of who they really are.

As for who your local land trust is, the Land Trust Alliance maintains a state-by-state list of organizations who meet their robust accreditation standards. Work with one of these groups if possible. I've included a link to the list in "Beyond the Book."

years, so you enjoy the full benefit of it even if the deduction is greater than your annual income.

- **Lower income taxes**: Beyond the charitable donation, some states will give you an income tax break if your land has a conservation easement.
- **Lower estate taxes**: In the next chapter, we'll talk about passing land to the next generation. Having an easement can lower the amount of estate tax your heirs have to pay, potentially making the difference regarding whether they can afford to keep the land after you're gone.
- **Lower property taxes**: Land is assessed on its "highest and best use," which is usually develop-

WATCH OUT!
PRESERVATION VS. CONSERVATION

At their core, easements are meant to do one job: keep land undeveloped. But that doesn't mean all easements are the same. From land trust to land trust and even from easement to easement, there can be differences in the way the easement is structured and in what you can and can't do on your property.

In the early days of easements, they typically prevented not only development, but any commercial use of the property. That meant you couldn't farm, cut trees, or even lease hunting rights. These easements were focused on preservation, turning the property into a nature preserve that just happened to be owned by a private landowner rather than the land trust itself.

While that might sound great, over time these preservation easements have become problematic for many easement holders. Suppose you want to follow my advice in the wildlife chapter and mimic old-growth habitat by cutting a few small patches. If your easement forbids tree cutting, you're out of luck. Even though your goal is to make your woodland better for nature, the easement language bars you from doing it.

Fortunately, more and more land trusts are recognizing that some farming and forestry can be compatible with nature. The preservation easement is becoming less common, and in its place are easements that allow for traditional land uses while only preventing development. You'll sometimes see these easements referred to as "working lands" easements; they are the only easements I recommend.

ment. But with an easement, development can't happen anymore. As a result, your land's assessment and property tax bill may go down. This doesn't always happen, but it's possible.

- **Big lump sum cash payment**: Most easements are donated, but there are a few cases in which land trusts purchase them. If you're fortunate enough to be in a place where you can sell your easement, you stand to gain a financial windfall from selling.

And of course, the land stays in your ownership, even though it's permanently protected from development. You can keep access private, continue farming or harvesting timber, and sell or pass on your land to someone else. You retain control of your property while ensuring that it remains open land.

How Do I Get an Easement?

Like any real estate transaction, getting an easement is a process, and it takes time. It can take even longer than selling property outright, because a lot of discussions and negotiations have to take place along the way to make sure both you and the land trust are satisfied.

Depending on where your property is, you'll have different options for land trusts. If it's in an area with a lot of development pressure or that has a rare natural feature, you may have lots of land trusts to pick from. In other cases you may have only one. Because most land trusts are small, they usually focus on specific places and generally try not to overlap each other. Before pursuing an easement, make sure the land trust you want to work with holds easements in your area.

Every land trust has different steps that take you from initial contact to signing the final paperwork, but the process generally works something like this. Once you identify a land trust you want to work with, get in touch with them. They'll ask you questions about your land. Again, because most land trusts are small, they aren't able to work with everyone. Instead they'll rank lands based on how valuable they are to the protection of the environment. For instance, my employer in the New York City Watershed eases land, but since we focus on water quality, we only select properties with streams. With our limited funds and staff, we don't have the resources to work with any other landowners, even though we'd like to.

Once the land trust confirms an interest in working with you, they'll schedule a visit so they can see your land in person. You'll walk the property together and talk about options for the easement. This is a good first chance to make sure you and the land trust are on the same page about what you want from the property and what the easement will—and won't—allow.

After this initial visit, the process becomes much like selling a house. An independent appraiser

WATCH OUT!
TERMS AND CONDITIONS MAY APPLY

Even though most easements have moved away from the preservation mindset, many still contain limitations beyond restricting development. As you go through the easement process, read everything carefully and make sure you know what you're signing.

Our easements in the New York City Watershed are great examples to study. Our focus is water quality, so while our easements allow farming and logging, we require the farmer or logger to use Best Management Practices. To make this requirement less burdensome, we work with the landowner to determine which BMPs to use, and then we provide funding to help offset installation costs.

Depending on which land trust you work with, you may find similar restrictions in your easement. Some of these restrictions are negotiable; others aren't. As with any contract, it's important to be honest with the land trust and find out what each of you is willing to live with.

Terms and conditions don't have to work against you. Our easements, for instance, have allowances for some level of development. Since we work a lot with farmers, our easements have designated areas of the property where farmers can build without restriction. In other spots, farmers can build farm-related structures only, while elsewhere no development is allowed. Under certain circumstances, we can carve out areas exempt from the easement so landowners can build a new house for a child who also wants to live on the land. All these designations are specific to the property and figured out in consultation with the landowner.

Of course there can be restrictions that rightfully cause you to rethink the easement. I've seen easement language stating that any tree cutting must receive prior approval from the land trust. I would avoid easements with this condition. To me, "prior approval" is just a nice way for a land trust to avoid saying that their easements create nature preserves. You get into the easement thinking it will be no problem for you to have a future timber harvest, and then, all too late, you find out the land trust won't approve anything.

The best way to avoid getting trapped by easement conditions is to get a second opinion on the easement contract. In fact, get a third and fourth opinion, too. Let other family members read it. Show it to a lawyer and your forester. Get beyond the legalese and make sure you know exactly what you're signing up for. Remember, you can back out any time before closing, but once you sign the final paperwork, the easement and all its terms will never go away.

assesses the land to figure out how much the property's development value is worth. Their appraisal will determine either how much money you'll make from selling your easement or how much you can deduct from your taxes if you donate it.

With the appraisal completed, the land trust will make an offer. At this point there's room for negotiation, though some land trusts are more open to it than others. You might discuss different terms, or arrange for certain areas to be excluded. This is the time to make sure that all the legal details are ironed out to your satisfaction.

The offer stage is also a good time to bring in an accountant. Your easement will result in a sizable check or charitable donation, and both have major tax implications. Having an accountant familiar with land and easements will help you navigate the stormy tax seas to get the most favorable outcome.

Once you and the land trust have settled all the terms, it's time for the final contract and closing. This gives you and the land trust one more chance to look everything over and make sure there aren't any last-minute issues. If both sides agree, the easement goes into effect.

How long this process takes varies from property to property and land trust to land trust. In the New York City Watershed, our easements commonly take two years from initial contact to closing.

While two years might sound extreme, I like the fact that it takes that long. That gives landowners lots of time to think about their decision and make sure it's the right one for their family and their land. If at any point they decide it isn't right for them, they can back out.

After Signing: Life Under Easement

Once you've eased your property, your interaction with the land trust isn't over. It's just beginning. As the holder of your easement, the land trust is legally obligated to ensure that the terms of your contract are carried out. Land trusts commonly refer to this requirement as "stewarding" an easement.

As with so much else with easements, stewarding may take several different shapes. At minimum it involves periodic property visits by someone from the land trust to confirm that you aren't violating any easement terms. For our easements, we do two annual checks: one by flyover and one on the ground. We're looking for signs of development (remember the easement's purpose is to limit development) as well as activities that require notification (like timber harvesting). If we spot violations, we work with the landowner to address them cooperatively. In theory we could sue the landowner for breach of contract, but that's a last-ditch option. It's far more important for us to maintain a working relationship with the landowner.

That's not to say ugly situations can't arise. I've

read horror stories of landowners having to watch their new home be demolished because they built it in an area where the easement forbids development. The possibility of such conflict turns a lot of people off to easements, and I can't blame them. It's one more reason why you need a thorough understanding up front of what your easement will and won't allow.

Aside from stewardship visits, life with an easement isn't all that different from life without one. You still own the land, so you can still hunt, fish, and recreate. When it comes time to sell or pass on the land, you can do so. The easement will go with the land to the new owners.

Having an easement will change your property, if in no other way than that you'll have an ongoing relationship with your local land trust. Speaking as someone who works at a land trust, I don't think that's a bad thing. Does it mean you might have a few hoops to jump through the next time you log? Probably. But it also means you have a partner for the future, someone you can fall back on for advice and assurance that you're making good decisions about your land.

CHAPTER 18

Leave a Legacy

We have not inherited this earth from our parents. We have borrowed it from our children.
—Numerous

There are moments that stay with you your whole life. Years later, you can recall every detail of where you were and what you were doing when the moment occurred. The JFK assassination. The moon landing. 9/11.

For me, one of those days is Sunday, August 7, 2011. As I cooked dinner (pancakes and bacon), the phone rang. It was Mom. My father had passed away suddenly.

He was 57.

In an instant, the lives of my family members were upended. No one had expected it. It seemed impossible.

We're all getting older. That's no secret. And landowners—sorry to say—are older than most. Almost 70 percent of US woodland owners are over 55. 40 percent are over 65. Those figures double the ones for the general population.

One of the hardest conversations to have with your family concerns what will happen to your land when you pass on. It's also one of the most important. Without a written plan, it's easy for your land to be broken up and sold for development to cover end-of-life expenses or to provide cash for heirs.

Three years before my dad died, my parents sat us kids down to talk about their will. I remember a fuzzy sound in my ears, like I couldn't let myself hear what they were saying. It was too much to face.

Looking back, though, I'm glad they took the time to think about those issues, plan ahead, and share their thoughts. Amid the grief of losing Dad, it was one less point of confusion, one less thing we all had to worry about.

My parents were fortunate in that a simple will

OPPOSITE: *Someday this land will be his. When the time comes, will he be ready?*

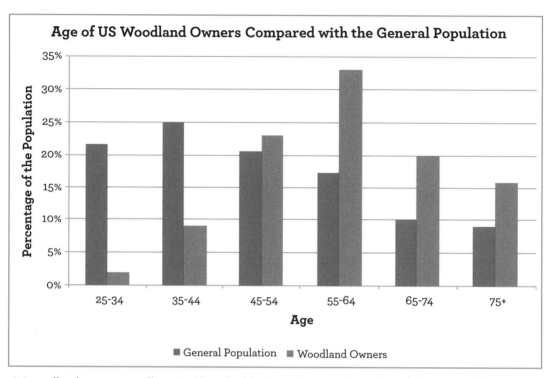

Age of US Woodland Owners Compared with the General Population

US woodland owners overall are significantly older than the general population.[1] As emotional as it is to think about, it's important to prepare for what will happen to your land when you're no longer able to take care of it.

was all they needed. For landowners, though, a will often isn't enough. Passing down the woods you've worked your life to care for is complicated. It can be hard even to know where to start.

That's what this chapter is: a starting point. Let me be clear on this. I'm a forester. I'm not a lawyer.

I'm not an accountant. I can't begin to give you all the information needed to make an effective estate plan in one chapter. Instead, I hope to give you things to think about, ways to get the conversation started, and ideas of professionals to engage when you're ready.

WATCH OUT!
THE ZOMBIE LANDOWNER

One of the most common arguments I hear from landowners who don't want to bother with legacy planning is what I call the Zombie Argument. "I don't want to limit my children's options," the landowner tells me. "I don't want to rule from beyond the grave."

This concern is valid. You may not want to tie your children's hands and force them to do something with the land that they have no interest in doing. That probably wouldn't result in the best outcome for either your family or your woods.

Yet this legitimate feeling is not an excuse to do nothing. Legacy planning doesn't mean you have to rule from beyond the grave. Even if you want your children to have full choice over what happens with the land, legacy planning still matters.

In fact, it's all the more important. If you die without a plan in place, the courts get to make your plan for you. They follow a prescribed set of rules called intestacy laws. These laws divide your assets in the manner the government thinks is best. Odds are that won't be what you or your heirs would have liked to see happen.

I Only Own Ten Acres. Can I Skip This Chapter?

Estate planning sounds like something only the mega-rich need to bother with. Many people hear the term and interpret it as "estate tax planning," as in, "How am I going to avoid estate taxes?"

For the vast majority of landowners, the federal estate tax isn't an issue anymore. Thanks to the American Taxpayer Relief Act of 2012, estates up to $5 million are exempt from federal estate tax. That amount is indexed to keep up with inflation, so as time goes by, that exemption will increase. From a tax perspective, then, you probably won't need to worry about estate planning.

But note the word I used for this chapter's title: legacy. Yes, estate planning can help you minimize your tax burden, but planning for your land's future is about much more than that. It's about ensuring that all the hard work you've put into nurturing your land doesn't crumble the moment you stop being around to take care of the property.

That's why, for the rest of this chapter, I won't use the phrase "estate planning." Rather, I'll refer to "legacy planning," a three-step process for passing not only your land but your passion and vision for it to the next generation. That's a process that's valuable for every landowner, no matter how much land you own or how much money you make.

Legacy Planning Step 1: Get Your Family Involved

There's a theme to the two Watch Out! sidebars in this chapter: the importance of family communication. You can't develop a good legacy plan in a bubble. How do you know your son isn't interested in the property? How do you know your daughter is interested? It's easy to envision a situation in which a daughter living close to the property would want nothing to do with it, while a son living far away would love to return home. You don't know unless you ask.

Talking with your heirs is also a great way to avoid becoming a Zombie Landowner. You won't be ruling from beyond the grave, because your heirs will be part of the decision process.

TALKING WITH YOUR HEIRS: THE FAMILY MEETING

Family meeting. There's a cringe-worthy phrase. It's hard enough just to get everyone together, and when you do, who knows what might happen? But open, honest communication between family members is the best way to ensure that everyone knows each other's needs and feelings related to the land.

Here are some tips for conducting a family meeting so that it (with a little luck) doesn't turn into a screaming match:

WATCH OUT!
FAIR AND EQUAL: NOT THE SAME

Another frequent concern landowners express in legacy planning is the desire to be fair to all their children. They don't want one child to get a larger share of the inheritance than the others. To be fair, they say, everything has to be equal.

As with the Zombie Argument, this is a valid feeling. I would caution you, though, that "fair" and "equal" aren't the same, especially when it comes to land.

Land isn't like stocks, bonds, or cash. It can't be equally divided. Yes, you could split the property and give the same number of acres to each child, but that wouldn't be equal. Your land likely isn't uniform. You might have some fields, some wooded areas, and maybe a stream. You might have some road frontage or a hilltop that could be leased for a cell tower. No matter how you chunk up the property, the parts won't be equal.

The parts also won't equal the whole. Whether your concerns are economic or environmental, bigger is better when it comes to land. A larger property has more options available to it, whether you want to attract loggers or wildlife.

Land also has this problem of being stationary. Your stocks and bonds don't have a place attached to them. You can divide them up, and it doesn't matter whether your kids live in Saginaw, Spokane, or San Francisco. Land doesn't work that way. It's stuck where it is. If it's in Wisconsin, your son in the Southwest might not care about it. It can't move to him, and he might not want to move to it.

But then, maybe your daughter lives in Green Bay. She might love the land and cherish the idea of taking care of it. If you give the land to her instead of splitting it between her and your son, that wouldn't be equal, but it might be fair. Your son never had an interest in it anyway.

This doesn't mean you have to cut your son out of an inheritance. If your daughter is really interested in the land, maybe your son would be more interested in other parts of your estate. Maybe there are family heirlooms he would enjoy. Maybe he's just interested in stocks. Finding other assets to pass down to him could make the final distribution fair—even if you aren't splitting everything evenly.

TRY THIS:
THE HEIRLOOM SCALE

What does your land mean to you? What does it mean to your heirs? Is it merely a financial asset, no more sentimental than the money in your savings account? Or is it a priceless heirloom, one to be kept in the family intact at all costs? Perhaps it's somewhere in between. Your answer would most likely be different from what your spouse or heirs would say.

Part of involving your family in legacy planning is learning how each person feels about the land and what they hope to get out of it. An easy way to start that conversation is with the Heirloom Scale, developed by Oregon Tree Farmer and CPA Clint Bentz.

Here's what you do. In your family meeting, give each person a piece of paper. Everyone then writes on that paper a number between 1 and 10. A "1" means they view the land with no emotional attachment; it's purely part of a financial portfolio. A "10" means they view the land as a priceless heirloom, one to be kept in the family and protected for future generations no matter what.

After everyone writes down their numbers, go around and share them. Each person should say the number they picked and why. Use this information as a starting point in your family discussions. Use it to talk about why you own this land and what you all would like to see happen to it over the next ten, twenty, even fifty or a hundred years.

As you have more family meetings, you can repeat the Heirloom Scale. You may find that as family members' lives change, their perspectives toward your land change too. In his *Tree Farmer* magazine article describing the Heirloom Scale, Clint talks about how some of his siblings rated the land as low as 3 when they first did this exercise on his family's woodlot. They were interested in the property, but it was mostly for the money it could yield. Over time, though, everyone in Clint's family became 10's, devoted to keeping the woods intact and in the family.

- As strange as it sounds, avoid the holidays if you can. Yes, they're a natural time to bring the family together, but they're also fraught with emotion and stress. Schedule a time specifically to talk about your land.
- Invite everyone, including spouses. Even if you want the land to stay only with the immediate family, it's a good idea to make sure everyone gets the same information at the same time.
- If there are family members who don't want to participate, that's all right. Do your best to include them to show you care about their perspective.

- Have at least your first meeting (yes, there will be more than one) in person. Even in the Internet Age, there's no substitute for that face-to-face connection.
- The best place to have the meeting is on the land itself. Land is real. It has a place. Let everyone experience it.
- Encourage everyone to keep an open mind and avoid making assumptions. This meeting isn't the place to air old grudges or sibling rivalries. Make sure everyone has a chance to express their opinions.
- Some families, for lots of reasons, just can't get along. If you're concerned your meeting might fall apart, consider hiring a professional mediator or counselor to guide it and keep everyone contributing in a positive way.

IT'S YOUR DECISION

In a perfect world, family meetings would lead to consensus. Everyone would realize what was in the land's and family's best interests, and everyone would come to the same conclusion about what to do.

But we don't live in a perfect world. There will be problems. That's OK. It's your land. You can make decisions even without family consensus.

I realize that recommendation treads close to the Zombie Landowner situation, but it's important to have a plan, even if there's disagreement. Time marches on, and avoiding decisions won't make the conflict go away. Instead, it will fester, and then, at a point when your heirs are grieving over your loss, it can explode.

My father witnessed these detonations many times in his career. He was a pastor, and he often counseled families as they navigated the emotional turmoil of losing a loved one. He had many horror stories about people who cared deeply for one another tearing their relationships apart over what was left behind.

Dad was determined for that not happen to our family. When he and Mom sat us down to talk about their will, he said something that stuck with me. He said, "At the end of the day, it's all stuff. Your relationship matters far more. Don't let stuff damage the love you have for each other."

Don't let stuff—even your land—ruin your family's relationships. The best ways to keep that from happening are to plan ahead and communicate.

Legacy Planning Step 2: Learn about Options for Passing Down Land

So you've had your family meeting, and you have an idea of what you'd like to happen to your land after you're gone. Excellent! That's the hardest, most emotional part of legacy planning. The rest is financial and legal paperwork, and thankfully, there are professionals who can handle that for you. They can identify the tools you need to make your vision a reality.

That said, it's helpful, when approaching a professional, if you have some idea of your options. Since I don't have a whole book to talk about legacy planning, I'm just going to give you an overview of a few tools you can use.

WILLS

Wills are legal documents that describe how to distribute your assets after you pass away. Without a will, the courts step in and make those decisions instead. If you do nothing else suggested in this chapter, at least have a will.

In your will, you can record not only who should get your land, but any desires you have concerning its treatment. Those desires can be general or specific, but the will is a good place to ensure they're written down and made clear.

Wills have the advantage of being cheap and relatively easy to assemble. They're an essential part of any legacy plan, even if you elect for some of the more complicated options described below.

By themselves, though, wills have limitations. Assets passed down through a will go through a public court process called probate, which can take months and cost thousands of dollars—if everything goes well. Wills are also a poor tool for passing your land to multiple heirs, as we'll discuss next.

DIFFERENT OWNERSHIP MODELS

A will can work if you're passing land to just one person, say the daughter in Green Bay from my earlier sidebar. But if you want to give your land to all your kids, a will won't be enough. Joint-owned real estate shouldn't be held as if it were held by individuals. For one, it complicates any decision-making about the property. It also leaves a lot of gray area concerning who's responsible for receiving income and paying costs like property taxes. In the worst-case scenario, joint ownership with a disinterested heir could force the other heirs to split up and sell the land.

Fortunately, there are ownership models that allow you to pass your land intact to multiple people while avoiding the drawbacks of individual ownership. The two most common approaches are limited liability corporations (LLCs) and trusts. In these ownership structures, you create a company that owns the land, rather than you or your heirs directly. You then pass down control of the company in the form of shares.

Now you may be thinking that this approach sounds too business-y for your woodlot, but those business aspects are what make these methods better than individual ownership. For instance, when you form an LLC or trust for your land, you establish rules for how decisions are made, how income is distributed, and how costs are paid. You can also set limitations, such as stating that the land shouldn't be subdivided or developed. These rules provide better, longer-lasting guidance than a will would provide by itself.

Which ownership structure is right for your family depends on your personal situation, so I won't go into detail on these structures. The best option if you want to pass land to multiple heirs is to speak to an attorney and get specific advice. In the next section, I'll talk about what to look for in a good legacy-planning attorney and where to find one.

If you'd like to dig more into ownership options before consulting an attorney, I recommend the *Your Land, Your Legacy* guide I've listed in "Beyond the Book." Pages 21–29 of that guide provide simple descriptions of the various ownership models.

CONSERVATION EASEMENTS

In the last chapter, I talked about conservation easements and their ability to permanently protect your land from development. Easements also play a powerful role in legacy planning. Few tools offer clearer management direction than an easement. A will or the founding documents of a trust might be misinterpreted, but an easement guarantees your land will never be chunked up into vacation homes or strip malls.

If you're concerned about estate taxes, easements also offer a chance to reduce your tax burden while keeping the land in the family. While the federal estate tax exemption has increased, many states have estate or inheritance taxes (or both!) with lower thresholds. Minnesota, for instance, exempts up to $2,000,000 in assets, less than half the federal exemption. That might still sound like a lot, but given how much land has increased in value, you'd be surprised how easy it is to hit that amount. At $5,000 an acre, for example, you would only need 400 acres to reach that level. And that assumes you own nothing else whatsoever—no home, no valuables, no retirement fund. When you account for everything else in your estate, you might be surprised at how quickly it all adds up.

Estate taxes are especially problematic because, again, land isn't like most other assets. If you owe estate tax on your stocks, it's easy to sell some to pay the tax. But with land, your only options to raise the needed cash may be to subdivide the property into house lots or pillage the timber with no thought to the future forest. Neither outcome is good for the land.

An easement can help. Because you no longer own the development rights, your land will typically receive a lower appraisal and therefore contribute less to your estate. That reduced value might be enough to put you below the estate tax threshold, or at least to lower your amount of tax due.

Remember, though, that an easement is permanent. It goes with the property from owner to owner. Make sure you talk it over with your heirs before committing.

One way to include the possibility of an easement while leaving your options open is to donate your easement through your will rather than doing it while you're alive. Since you can change your will whenever you like, you can always remove the donation from it if you need to sell your property to cover, say, medical expenses. But if you wind up not needing the cash, you'll still reduce your heirs' estate tax burden, since the easement is a charitable donation.

Legacy Planning Step 3: Get the Pros You Need

I've emphasized DIY activities throughout this book, but your legacy plan isn't one of them. The legal documents you need for a will, trust, or con-servation easement all require professional help. The price can be steep; forming a trust can cost thousands of dollars. Compared with the costs of probate and estate taxes, though, these fees are minimal. Like a good forester in a timber sale, the right legacy planning professionals will more than pay for themselves.

LAWYER

You might already have a lawyer, but with all respect to that person, you will probably want someone else for your legacy plan. Estate transfer is a specialized branch of law, and you want someone who knows it inside and out. A generalist lawyer won't be able to give you the same level of service or offer you the range of options that one focused on legacy planning can provide.

Your best choice—if you can find one—is an estate lawyer who has worked with landowners who want to keep the land in their families. Farmers and woodland owners should be on the lawyer's client list. In an ideal world, the lawyer would have experience physically being on land, perhaps growing up on a farm or being a woodland owner.

Why is a land connection so important for your lawyer to have? A lot of estate lawyers have two overriding goals in their process: minimize any tax burdens and convert as many assets to cash as possible to divide among the heirs. That strategy works if all your assets are paper, like stocks and bonds, but it falls apart if you want to keep land intact for the family. A lawyer who works with landowning clients is more likely to understand your desires and have experience with the tools needed to make them realities.

These lawyers can be difficult to find, so shop around and ask multiple lawyers about their client lists and experiences. If you can't find anyone with a land background, a good alternate option is a lawyer who has worked with the passing down of family businesses. Many of the same tools that apply to land transfer also work for business transfer, so a lawyer with experience in this arena can work and may be more common than a land-focused one.

Where do you find these lawyers? There are online databases, and I've provided a link to one in "Beyond the Book." Because land experience is so essential with whomever you find, I recommend seeking referrals first. Reach out to other landowners near you and see who they use, if anyone. Also check with your state's woodland owner association to see if they have contacts.

If you search online, make sure you do thorough research and ask a lot of questions. Have each lawyer you contact describe a typical client, and most important, get references.

CERTIFIED PUBLIC ACCOUNTANT

I mentioned the usefulness of CPAs back in the chapter on taxes, so I'll be brief here. Particularly in states with estate or inheritance taxes, having a CPA or other tax pro on your legacy planning team can come in handy. He or she can help you identify ways to reduce your estate tax burden as well as other potential end-of-life costs like long-term care.

Just as with lawyers, it helps to have a CPA familiar with land and land conservation. There are whole sections of the tax code specific to woodland owners, and you want someone knowledgeable about them all. See "Beyond the Book" for a link to a CPA database.

FORESTER

A forester won't be able to help you much with law or tax matters, but they can help identify information about your land that will be relevant to your legacy plan. When you sit down to discuss your land's future with your family, it will be useful to know how much land you own and what natural resources are on it. A forester can help with both these needs.

As I mentioned in "Timber!," several states have forester licensing, and these states often publish those lists online. I've included links in the "State Resources" appendix to help you locate foresters in your state.

QUALIFIED INDEPENDENT APPRAISER

How much is your land worth? If you bought it decades ago—or if you inherited it—it could be worth more than you realize. No one is making more land, and land values have risen a lot in recent decades. Without an official appraisal, it's hard to know if your heirs will be subject to estate tax.

The IRS only recognizes appraisals performed

by Qualified Independent Appraisers, so look for this designation when seeking someone. You can find a link to an appraiser database in "Beyond the Book."

The Best Thing You Can Do to Secure Your Land's Future

I've offered a lot of suggestions in this book, and I'm sure not all of them have made sense for your situation. That's OK. I'd like to end, though, with what I believe is the single best way to do right by your land: get your kids involved.

I don't just mean get them involved in your legacy planning. Get them involved in your land. If you want them to take over the family land some day, it's worth spending as much time as possible with them on the property so they can learn about it and its care. Encourage them to take part in meetings with your forester, and to observe a timber sale if you have one. You still make the final decisions, but show your heirs that you value their input and that you want them to learn why this place is so important.

In a way it's like grooming a child to take over the family business. Help your heirs learn about owning woodland by giving them small responsibilities. Let them make decisions about a section of the property, or have them plan a timber harvest for a portion of woods. It's a little scary, but let them make mistakes. That's how you improve. The more time your kids can spend learning about your property's care while you're around to teach them, the better.

I've seen the importance of this involvement firsthand. In early 2015, I did a survey of New York landowners for a research project. I put my contact information on it in case landowners had questions.

One morning, a woman called me. She had that fast, shrill voice of someone both panicked and hopeful. She had just moved to New York from New Mexico after her mother had fallen ill. She was taking care of her now-dying mother and trying to look after the family land all by herself. She'd lived in New Mexico most of her life; she knew nothing about forests, certainly not wet eastern forests. Now her mother was in no position to teach her, and she feared she wouldn't be able to hold on to the property.

She and I talked for a while, and I gave her some ideas of places she could go for help. I gave her phone numbers for a local landowner group and some foresters. I also pointed her in the direction of some volunteer long-time landowners who were willing to visit her property and share their experiences owning New York woodlands.

I don't know the circumstances before this woman's mother fell ill, but I got the sense the two of them never talked about the land or what this woman would do when she found herself in charge of all the decisions. As a result she had a trial by fire, and only a happy coincidence—me sending her a survey—gave her a lifeline.

Even though I was able to help her, neither I nor any of the people I pointed her toward could have given this woman as much insight into her family's land as her mother could have. That's why it's so crucial to engage your kids with your woods as early and as often as possible.

Getting your kids involved doesn't have to be all business. It can and should be fun too. If you want your family to care about the property, do it by creating memories together. Encourage your kids and grandkids to explore your land and see the trees, streams, and wildlife for themselves. Share your knowledge with them on hikes. Point out different features and tell stories.

If your kids live far away, send them photos of your land. This activity can work especially well as the seasons change, because your woods will be changing right alongside them. And if you can, get the whole family to the property at least once a year for a picnic or holiday.

It's your land, but only for a little while. You've borrowed it from the next generation, and eventually you have to give it back. When you do, make sure they're as devoted to it as you are.

ACKNOWLEDGMENTS

This book has taken a long journey from basic idea to finished product, and it wouldn't have made it to your hands without the help of an amazing group of people. I want to start by acknowledging my mentors, a group of authors and friends who have taught and encouraged me on this marathon called writing: Shannon Delany, John Elder, Rowan Jacobsen, Clare Walker Leslie, and Ginger Strand. I also want to thank Sterling College, who hosted the nature-writing seminar where I was fortunate enough to meet four of these incredible authors.

Writing may seem like a lonely pursuit, but many fingerprints are on this book. Ginger Strand reviewed my proposal and gave me great tips to refine my ideas. My coworkers at the Watershed Agricultural Council have been brilliant: reviewing drafts, checking facts, supplying photos, and feeding me more ideas for woodsy projects than I could ever have hoped to fit in one book. In particular I want to thank Tom Foulkrod, Heather Hilson, Brendan Murphy, Tom Pavlesich, and Karl VonBerg, all of whom contributed directly to this book in one form or another.

In addition to this writing support crew, I've been blessed with an equally talented team on the publishing side. My agent Jennifer Unter, of the Unter Agency, has been wonderful, sticking with me and fighting hard on my behalf. The editors at The Countryman Press have all shown their commitment, both to this project in particular and to writing in general. I want to thank those editors who were involved in assembling this book: Dan Crissman and Ann Treistman. I'd like to also thank the copyeditor, Max Winter. All of them helped refine *Your Backyard Forest*'s content, tone, and language to make it a more useful and enjoyable read.

Finally, I want to thank my wife, Christine. Writing this book has meant many hours of reading, researching, writing, and rewriting. I'm beyond grateful to be married to someone who understands my love for helping others through the written word, and who makes sure I keep up the discipline to write every day.

CHAPTER 1: PRIVATE LANDOWNERS RULE!

mylandplan.org: This free nationwide, interactive woodland planning tool lets you map your land, identify activities to complete, and find resources to get the work done.

mywoodlot.com: This free woodland site is focused on the northeastern United States, but it provides a wealth of projects you can do on your land. I curate this site's content, and it inspired me to write this book.

tinyurl.com/forestry-ed-sites: You can learn a lot about caring for your woods from books, but nothing beats getting outside and seeing on-the-ground projects. This national map shows demonstration forests you can visit to learn firsthand how different people look after the land.

CHAPTER 2: WHERE DO I START?

tinyurl.com/Sand-County-Almanac-Leopold: Aldo Leopold was one of America's strongest voices for land and landowners. Though he wrote many works, *A Sand County Almanac* is his most famous. In it he chronicles his observations about his Wisconsin farm over a full year, and he champions the idea of a land ethic where we see the land as part of our community.

CHAPTER 3: NATURE'S BEAUTY

tinyurl.com/Reading-the-Forest: If you want to get more out of your woods walks, particularly if you live in the Northeast, I highly recommend Tom Wessels' book *Reading the Forested Landscape: A Natural History of New England.*

leafsnap.com: This free app tells you what tree you're looking at simply by having you take a picture of a leaf with your smartphone.

tinyurl.com/Birding-by-Ear-Eastern: Put simply, *Birding by Ear* is the best way I've found to learn the major bird calls of North America. This link is for the eastern half of the continent.

tinyurl.com/Birding-by-Ear-Western: If you live in a western state, here's the *Birding by Ear* link for western North America.

CHAPTER 4: GET OUT AND PLAY!

tinyurl.com/NWF-Family-Fun: I only had space to talk about a couple kid-friendly outdoor ideas. This website from the National Wildlife Federation provides a searchable database of more than 600 nature-related activities for families. You can search based on the age of your kids, the topic you'd like to explore, and even by season.

tinyurl.com/Red-Flag-Map: This automatically updated map from the National Weather Service shows current red flag warnings and fire watches for the United States.

tinyurl.com/Macroinvertebrate-Key: This easy key will help you identify macroinvertebrates. You can also use it to figure out your stream's water quality based on the kinds of critters you find. In the key, the letters represent how tolerant to pollution a species is: "S" for sensitive, "F" for fairly tolerant, and "T" for tolerant.

tinyurl.com/Topo-Map-Downloads: The US Geological Survey produces topographic maps for the country. This mapper lets you zoom in on your property (or anywhere else in the United States), pick the topo map you want, and then download it for free.

tinyurl.com/Compass-Tutorial: Aerial photos and topo maps help you get where you're going, but to really stay on track in the woods, learn to use a compass. This video teaches the basics of choosing a travel direction and then sticking to it while hiking.

tinyurl.com/Trail-Markers: Voss Signs is an example of a company that allows you to purchase trail markers in a variety of colors.

tinyurl.com/Ben-Meadows-Tree-Paint: Ben Meadows is a forestry supply company with lots of products for work and play in the woods. This link takes you to their tree paint selection.

CHAPTER 5: HEALTH AND WELLNESS

tickencounter.org: The Tick Encounter Resource Center at the University of Rhode Island is the best source I've found online for all things tick-related. It has great resources on topics like tick identification and removal, bite prevention, and disease symptoms and treatments.

tinyurl.com/Insect-Shield: In addition to DEET,

another way to protect yourself from ticks is to buy clothing pretreated with insect repellent. This link lists stores that sell pretreated clothing. More impressive, it has a feature where you can send in your current outdoor clothing and get it treated for a fee.

CHAPTER 6: WONDERFUL WOODLAND WILDLIFE

tinyurl.com/Food-Plot-Video: This video by Wisconsin landowner Nate Francois is the first in a series of three. Together they show how to build and maintain a food plot on your land.

nacdnet.org/about/districts/directory: This mapper from the National Association for Conservation Districts can help you find contact information for your district's office.

tinyurl.com/Brush-Piles: This page from the Humane Society offers tips on building brush piles, and it includes a video demonstration of a woman building one in her backyard.

CHAPTER 7: THE WORLD'S BIGGEST WATER FILTER

tinyurl.com/BMP-Tips-Video: There's more to BMPs than waterbars and stream crossings. This brief video outlines basic BMPs you and your logger should consider when harvesting timber.

stateforesters.org/state-forestry-BMPs-map: Every state has different BMPs and ways of enforcing them. The National Association of State Foresters created this interactive map that lets you choose your state, find out whether BMPs are voluntary or mandatory there, and access your state's BMP guidelines.

tinyurl.com/Tree-Planting-Video: This National Gardening Association video shows you how to plant a tree. It's geared toward yard trees, but the techniques apply to most tree-planting situations.

arborday.org/trees/planting/bare-root.cfm: Planting bare-root trees is tougher than planting ones that come in containers, but bare-root trees are cheaper. If you want to plant bare-root trees, check out this resource from the Arbor Day Foundation that includes step-by-step instructions and a video.

tinyurl.com/Tree-Tubes: If you need tree tubes, here's an example of a place where you can purchase them.

tinyurl.com/Bark-Protectors: Once the tree tubes come off, bark protectors can help keep deer and other animals from damaging your young trees. Here's an example of one kind of bark protector.

CHAPTER 8: CHANGING CLIMATE, CHANGING WOODLAND

gameoflogging.com/upcoming_events.php: Game of Logging is a professional chainsaw safety course, and its lessons have been credited with saving hundreds of loggers from injury or death in the woods. If you plan to cut your own firewood, you owe it to yourself and your family to attend a chainsaw safety course like Game of Logging first.

tinyurl.com/Tree-Felling-Video: While no substitute for an in-person training, this video from *The Progressive Farmer* will introduce you to safer tree cutting techniques.

tinyurl.com/Firewood-Stacking: I touched on firewood stacking, but this article from *Mother Earth News* walks you through the techniques to a firewood pile that will both dry well and look great.

epa.gov/burnwise: The US Environmental Protection Agency's Burn Wise website provides tips on cleaner, more efficient wood burning and lists of certified wood heating appliances.

tinyurl.com/Yale-Wood-Study-1 and **tinyurl.com/Yale-Wood-Study-2**: Don't believe me about wood's potential as a climate change fighter? Here are two links to the Yale study I referenced so you can check out the numbers for yourself.

CHAPTER 9: THE TAXMAN COMETH

tinyurl.com/Timber-Tax-Tips: The US Forest Service publishes the *Federal Income Tax on Timber: A Quick Guide for Woodland Owners* every few years. This link is for the latest edition as of the time I wrote this chapter, but keep in mind that tax rules change often. Make sure you have the most up-to-date information when making tax decisions.

tinyurl.com/Tax-Preparer-Tips: These tips from the IRS on finding and choosing the right tax preparer are general, but they're solid advice regardless.

tinyurl.com/find-CPA: The American Institute of CPA's maintains this searchable, nationwide CPA database.

tinyurl.com/find-Enrolled-Agent: Enrolled Agents are IRS-licensed tax specialists. The National Association of Enrolled Agents maintains this searchable, nationwide Enrolled Agent database.

srs.fs.usda.gov/econ/data/forestincentives: While I'm not covering funding programs because of their high competition, there are federal, state, and private grants for certain woodland practices. If you want to try your luck with them, this US Forest Service site lets you find programs in your state with links where possible. The links don't all work anymore—the resource was assembled in 2006 and hasn't been updated—but the information on the site can still provide the keywords to fuel an Internet search about a particular program.

CHAPTER 10: POSTED

tinyurl.com/Boundary-Line-Marking: This article by Chris Mead of the Alabama Forest Commission describes how to mark the boundaries of both your property and a timber harvest.

nelsonpaint.com: The Nelson Paint Company is an example of a site where you can purchase paint specifically designed for use on trees.

vosssigns.com/products: Voss Signs is an example of a company that provides both stock and custom posted signs.

CHAPTER 11: A BURNING PROBLEM

tinyurl.com/Firewise-Resources: This Firewise website includes links to more information about protecting your home from wildfire, including more landscape and construction tips, as well as videos on fire behavior and safety.

tinyurl.com/Timber-Salvage-Resources: This collection of fact sheets, most developed by the University of Kentucky, offers suggestions on safety and salvage decisions following a natural disaster. It even includes tips for reporting timber losses on your income taxes. Though the fact sheets focus on ice storms, their lessons apply to other natural disasters too.

CHAPTER 12: CHOWING DOWN

tinyurl.com/Invasive-Species-Map: Which forest pests affect your woodlot? The Forest Service created this interactive map that lets you zoom in to your land and see which species threaten it.

invasive.org: Once you know which forest pests are near you, you can use this website from the Center for Invasive Species and Ecosystem Health to find out more about those species, including control options where available.

tinyurl.com/EAB-Map: Because the emerald ash borer spreads so rapidly, I haven't included a range map in this book. Instead, this link takes you to the most current map of known US emerald ash borer infestations.

tinyurl.com/EAB-Symptoms: How do you know if you have emerald ash borers on your land? This two-page fact sheet from Michigan State University reviews the symptoms of an infestation.

tinyurl.com/Arborist-Search: If you want to treat a few trees with insecticide to protect them from pests like the emerald ash borer, get an arborist to help. Arborists can also help you remove diseased or dead trees that threaten your home or cabin. This website from the International Society of Arborists provides a searchable database of certified arborists.

CHAPTER 13: TIMBER!

tinyurl.com/Choosing-a-Forester: You should always work with a forester when having a timber harvest, but what should you look for in a forester? Cornell University provides some tips on this website.

tinyurl.com/Sample-Timber-Prospectus: While most foresters will have their own prospectus sheets, this example prospectus will show you what to expect and what information you and your forester will need to gather.

tinyurl.com/Sample-Timber-Contract: I provided an overview of timber contract clauses, but this sample contract from the University of New Hampshire gives examples of contract language as well as explanations of why each clause matters.

CHAPTER 14: FARM THE FOREST

farmingthewoods.com: Written by two educators and forest farmers, *Farming the Woods* is a great book for the would-be forest farmer who is deciding where to start. With numerous photographs, diagrams, and examples of real people forest farming, this book provides an overview of dozens of potential crops.

youtube.com/user/exforestfarming: This YouTube channel by Extension features dozens of videos on forest farming crops and techniques.

tinyurl.com/Home-Maple-Syrup-Video: If you want to make maple syrup at home for personal use, this video walks you through how to do it, using a turkey fryer and stove. It also includes a section on tapping trees.

bascommaple.com and **tapmytrees.com /starter-kit.html**: When you're ready to start tapping trees, here are two online retailers where you can purchase maple supplies, from the basics to professional equipment.

tinyurl.com/Ginseng-Assessment: This ginseng site assessment by ginseng expert Bob Beyfuss of Cornell Cooperative Extension provides an objective way of evaluating whether part of your land might be suitable for ginseng cultivation.

tinyurl.com/Silvopasture-Site-Eval: Similar to the ginseng site assessment, this scoring rubric will help you determine if your land is a good candidate for silvopasture.

CHAPTER 15: OTHER INCOME SOURCES

finitecarbon.com: Finite Carbon is a national company that works with landowners to negotiate carbon credit payments. Their website is a good place to learn more about carbon credits and how to get started pursuing them.

nationalhuntingleases.com. The Hunting Lease Network offers a real estate-like service for hunters and landowners looking to lease hunting rights.

tinyurl.com/Hunting-Lease-Sample: This publication from the University of Georgia gives more tips on hunting lease contracts and includes sample clauses.

tinyurl.com/Fishing-Lease-Info: Though written in 1992, this publication from the Southern Regional Aquaculture Center is one of the few reliable sources on fishing leases.

airbnb.com: Airbnb is known as a way for property owners to rent their homes to vacationers. It has also become popular with landowners who wish to advertise their land or cabin for camping.

CHAPTER 16: START A NEW FOREST

tinyurl.com/How-Wolves-Change-Rivers: Narrated by British author George Monbiot, this remarkable video explains in four short minutes how the reintroduction of wolves and resulting reduction in deer herds improved not only Yellowstone's biology but the physical characteristics of its waterways.

tinyurl.com/Tree-Planting-Programs: Even though natural regrowth is preferred over plantations, sometimes tree planting is the fastest, best way to start a new forest. This interactive map shows tree-planting programs across the United States and features links to information and assistance to landowners interested in planting trees.

tinyurl.com/Deer-Fence-Tips: I barely touched on the variety of deer fence types and materials available. This publication from Michigan State University gives more details on the various options and includes photos of examples.

CHAPTER 17: KEEP YOUR WOODS AS WOODS

conservationeasement.us: Are there eased lands near your property? This national map shows the location of easements throughout the United States. Participation in the map is voluntary, so it doesn't show everything. Still, you might be surprised at how many landowners near you have eased their land.

tinyurl.com/Accredited-Land-Trusts: While there are more than 1,700 land trusts across the United States, only about 300 have earned accreditation by the Land Trust Alliance. When deciding whether to pursue an easement, start with this list of established organizations.

tinyurl.com/Easement-Case-Study-1 and **tinyurl.com/Easement-Case-Study-2**: Before getting an easement, talk to other landowners who have easements and learn from their experiences. These two videos let you hear from a few landowners about why they chose easements to protect their properties.

CHAPTER 18: LEAVE A LEGACY

tinyurl.com/land-legacy: *Your Land, Your Legacy* is a legacy planning primer from the University of Massachusetts. Though it's written with a Massachusetts landowner in mind, its step-by-step approach and numerous case studies will be helpful no matter where your woods are.

tinyurl.com/the-heirloom-scale: This *Tree Farmer* magazine article by landowner and CPA Clint Bentz discusses the Heirloom Scale and one family's experience using it.

tinyurl.com/Estate-Lawyer-Search: This searchable database of estate planning lawyers lets you search by state, then by city to find someone local.

tinyurl.com/find-appraiser: The Appraisal Institute maintains this searchable, nationwide appraiser database.

NATIONAL RESOURCES

Forester Lists: Society of American Foresters (SAF) Certified Foresters (safnet.org/certifiedforester/findcertifiedforester.cfm); Association of Consulting Foresters (acf-foresters.org); Forest Guild (forestguild.org/find-a-forester)

Landowner Organization: National Woodland Owners Association (woodlandowners.org)

Cooperative Extension: I realize this map is on a website about pesticide use, but it's a great resource that provides phone numbers and web addresses for every US county's Cooperative Extension office. (npic.orst.edu/pest/countyext.htm)

Forestry Agency: US Forest Service—State and Private Forestry (fs.fed.us/spf)

ALABAMA

Tree Guide: *A Key to Common Native Trees of Alabama* (tinyurl.com/Alabama-tree-guide)

Property Tax Program: Current Use (tinyurl.com/Alabama-current-use)

Forester List: Alabama State Board of Registration for Foresters (tinyurl.com/Alabama-forester-list)

Natural Heritage Program: Alabama Natural Heritage Program (alnhp.org)

Landowner Organization: Alabama Forest Owners Association (afoa.org)

Cooperative Extension: Alabama A&M and Auburn Universities Cooperative Extension (aces.edu/main)

State Forestry Agency: Alabama Forestry Commission (forestry.alabama.gov)

ALASKA

Tree Guide: *Common Trees of Alaska* (tinyurl.com/Alaska-tree-guide)

Property Tax Program: Automatic exemption for forestland

Forester List: None available; use national lists

Natural Heritage Program: Alaska Natural Heritage Program (aknhp.uaa.alaska.edu)

Landowner Organization: Alaska Forest Association (akforest.org)

Cooperative Extension: University of Alaska-Fairbanks Extension (uaf.edu/ces)

State Forestry Agency: Alaska Division of Forestry (forestry.alaska.gov)

ARIZONA

Tree Guide: *Trees of Arizona Field Guide* (tinyurl.com/Arizona-tree-guide)

Property Tax Program: Automatic reduction for forestland

Forester List: None available; use national lists

Natural Heritage Program: Arizona Heritage Data

Management System (tinyurl.com/Arizona-natural-heritage)

Landowner Organization: None, use National Woodland Owners Association

Cooperative Extension: University of Arizona Extension (extension.arizona.edu)

State Forestry Agency: Arizona State Forestry Division (azsf.az.gov)

ARKANSAS

Tree Guide: *Trees of Arkansas* (https://www.ark.org/afc/index.php)

Property Tax Program: Automatic reduction for forestland

Forester List: Arkansas Board of Registration for Foresters (arkansas.gov/abof)

Natural Heritage Program: Arkansas Natural Heritage Commission (naturalheritage.com)

Landowner Organization: Arkansas Forestry Association (arkforests.org); see also Ozark Woodland Owner's Association (ozarkforestry.org/owoa.html)

Cooperative Extension: University of Arkansas Cooperative Extension Service (uaex.edu)

State Forestry Agency: Arkansas Forestry Commission (forestry.arkansas.gov)

CALIFORNIA

Tree Guide: *National Audubon Society Field Guide to California* (tinyurl.com/California-tree-guide)

Property Tax Program: California Land Conservation Act/Williamson Act (conservation.ca.gov/dlrp/lca/Pages/Index.aspx)

Forester List: California Registered Professional Foresters (tinyurl.com/California-forester-list)

Natural Heritage Program: California Natural Diversity Database (tinyurl.com/California-natural-heritage)

Landowner Organization: Forest Landowners of California (forestlandowners.org)

Cooperative Extension: University of California Cooperative Extension (ucanr.edu)

State Forestry Agency: California Board of Forestry and Fire Protection (bof.fire.ca.gov)

COLORADO

Tree Guide: *The Native Trees of Colorado* (western-explorers.us/ColoradoTrees.html)

Property Tax Program: Forest Ag Program (csfs.colostate.edu/forest-ag-program)

Forester List: None available; use national lists

Natural Heritage Program: Colorado Natural Heritage Program (cnhp.colostate.edu)

Landowner Organization: Colorado Forestry Association (coloradoforestry.org) and Colorado Tree Farmers (treefarmer.com)

Cooperative Extension: Colorado State University Extension (www.ext.colostate.edu/index.html)

State Forestry Agency: Colorado State Forest Service (csfs.colostate.edu)

CONNECTICUT

Tree Guide: *Connecticut Trees & Wildflowers Pocket Guide* (tinyurl.com/Connecticut-tree-guide)

Property Tax Program: Public Act 490 (tinyurl.com/Connecticut-490)

Forester List: Connecticut Certified Forest Practitioners (tinyurl.com/Connecticut-forester-list)

Natural Heritage Program: Recreation and Natural Heritage Trust Program (tinyurl.com/Connecticut-natural-heritage)

Landowner Organization: Connecticut Forest & Park Association (ctwoodlands.org) and Eastern Connecticut Forest Landowners Association (ecfla.org)

Cooperative Extension: University of Connecticut Extension Forestry (canr.uconn.edu/ces/forest)

State Forestry Agency: Connecticut Department of Energy & Environmental Protection—Forestry (tinyurl.com/Connecticut-DEEP-forestry)

DELAWARE

Tree Guide: *Native Trees of Delaware* (tinyurl.com/Delaware-tree-guide) Note: This is just a list, so pair it with a general guide like the Virginia Tech tree ID website listed in Chapter 3's Beyond the Book.

Property Tax Program: Commercial Forest Plantation Act (dda.delaware.gov/forestry/conser.shtml; scroll down to "Property Tax Exemptions")

Forester List: dda.delaware.gov/forestry/conser.shtml (see "Free Forest Management Plans/Timber Harvest Assistance" for contact info)

Natural Heritage Program: Wildlife Species Conservation & Research Program (www.dnrec.delaware.gov/fw/nhesp)

Landowner Organization: Delaware Forestry Association (delawareforest.com)

Cooperative Extension: University of Delaware Cooperative Extension (extension.udel.edu)

State Forestry Agency: Delaware Forest Service (dda.delaware.gov/forestry/conser.shtml)

FLORIDA

Tree Guide: *Forest Trees of Florida* (ftof.freshfromflorida.com)

Property Tax Program: Greenbelt Law (tinyurl.com/Florida-Greenbelt-1; see also tinyurl.com/Florida-Greenbelt-2)

Forester List: Florida County Foresters (tinyurl.com/Florida-forester-list)

Natural Heritage Program: Florida Natural Areas Inventory (fnai.org)

Landowner Organization: Florida Forestry Association (floridaforest.org)

Cooperative Extension: University of Florida Extension (sfrc.ufl.edu/extension/index.html)

State Forestry Agency: Florida Forest Service (freshfromflorida.com/Divisions-Offices/Florida-Forest-Service)

GEORGIA

Tree Guide: *Native Trees of Georgia* (tinyurl.com/Georgia-tree-guide)

Property Tax Program: Conservation Use Assessment (dor.georgia.gov/conservation-use -assessment-information)

Forester List: Georgia Forestry Commission consulting forester list (gfc.state.ga.us/resources /directories/consulting-foresters)

Natural Heritage Program: Georgia Rare Species and Natural Community Data (georgiawildlife.com /node/1370)

Landowner Organization: Georgia Forestry Association (gfagrow.org)

Cooperative Extension: University of Georgia Extension (extension.uga.edu/agriculture/forestry; see also warnell.uga.edu/outreach)

State Forestry Agency: Georgia Forestry Commission (gfc.state.ga.us)

HAWAII

Tree Guide: *Common Forest Trees of Hawaii* (tinyurl .com/Hawaii-tree-guide)

Property Tax Program: Each county has its own. Visit tinyurl.com/Hawaii-forest-incentives, then scroll down to "Reduce your property taxes" and click on your county for more information about its program.

Forester List: None available; use national lists

Natural Heritage Program: Hawaii Natural Heritage Program (www2.hawaii.edu/~hinhp/staff.html)

Landowner Organization: Hawaii Forest Institute (hawaiiforestinstitute.org)

Cooperative Extension: University of Hawaii Forestry Extension (www2.ctahr.hawaii.edu/forestry)

State Forestry Agency: Hawaii Division of Forestry and Wildlife (dlnr.hawaii.gov/forestry)

IDAHO

Tree Guide: *Trees of Idaho* (idahoforests.org/img /pdf/treesofidaho.pdf)

Property Tax Program: Productivity Tax or Bare Land and Yield Tax (tinyurl.com/ Idaho-forest-tax-law)

Forester List: Idaho Department of Lands Supervisory Areas (www.idl.idaho.gov/areas/index.html)

Natural Heritage Program: Idaho Natural Heritage Program (tinyurl.com/Idaho-natural-heritage)

Landowner Organization: Idaho Forest Owners Association (idahoforestowners.org)

Cooperative Extension: University of Idaho Extension (www.extension.uidaho.edu/forestry.asp)

State Forestry Agency: Idaho Department of Lands (www.idl.idaho.gov/forestry/service)

ILLINOIS

Tree Guide: *Illinois Trees: An Identification and Activity Book* (tinyurl.com/Illinois-tree-guide-1); see also *Illinois Trees* (tinyurl.com/Illinois-tree-guide-2)

Property Tax Program: Conservation Stewardship Program (dnr.state.il.us/stewardship)

Forester List: Directory of Professional Consulting Foresters (tinyurl.com/Illinois-forester-list)

Natural Heritage Program: Illinois Natural Heritage Database (tinyurl.com/Illinois-natural-heritage)

Landowner Organization: Illinois Forestry Association (ilforestry.org); see also Northwest Illinois Forestry Association (www.nifatrees.org)

Cooperative Extension: University of Illinois Extension (web.extension.illinois.edu/forestry /home.html)

State Forestry Agency: Division of Forest Resources (dnr.state.il.us/conservation/forestry)

INDIANA

Tree Guide: *22 Trees of Indiana State Parks and Reservoirs* (in.gov/dnr/files/22_trees.pdf)

Property Tax Program: Classified Forest & Wildlands (state.in.us/dnr/forestry/4801.htm)

Forester List: Directory of Professional Foresters (findindianaforester.org)

Natural Heritage Program: Natural Heritage Data Center (in.gov/dnr/naturepreserve/4746.htm)

Landowner Organization: Indiana Forestry & Woodland Owners Association (ifwoa.org)

Cooperative Extension: Purdue Extension (ag.purdue.edu/fnr/Extension)

State Forestry Agency: Indiana Department of Natural Resources (state.in.us/dnr/forestry)

IOWA

Tree Guide: *Trees of Iowa: An Interactive Key* (tinyurl.com/Iowa-tree-guide)

Property Tax Program: Forest Reserve Law (tinyurl .com/Iowa-forest-reserve-law)

Forester List: District Forester Contacts (tinyurl .com/Iowa-forester-list)

Natural Heritage Program: Natural Heritage Foundation (inhf.org)

Landowner Organization: Iowa Woodland Owners Association (iowawoodlandowners.org)

Cooperative Extension: Iowa State University Extension (extension.iastate.edu/forestry)

State Forestry Agency: Iowa Forestry Bureau (iow-adnr.gov/Environment/Forestry.aspx)

KANSAS

Tree Guide: *Kansas Native Plants* (tinyurl.com /Kansas-tree-guide)

Property Tax Program: Automatic reduction for forestland

Forester List: Consultants & Contractors (tinyurl .com/Kansas-forester-list)

Natural Heritage Program: Natural Heritage Inventory (biosurvey.ku.edu/ksnhi)

Landowner Organization: Rural Forestry Program (www.kansasforests.org/rural_forestry)

Cooperative Extension: Kansas State Research and Extension (tinyurl.com/Kansas-forestry -extension)

State Forestry Agency: Kansas Forest Service (www.kansasforests.org)

KENTUCKY

Tree Guide: *Leaves of Typical Kentucky Tree Species* (tinyurl.com/Kentucky-tree-guide)

Property Tax Program: Automatic reduction for forestland

Forester List: Kentucky Association of Consulting Foresters (kacf.org/index.php/find-a-forester)
Natural Heritage Program: Natural Heritage Database (naturepreserves.ky.gov/data)
Landowner Organization: Kentucky Woodland Owners Association (kwoa.net)
Cooperative Extension: University of Kentucky Forestry Extension (www2.ca.uky.edu/forestry extension)
State Forestry Agency: Kentucky Division of Forestry (forestry.ky.gov)

LOUISIANA
Tree Guide: *Leaf Key to Common Trees in Louisiana* (tinyurl.com/Louisiana-tree-guide)
Property Tax Program: Automatic reduction for forestland
Forester List: Consulting Foresters of Louisiana (tinyurl.com/Louisiana-forester-list)
Natural Heritage Program: Natural Heritage Program (wlf.louisiana.gov/wildlife/louisiana-natural-heritage-program)
Landowner Organization: Louisiana Forestry Association (laforestry.com)
Cooperative Extension: Louisiana State University AgCenter (lsuagcenter.com/en/environment/forestry)
State Forestry Agency: Louisiana Department of Agriculture and Forestry (ldaf.state.la.us/forestry)

MAINE
Tree Guide: *Forest Trees of Maine* (tinyurl.com/Maine-tree-guide)
Property Tax Program: Tree Growth Tax Law (tinyurl.com/Maine-tree-growth)
Forester List: Maine Licensed Foresters (tinyurl.com/Maine-forester-list)
Natural Heritage Program: Natural Areas Program (maine.gov/dacf/mnap)
Landowner Organization: Small Woodland Owners Association of Maine (swoam.org)
Cooperative Extension: University of Maine Extension (extension.umaine.edu)
State Forestry Agency: Maine Forest Service (maine.gov/dacf/mfs)

MARYLAND
Tree Guide: *Leaf Key to Common Trees in Maryland* (tinyurl.com/Maryland-tree-guide)
Property Tax Program: Forest Conservation and Management (tinyurl.com/Maryland-Forest-Conservation)
Forester List: Maryland Consulting and Industrial Foresters (tinyurl.com/Maryland-consulting-foresters); If your property is less than 10 acres, see the Small Acreage Foresters Directory (tinyurl.com/Maryland-foresters-small).
Natural Heritage Program: Natural Heritage Program (tinyurl.com/Maryland-natural-heritage)
Landowner Organization: Maryland Forests Association (mdforests.org)

Cooperative Extension: University of Maryland Extension (extension.umd.edu/woodland)
State Forestry Agency: Maryland Forest Service (dnr2.maryland.gov/forests)

MASSACHUSETTS

Tree Guide: *GoBotany Simple Key: Woody Plants* (gobotany.newenglandwild.org/simple /woody-plants)
Property Tax Program: Forest Tax Program Chapter 61 (tinyurl.com/Massachusetts-chapter-61)
Forester List: Massachusetts Licensed Foresters (tinyurl.com/Mass-licensed-foresters)
Natural Heritage Program: Natural Heritage & Endangered Species Program (mass.gov/eea /agencies/dfg/dfw/natural-heritage)
Landowner Organization: Massachusetts Forest Alliance (massforestalliance.org)
Cooperative Extension: MassWoods Forest Conservation Program (masswoods.net)
State Forestry Agency: Massachusetts Bureau of Forestry (tinyurl.com/Massachusetts-forestry -bureau)

MICHIGAN

Tree Guide: *Identifying Trees of Michigan* (tinyurl .com/Michigan-tree-guide)
Property Tax Program: Qualified Forest Property Tax Program (tinyurl.com/Michigan-qualified -forest) and the Commercial Forest Program (tinyurl .com/Michigan-commercial-forest)

Forester List: Qualified Foresters by County (tinyurl.com/Michigan-forester-list)
Natural Heritage Program: Natural Features Inventory (mnfi.anr.msu.edu)
Landowner Organization: Michigan Forest Association (michiganforests.com)
Cooperative Extension: Michigan State University Extension (www.msue.anr.msu.edu/topic/info /forestry)
State Forestry Agency: Michigan Department of Natural Resources (tinyurl.com/Michigan-DNR)

MINNESOTA

Tree Guide: *A Beginner's Guide to Minnesota Trees* (tinyurl.com/Minnesota-tree-guide)
Property Tax Program: Sustainable Forest Incentive Act (tinyurl.com/Minnesota-sustainable -forest) and 2c Managed Forest Land (tinyurl.com /Minnesota-2c)
Forester List: Approved Minnesota Stewardship Plan Preparers (tinyurl.com/Minnesota-forester-list)
Natural Heritage Program: Natural Heritage and Nongame Research Program (dnr.state.mn.us /nhnrp)
Landowner Organization: Minnesota Forestry Association (minnesotaforestry.org)
Cooperative Extension: University of Minnesota Forest Resources Extension (myminnesotawoods .umn.edu)
State Forestry Agency: Minnesota Division of Forestry (dnr.state.mn.us/forestry)

MISSISSIPPI

Tree Guide: *Know Your Trees* (tinyurl.com /Mississippi-tree-guide-1); see also *Mississippi Tree Identification Interactive Search Tool* (tinyurl.com /Mississippi-tree-guide-2)

Property Tax Program: Automatic reduction for forestland

Forester List: Mississippi Board of Registration for Foresters (cfr.msstate.edu/borf)

Natural Heritage Program: Natural Heritage Program (mdwfp.com/seek-study/heritage-program .aspx)

Landowner Organization: Mississippi Forestry Association (msforestry.net)

Cooperative Extension: Mississippi State University Forestry Extension (msucares.com/forestry /index.html)

State Forestry Agency: Mississippi Forestry Commission (mfc.ms.gov)

MISSOURI

Tree Guide: *Fifty Common Trees of Missouri* (tinyurl .com/Missouri-tree-guide)

Property Tax Program: Forest Crop Land (tinyurl .com/Missouri-forest-crop)

Forester List: Missouri Consulting Foresters Association (missouriforesters.com/roster.php)

Natural Heritage Program: Natural Heritage Program (tinyurl.com/Missouri-natural-heritage)

Landowner Organization: Forest & Woodland Association of Missouri (forestandwoodland.org)

Cooperative Extension: University of Missouri Forestry Extension (snr.missouri.edu/forestry /extension)

State Forestry Agency: Missouri Department of Conservation (mdc.mo.gov/your-property)

MONTANA

Tree Guide: *Trees and Shrubs in Montana* (tinyurl .com/Montana-tree-guide)

Property Tax Program: Forest Lands Tax Act (tinyurl.com/Montana-forest-land)

Forester List: Department of Natural Resources Service Foresters (tinyurl.com/Montana-forester-list)

Natural Heritage Program: Natural Heritage Program (mtnhp.org)

Landowner Organization: Montana Forest Owners Association (forestsmontana.com)

Cooperative Extension: Montana State University Extension Forestry (msuextension.org/forestry)

State Forestry Agency: Forestry Division (dnrc .mt.gov/divisions/forestry)

NEBRASKA

Tree Guide: *Trees of Nebraska* (nfs.unl.edu /documents/TreesofNebraska.pdf)

Property Tax Program: Automatic reduction for forestland

Forester List: District Foresters (nfs.unl.edu /nfs-districts); see also Nebraska Forestry Consultants (tinyurl.com/Nebraska-forester-list)

Natural Heritage Program: Natural Heritage Program (outdoornebraska.ne.gov/wildlife/programs /nongame/Heritage.asp)

Landowner Organization: None—use National Woodland Owners Association or contact a state District Forester

Cooperative Extension: Nebraska Extension (extension.unl.edu)

State Forestry Agency: Nebraska Forest Service (nfs.unl.edu)

NEVADA

Tree Guide: *Southern Nevada Guide: Tree Selection and Care* (tinyurl.com/Nevada-tree-guide)

Property Tax Program: Agricultural or Open Space Use (tinyurl.com/Nevada-ag-bulletins, then click on the most recent "Ag Bulletin" to find out more)

Forester List: None available; use national lists

Natural Heritage Program: Natural Heritage Program (heritage.nv.gov)

Landowner Organization: None—use National Woodland Owners Association

Cooperative Extension: University of Nevada Cooperative Extension (www.unce.unr.edu)

State Forestry Agency: Nevada Division of Forestry (forestry.nv.gov)

NEW HAMPSHIRE

Tree Guide: *Gallery & Guide to NH Trees* (amc-nh.org/resources/guides/trees)

Property Tax Program: Current Use Taxation Program (nh.gov/btla/appeals/currentuse.htm)

Forester List: Directory of Licensed Foresters (extension.unh.edu/fwt/dir/index.cfm)

Natural Heritage Program: Natural Heritage Bureau (tinyurl.com/New-Hampshire-natural -heritage)

Landowner Organization: New Hampshire Timberland Owners Association (nhtoa.org)

Cooperative Extension: University of New Hampshire Cooperative Extension (extension.unh.edu /Natural-Resources/Forests-Trees)

State Forestry Agency: Division of Forests and Lands (nhdfl.org)

NEW JERSEY

Tree Guide: *Trees of New Jersey & the Mid-Atlantic States* (state.nj.us/dep/parksandforests/forest /materials3.htm)

Property Tax Program: Farmland Assessment (state.nj.us/agriculture/home/farmers/farmland assessment.html)

Forester List: List of Approved Foresters (state. nj.us/dep/parksandforests/forest/ACF.pdf)

Natural Heritage Program: Natural Heritage Program (state.nj.us/dep/parksandforests/natural /heritage)

Landowner Organization: New Jersey Forestry Association (njforestry.org)

Cooperative Extension: Rutgers New Jersey Agricultural Experiment Station (njaes.rutgers.edu /environment)

State Forestry Agency: New Jersey State Forestry Services (nj.gov/dep/parksandforests/forest)

NEW MEXICO

Tree Guide: *New Mexico Envirothon Tree Identification* (tinyurl.com/New-Mexico-tree-guide)

Property Tax Program: Automatic reduction for forestland

Forester List: State Forestry Contact Information (emnrd.state.nm.us/SFD/contact.html)

Natural Heritage Program: Natural Heritage New Mexico (nhnm.unm.edu)

Landowner Organization: New Mexico Forest and Watershed Restoration Institute (nmfwri.org)

Cooperative Extension: New Mexico State University Cooperative Extension Service (aces.nmsu.edu/ces/forestry)

State Forestry Agency: New Mexico State Forestry Division (emnrd.state.nm.us/SFD)

NEW YORK

Tree Guide: *Know Your Trees* (tinyurl.com/New-York-tree-guide)

Property Tax Program: Forest Tax Law Program 480-a (www.dec.ny.gov/lands/5236.html)

Forester List: Cooperating Forester Program (www.dec.ny.gov/lands/5230.html)

Natural Heritage Program: Natural Heritage Program (nynhp.org)

Landowner Organization: New York Forest Owners Association (nyfoa.org)

Cooperative Extension: Cornell Cooperative Extension (tinyurl.com/New-York-extension)

State Forestry Agency: Division of Lands and Forests (www.dec.ny.gov/about/650.html)

NORTH CAROLINA

Tree Guide: *Common Forest Trees of North Carolina* (ncforestservice.gov/publications/IE0112.pdf)

Property Tax Program: Present-use Value Program (tinyurl.com/North-Carolina-present-use) and the Wildlife Conservation Land Program (tinyurl.com/North-Carolina-conservation)

Forester List: Registered Consulting Foresters (tinyurl.com/North-Carolina-forester-list)

Natural Heritage Program: Natural Heritage Program (ncnhp.org)

Landowner Organization: NCWoodlands (ncwoodlands.org); *see also* North Carolina Forestry Association (ncforestry.org)

Cooperative Extension: North Carolina Cooperative Extension (forestry.ces.ncsu.edu)

State Forestry Agency: North Carolina Forest Service (ncforestservice.gov/index.htm)

NORTH DAKOTA

Tree Guide: *Trees and Shrubs of North Dakota* (tinyurl.com/North-Dakota-tree-guide)

Property Tax Program: Forest Stewardship Tax Law (tinyurl.com/North-Dakota-forest-tax)

Forester List: none available; use national lists

Natural Heritage Program: Natural Heritage (parkrec.nd.gov/nature/heritage.html)

Landowner Organization: North Dakota Urban & Community Forestry Association (nducfa.com)

Cooperative Extension: North Dakota State University Extension Service (tinyurl.com/North-Dakota-extension)

State Forestry Agency: North Dakota Forest Service (tinyurl.com/North-Dakota-forest-service)

OHIO
Tree Guide: *Leaf Identification Key to Eighty-Eight Ohio Trees* (tinyurl.com/Ohio-tree-guide)
Property Tax Program: Forest Tax Law (forestry.ohiodnr.gov/oftl)
Forester List: Ohio Society of American Foresters Directory (osafdirectory.com)
Natural Heritage Program: Natural Heritage Database (tinyurl.com/Ohio-natural-heritage)
Landowner Organization: The Ohio Forestry Association (ohioforest.org)
Cooperative Extension: Ohio State University Extension (woodlandstewards.osu.edu)
State Forestry Agency: Division of Forestry (forestry.ohiodnr.gov)

OKLAHOMA
Tree Guide: *Forest Trees of Oklahoma* (www.forestry.ok.gov/forest-trees-of-oklahoma-book)
Property Tax Program: Automatic reduction for forestland
Forester List: Find a Forester Near You (www.forestry.ok.gov/county-contacts)
Natural Heritage Program: Natural Heritage Inventory (oknaturalheritage.ou.edu)
Landowner Organization: Oklahoma Forestry Association (oklahomaforestry.org)
Cooperative Extension: Oklahoma State University Extension (nrem-old.okstate.edu/Extension)

State Forestry Agency: Oklahoma Forestry Services (www.forestry.ok.gov)

OREGON
Tree Guide: *Common Trees of the Pacific Northwest* (oregonstate.edu/trees/name_common.html)
Property Tax Program: Oregon has multiple tax reduction programs with varying requirements. Visit tinyurl.com/Oregon-Forest-Tax to learn about them.
Forester List: Oregon Forest Industry Directory (orforestdirectory.com)
Natural Heritage Program: Biodiversity Information Center (orbic.pdx.edu)
Landowner Organization: Oregon Small Woodlands Association (oswa.org)
Cooperative Extension: Oregon State University Forestry & Natural Resources Extension Program (extensionweb.forestry.oregonstate.edu)
State Forestry Agency: Oregon Department of Forestry (oregon.gov/ODF)

PENNSYLVANIA
Tree Guide: *Common Trees of Pennsylvania* (tinyurl.com/Pennsylvania-tree-guide)
Property Tax Program: Clean and Green (conservationtools.org/guides/44-clean-and-green)
Forester List: Consulting Foresters (dcnr.state.pa.us/forestry/yourwoods/consultingforesters)
Natural Heritage Program: Natural Heritage Program (www.naturalheritage.state.pa.us)
Landowner Organization: Pennsylvania Woodland

Owners Associations (tinyurl.com
/Pennsylvania-woodland-assoc)
Cooperative Extension: Penn State Extension
(extension.psu.edu/natural-resources/forests)
State Forestry Agency: Bureau of Forestry
(dcnr.state.pa.us/forestry)

RHODE ISLAND

Tree Guide: *Rhode Island Native Plant Guide* (web
.uri.edu/rinativeplants)
Property Tax Program: Farm, Forest, and Open
Space Act (tinyurl.com/Rhode-Island-open-space)
Forester List: Forestry Consultants List (tinyurl.
com/Rhode-Island-forester-list)
Natural Heritage Program: Natural Heritage
Program (tinyurl.com/Rhode-Island-natural
-heritage)
Landowner Organization: Rhode Island Forest
Conservators Organization (rifco.org)
Cooperative Extension: University of Rhode Island
Extension (web.uri.edu/forestry)
State Forestry Agency: Division of Forest Environ-
ment (tinyurl.com/Rhode-Island-DEM)

SOUTH CAROLINA

Tree Guide: *Familiar Trees of South Carolina* (clem
son.edu/extfor/publications/bul117)
Property Tax Program: Agricultural Assessment
Reform Act of 2009 (tinyurl.com/South-Carolina
-ag-assessment)
Forester List: Consulting Forester list (www.state
.sc.us/forest/consult.htm)

Natural Heritage Program: Heritage Trust Pro-
gram (dnr.sc.gov/mlands/hpprogram.html)
Landowner Organization: South Carolina Forestry
Association (scforestry.org)
Cooperative Extension: Clemson Cooperative
Extension (clemson.edu/extension/natural
_resources/index.html)
State Forestry Agency: South Carolina Forestry
Commission (www.state.sc.us/forest)

SOUTH DAKOTA

Tree Guide: *South Dakota Tree List* (tinyurl.com
/South-Dakota-tree-guide)
Property Tax Program: Automatic reduction for
forestland
Forester List: South Dakota Register of Private Pro-
fessional Foresters (tinyurl.com
/South-Dakota-forester-list)
Natural Heritage Program: Wildlife Diversity Pro-
gram (gfp.sd.gov/wildlife/management/diversity)
Landowner Organization: Black Hills Forest
Resource Association (bhfra.org)
Cooperative Extension: South Dakota State Univer-
sity Extension (sdstate.edu/sdsuextension)
State Forestry Agency: Department of Agricul-
ture   Conservation & Forestry (sdda.sd.gov
/conservation-forestry)

TENNESSEE

Tree Guide: *The All Season Pocket Guide to Identifying Common Tennessee Trees* (tinyurl.com
/Tennessee-tree-guide)

Property Tax Program: Greenbelt (tinyurl.com/Tennessee-greenbelt)

Forester List: Cooperating Forester List (forestcertificationcenter.org/CF_List)

Natural Heritage Program: Natural Heritage Inventory Program (tinyurl.com/Tennessee-natural-heritage)

Landowner Organization: Tennessee Forestry Association (tnforestry.com)

Cooperative Extension: University of Tennessee Institute of Agriculture (fwf.ag.utk.edu/Extension/forestry.htm)

State Forestry Agency: Tennessee Department of Agriculture (tennessee.gov/agriculture/section/forests)

TEXAS

Tree Guide: *Trees of Texas* (texastreeid.tamu.edu)

Property Tax Program: Open Space (tinyurl.com/Texas-open-space)

Forester List: Professional Management Services List (tinyurl.com/Texas-forester-list)

Natural Heritage Program: Wildlife Diversity Program (tpwd.texas.gov/huntwild/wild/wildlife_diversity)

Landowner Organization: Texas Forestry Association (texasforestry.org)

Cooperative Extension: Texas A&M AgriLife Extension (agrilifeextension.tamu.edu)

State Forestry Agency: Texas Forest Service (txforestservice.tamu.edu)

UTAH

Tree Guide: *Native and Naturalized Trees of Utah* (forestry.usu.edu/htm/treeid)

Property Tax Program: Utah Farmland Assessment Act (tinyurl.com/Utah-farmland-assessment)

Forester List: none available, use national lists

Natural Heritage Program: Conservation Data Center (dwrcdc.nr.utah.gov/ucdc)

Landowner Organization: none available, use National Woodland Owners Association

Cooperative Extension: Utah State University Extension (forestry.usu.edu)

State Forestry Agency: Utah Division of Forestry, Fire, and State Lands (ffsl.utah.gov)

VERMONT

Tree Guide: *Identify the Leaves of Vermont Foliage* (tinyurl.com/Vermont-tree-guide)

Property Tax Program: Use Value Appraisal (tinyurl.com/Vermont-use-value)

Forester List: Vermont County Foresters (tinyurl.com/Vermont-forester-list)

Natural Heritage Program: Natural Resources Atlas (anr.state.vt.us/site/html/maps.htm)

Landowner Organization: Vermont Woodlands Association (vermontwoodlands.org)

Cooperative Extension: University of Vermont Extension (uvm.edu/extension/environment/forestry)

State Forestry Agency: Vermont Department of Forests, Parks, and Recreation (fpr.vermont.gov)

VIRGINIA

Tree Guide: *Common Native Trees of Virginia* (tinyurl.com/Virginia-tree-guide)

Property Tax Program: Use Value Assessment Program (usevalue.agecon.vt.edu)

Forester List: Consultant Foresters (dof.virginia.gov/services/consultant-forester.htm)

Natural Heritage Program: Natural Heritage Program (dcr.virginia.gov/natural_heritage)

Landowner Organization: Virginia Forestry Association (www.vaforestry.org)

Cooperative Extension: Virginia Cooperative Extension (ext.vt.edu)

State Forestry Agency: Virginia Department of Forestry (dof.virginia.gov)

WASHINGTON

Tree Guide: *Trees of Washington* (tinyurl.com/Washington-tree-guide)

Property Tax Program: Designated Forest Land (tinyurl.com/Washington-designated-forest)

Forester List: Consulting Forester Directory (tinyurl.com/Washington-forester-list)

Natural Heritage Program: Natural Heritage Program (www.dnr.wa.gov/natural-heritage-program)

Landowner Organization: Washington Farm Forestry Association (wafarmforestry.com)

Cooperative Extension: Washington State University Extension Forestry (forestry.wsu.edu)

State Forestry Agency: Washington State Department of Natural Resources (www.dnr.wa.gov/programs-and-services/forest-practices)

WEST VIRGINIA

Tree Guide: *West Virginia Trees* (tinyurl.com/West-Virginia-tree-guide)

Property Tax Program: Managed Timberland Program (tinyurl.com/West-Virginia-timberland)

Forester List: Board of Registration for Foresters—Roster of Current Licenses (wvlicensingboards.com/foresters/roster.cfm)

Natural Heritage Program: Wildlife Diversity Program (wvdnr.gov/wildlife/wdpintro.shtm)

Landowner Organization: WV Woodland Stewards (wvstewards.ning.com)

Cooperative Extension: West Virginia University Extension Service (anr.ext.wvu.edu)

State Forestry Agency: West Virginia Division of Forestry (wvforestry.com)

WISCONSIN

Tree Guide: *Key to the Trees of Wisconsin* (tinyurl.com/Wisconsin-tree-guide)

Property Tax Program: Managed Forest Law (tinyurl.com/Wisconsin-managed-forest)

Forester List: Forestry Assistance Locator (dnr.wi.gov/topic/ForestLandowners/assist.html)

Natural Heritage Program: Natural Heritage Inventory (dnr.wi.gov/topic/nhi)

Landowner Organization: Wisconsin Woodland Owners Association (wisconsinwoodlands.org)

Cooperative Extension: University of Wisconsin–Extension (mywisconsinwoods.org)

State Forestry Agency: Wisconsin Department of Natural Resources (dnr.wi.gov/topic/Forest landowners)

WYOMING

Tree Guide: *Trees for Wyoming* (tinyurl.com /Wyoming-tree-guide)

Property Tax Program: Automatic reduction for forestland

Forester List: Wyoming State Forestry Division Contact List (wsfd.wyo.gov/home/staff-directory)

Natural Heritage Program: Natural Diversity Database (uwyo.edu/wyndd)

Landowner Organization: Wyoming Association of Conservation Districts (conservewy.com /FORESTRY.html)

Cooperative Extension: University of Wyoming Extension (uwyo.edu/uwe)

State Forestry Agency: Wyoming State Forestry Division (wsfd.wyo.gov)

CHAPTER 1: PRIVATE LANDOWNERS RULE!

1 Jacek Siry, Frederick Cubbage, and David Newman. "Global Forest Ownership: Implications for Forest Production, Management, and Protection." (Buenos Aires, Argentina: XIII World Forestry Congress, 2009), 10.

2 Ibid.

3 Brett Butler, *Family Forest Owners of the United States, 2006*, (Newtown Square, PA: US Forest Service, 2008), 72.

4 Data used to create this map is from Jaketon Hewes and others, "Public and Private Forest Ownership in the Conterminous United States: Distribution of Six Ownership Types—Geospatial Dataset," (Fort Collins, CO: US Forest Service, 2014), dx.doi.org/10.2737/RDS-2014-0002.

5 Butler, 2008.

6 Brad Smith and others, *Forest Resources of the United States, 2007*, (Washington, DC: US Forest Service, 2009), 336.

7 US Natural Resources Conservation Service, *America's Private Land: A Geography of Hope*, (Washington, DC: US Department of Agriculture, 1997), 80.

8 Delwin Benson, Ross Shelton, and Don Steinbach, *Wildlife Stewardship and Recreation on Private Lands*, (College Station, TX: Texas A&M University Press, 2005), 184.

9 US Fish and Wildlife Service, "Our Endangered Species Program and How It Works with Landowners," July 2009, fws.gov/endangered/esa-library/pdf/landowners.pdf.

10 Climate Change Program Office, Office of the Chief Economist, *U.S. Agriculture and Forestry Greenhouse Gas Inventory: 1990–2008*, (Washington, DC: US Department of Agriculture, 2011), 162.

11 Yang Wan and Mike Fiery, *The Economic Impact of Privately-Owned Forests in the United States*, (Charlotte, NC: Forest2Market, 2013), 48.

12 Southwick Associates, Inc., "The Outdoor Recreation Economy," (Boulder, CO: Outdoor Industry Association, 2012), 18.

13 US Fish and Wildlife Service, *2011 National Survey of Fishing, Hunting, and Wildlife-Associated Recreation*, (US Department of the Interior, 2012), 131.

CHAPTER 2: WHERE DO I START?

1 Brett Butler, *Family Forest Owners of the United States, 2006*, (Newtown Square, PA: US Forest Service, 2008), 72.

2 David Kittredge and William Haslam, "The Spread in Lump Sum Stumpage Price Bids," *Northern Journal of Applied Forestry* 17, no. 1 (2000).

7–8. See also Philip Bailey and others, "Income Tax Considerations for Forest Landowners in the South," *Journal of Forestry* 99, no. 4 (1999), 10–15.

3   For examples of these phenomena, see Corey Bradshaw and others, "Global Evidence that Deforestation Amplifies Flood Risk and Severity in the Developing World," *Global Change Biology* 13, no. 11 (2007), 2379–2395; Jason Johnston and Jonathan Klick, "Fire Suppression Policy, Weather, and Western Wildland Fire Trends," 159–177 in Karen Bradshaw and Dean Lueck, ed., *Wildfire Policy: Law and Economics Perspective*, (New York: RFF Press, 2012), 224; and David Theobald, James Miller, and N. Thompson Hobbs, "Estimating the Cumulative Effects of Development on Wildlife Habitat," *Landscape and Urban Planning* 39, (1997), 25–36.

CHAPTER 3: NATURE'S BEAUTY

1   Brett Butler, *Family Forest Owners of the United States, 2006*, (Newtown Square, PA: US Forest Service, 2008), 72.

2   Hoosier Heartland Resource Conservation and Development Council, "Edge Feathering for Native Habitat," accessed July 14, 2015, hhrcd.org/pdf/Edge%20Feathering%20Fact%20Sheet-final.pdf.

3   Center for Invasive Species and Ecosystem Health, "Invasive and Exotic Species of North America," September 15, 2015, invasive.org.

CHAPTER 4: GET OUT AND PLAY!

1   US Fish and Wildlife Service, *2011 National Survey of Fishing, Hunting, and Wildlife-Associated Recreation*, (Washington, DC: US Department of the Interior, 2012), 131.

2   Ibid.

CHAPTER 5: HEALTH AND WELLNESS

1   Bum Jin Park and others, "The Physiological Effects of *Shinrin-yoku* (Taking in the Forest Atmosphere or Forest Bathing): Evidence from Field Experiments in 24 Forests across Japan," *Environmental Health and Preventive Medicine* 15 (2010), 18–26.

2   Yoshifumi Miyazaki and others, "Forest Medicine Research in Japan," *Japanese Journal of Hygiene* 69 (2014), 122–135. See also Q. Li and others, "A Forest Bathing Trip Increases Human Natural Killer Activity and Expression of Anti-cancer Proteins in Female Subjects," *Journal of Biological Regulators and Homeostatic Agents* 22, no. 1 (2008), 45–55.

3   Brian Wu, "'Forest Bath' Is Way to Let Nature Cleanse Away Stress," *Los Angeles Times*, Feb. 20, 2015, latimes.com/health/mentalhealth/la-he-forest-20150221-story.html.

4   Christopher Ingraham, "Chart: The Animals That Are Most Likely to Kill You This Summer," *Washington Post*, June 16, 2015, www.washingtonpost.com/news/wonk/wp/2015/06/16/chart-the-animals-that-are-most-likely-to-kill-you-this-summer.

5   Centers for Disease Control and Prevention, "Lyme Disease: Transmission," March 4, 2015, cdc.gov/lyme/transmission.

6   Centers for Disease Control and Prevention, "Stop Ticks," April 21, 2015, cdc.gov/features/stopticks. See also US Environmental Protection Agency, "DEET," February 20, 2015, www2.epa.gov/insect-repellents/deet.

CHAPTER 6: WONDERFUL WOODLAND WILDLIFE

1 David King and Scott Schlossberg, "Synthesis of the Conservation Value of the Early-Successional Stage in Forests of Eastern North America," *Forest Ecology and Management* 324, (2014), 186–195. See also Mark Swanson, "Early Seral Forest in the Pacific Northwest: A Literature Review and Synthesis of Current Science," report for the Central Cascades Adaptive Management Partnership, January 11, 2012, ncfp.files.wordpress.com/2012/06/swanson_20120111.pdf.

2 Matthew Wilson, Winsor Lowe, and Keith Nislow, "Family Richness and Biomass of Understory Invertebrates in Early and Late Successional Habitats of Northern New Hampshire," *Journal of Forestry* 112, no. 4 (2014), 337–345.

3 Audubon New York, *Wildlife and Forestry in New York Northern Hardwoods: A Guide for Forest Owners and Managers*, (Albany, NY: Audubon New York, 2002), 40.

4 Scott Stoleson, "Condition Varies with Habitat Choice in Postbreeding Forest Birds," *The Auk* 130, no. 3 (2013), 417–428.

5 The data for this graph come from New York City's 2011 Watershed Forest Management Plan, available online at nyc.gov/html/dep/pdf/watershed_protection/dep_forest_management_plan_2011.pdf.

CHAPTER 7: THE WORLD'S BIGGEST WATER FILTER

1 New York State Department of Environmental Conservation, "Facts about the New York City Watershed," accessed July 15, 2015, dec.ny.gov/lands/58524.html.

2 Thomas Brown and others, "Spatial Distribution of Water Supply in the Coterminous United States," *Journal of the American Water Resources Association* 44, no. 6 (2008), 1474–1487.

3 Todd Gartner and others, *Natural Infrastructure: Investing in Forested Landscapes for Source Water Protection in the United States*, (Washington, DC: World Resources Institute, 2013), 132.

4 Caryn Ernst, *Land Conservation and the Future of America's Drinking Water: Protecting the Source*, (San Francisco, CA: Trust for Public Land, 2004), 52.

5 W.R. Osterkamp and others, "Economic Considerations of a Continental Sediment-Monitoring Program," *International Journal of Sediment Research* 13, no. 4 (1998), 12–24.

6 US Environmental Protection Agency, "Polluted Runoff: Forestry," October 22, 2012, water.epa.gov/polwaste/nps/forestry.cfm.

CHAPTER 8: CHANGING CLIMATE, CHANGING WOODLAND

1 Bill Lascher, "If You Plant Different Trees in the Forest, Is It Still the Same Forest?" *The Guardian*, October 19, 2014, theguardian.com/vital-signs/2014/oct/19/-sp-forests-nature

-conservancy-climate-change-adaptation-minnesota
-north-woods.

2   John Fleck, "Las Conchas Fire Recovery a Daunting Task," *Albuquerque Journal*, May 6, 2012, abq journal.com/104174/news/las-conchas-fire
-recovery-a-daunting-task.html.

3   Jason Funk and Stephen Saunders, *Rocky Mountain Forests at Risk: Confronting Climate-Driven Impacts from Insects, Wildfires, Heat, and Drought*, (Cambridge, MA: Union of Concerned Scientists and Louisville, CO: Rocky Mountain Climate Organization, 2014), 54.

4   Sebastian Luyssaert and others, "Old-Growth Forests As Global Carbon Sinks," *Nature* 455, (2008), 213–215.

5   Bruce Lippke and others, "Life Cycle Impacts of Forest Management and Wood Utilization on Carbon Mitigation: Knowns and Unknowns," *Carbon Management* 2, no. 3 (2011), 303–333.

6   US Energy Information Administration, "Heating and Cooling No Longer Majority of U.S. Home Energy Use," March 7, 2013, eia.gov/todayin energy/detail.cfm?id=10271&src=%E2%80%B9%20 Consumption%20%20%20%20%20%20Residential %20Energy%20Consumption%20Survey%20 %28RECS%29-b1. See also US Energy Information Administration, "2009 RECS Survey Data," accessed January 19, 2015, eia.gov/consumption/residential /data/2009/index.cfm?view=consumption#end-use.

7   Jacquelyn Smith, "America's 10 Deadliest Jobs," *Forbes*, August 22, 2013, forbes.com/sites /jacquelynsmith/2013/08/22/americas-10-deadliest -jobs-2.

8   Bruce Lippke and others, "CORRIM: Life-Cycle Environmental Performance of Renewable Building Materials," *Forest Products Journal* 54, no. 6 (2004), 8–19.

9   Chadwick Oliver and others, "Carbon, Fossil Fuel, and Biodiversity Mitigation with Wood and Forests," *Journal of Sustainable Forestry* 33, (2014), 248–275.

CHAPTER 9: THE TAXMAN COMETH

1   Catherine Mater, *The Forest Health-Human Health Initiative: Linking Landowners, Carbon Markets, and Health Care to Conserve and Sustainably Manage Family Forests*, (Washington, DC: The Pinchot Institute for Conservation, 2012), 33. See also Rebecca Stone and Mary Tyrrell, "Motivations for Family forestland Parcelization in the Catskill /Delaware Watersheds of New York," *Journal of Forestry* 110, no. 5 (2012), 267–274.

2   Stone and Tyrrell, 2012.

3   Anthony D'Amato and others, "Are Family Forest Owners Facing a Future in which Forest Management Is Not Enough?," *Journal of Forestry* 108, no. 1 (2010), 32–38.

4   Farmland Information Center, "Cost of Community Services Studies," (Washington, DC: American Farmland Trust, 2010), 6.

5   Philip Bailey and others, "Income Tax Considerations for Forest Landowners in the South," *Journal of Forestry* 99, no. 4 (1999), 10–15.

6 Brett Butler and others, "Effectiveness of Land-owner Assistance Activities: An Examination of the USDA Forest Service's Forest Stewardship Program," *Journal of Forestry* 112, no. 2 (2014), 187–197. See also Joshua VanBrakle and others, "Do Forest Management Plans Increase Best Management Practices on Family Forests? A Formative Evaluation in the New York City Watershed," *Journal of Forestry* 111, no. 2 (2013), 108–114.

7 Debra Groom, "Timber Theft Continues in Central New York Despite Tougher Law," *Post-Standard*, December 22, 2009, syracuse.com/news /index.ssf/2009/12/timber_theft_continues_in _cent.html.

CHAPTER 11: A BURNING PROBLEM

1 Russell Graham, ed., *Hayman Fire Case Study*, (Ogden, UT: US Forest Service, 2003), 396.

2 National Interagency Fire Center, "Total Wildland Fires and Acres," 2013, nifc.gov/fireInfo /fireInfo_stats_totalFires.html.

3 Data for this chart comes from National Interagency Fire Center, 2013.

4 Sierra Nevada Conservancy, "Sierra Nevada Watershed Facts," accessed July 17, 2015, sierra nevada.ca.gov/our-work/sierra-nevada-wip/SNWIP FactSheet.pdf.

5 Denver Water, "From Forests to Faucets," accessed July 17, 2015, denverwater.org/ SupplyPlanning/WaterSupply/PartnershipUSFS.

6 Pam Bostwick, Jim Menakis, and Tim Sexton, "How Fuel Treatments Saved Homes from the 2011 Wallow Fire," US Forest Service Fuel Treatment Effectiveness Assessment, 14.

7 David Foster and David Orwig, "Preemptive and Salvage Harvesting of New England Forests: When Doing Nothing Is a Viable Alternative," *Conservation Biology* 20, no. 4 (2006), 959–970.

8 NYC Department of Environmental Protection, "Department of Environmental Protection Provides Update on Forestry Management Project at Kensico Reservoir," November 20, 2013, nyc.gov/html/dep /html/press_releases/13-112pr.shtml.

CHAPTER 12: CHOWING DOWN

1 Center for Invasive Species and Ecosystem Health, "Invasive and Exotic Species of North America," September 15, 2015, invasive.org.

2 Andrew Liebhold and others, "A Highly Aggregated Geographical Distribution of Forest Pest Invasions in the USA," *Diversity and Distributions* 19 (2013), 1208–1216.

3 World Health Organization, "WHO Definition of Health," accessed September 4, 2015, who.int/about /definition/en/print.html.

4 Wendy Klooster and others, "Ash (*Fraxinus* spp.) Mortality, Regeneration, and Seed Bank Dynamics in Mixed Hardwood Forests Following Invasion by Emerald Ash Borer," *Biological Invasions* 16 (2014), 859–873.

CHAPTER 13: TIMBER!

1 Laura Kenefic and Ralph Nyland, "Diameter-Limit Cutting and Silviculture in Northeastern Forests: A Primer for Landowners, Practitioners, and Policy-makers," (Newtown Square, PA: US Forest Service, 2005), 18.

2 Ralph Nyland, "Diameter-Limit Cutting and Silviculture: A Comparison of Long-Term Yields and Values for Uneven-Aged Sugar Maple Stands," *Northern Journal of Applied Forestry* 22, no. 2 (2005), 111–116.

3 Ibid. See also Paul Catanzaro and Anthony D'Amato, "High Grade Harvesting: Understand the Impacts, Know Your Options," University of Massachusetts-Amherst, accessed July 20, 2015, masswoods.net/sites/masswoods.net/files/pdf-doc -ppt/High_Grade_Harvesting.pdf.

4 David Kittredge and William Haslam, "The Spread in Lump Sum Stumpage Price Bids," *Northern Journal of Applied Forestry* 17, no. 1 (2000), 7–8.

CHAPTER 14: FARM THE FOREST

1 National Agroforestry Center, "What Is Forest Farming?" January 2012, nac.unl.edu/documents /workingtrees/infosheets/WT_Info_forest _farming.pdf.

2 National Agriculture Statistics Service, "Maple Syrup Production," June 11, 2014, nass.usda.gov /Statistics_by_State/New_England_includes /Publications/0605mpl.pdf.

3 Larry Godsey, "Silvopasture Economics: Three Case Studies," The Center for Agroforestry, University of Missouri, accessed July 20, 2015, www2.dnr .cornell.edu/ext/info/pubs/silvopasturing/Silvo pasture_economics_L.Godsey.UMCA.pdf.

CHAPTER 15: OTHER INCOME SOURCES

1 Nathaniel Gronewold, "Chicago Climate Exchange Closes Nation's First Cap-And-Trade System but Keeps Eye to the Future," *New York Times*, January 3, 2011, nytimes.com/cwire/2011/01/03 /03climatewire-chicago-climate-exchange-closes -but-keeps-ey-78598.html.

2 Climate Policy Initiative, "California Carbon Dashboard," September 23, 2015, calcarbondash.org.

3 US Fish and Wildlife Service, *2011 National Survey of Fishing, Hunting, and Wildlife-Associated Recreation*, (Washington, DC: US Department of the Interior, 2012), 131.

4 Ibid.

5 US Forest Service, *National Report on Sustainable Forests—2010*, (Washington, DC: US Department of Agriculture, 2011), 214.

6 Michael Mengak, "Tips for Creating a Hunting Lease," University of Georgia Cooperative Extension, June 2012, extension.uga.edu/publications /files/pdf/C%20971_2.PDF.

7 US Fish and Wildlife Service, 2012.

8 US Census Bureau, "2010 Census Urban and Rural Classification and Urban Area Criteria," February 9, 2015, census.gov/geo/reference/ua /urban-rural-2010.html. See also National Agricultural Statistics Service, *2012 Census of Agriculture: United States Summary and State Data*, (Washington, DC: US Department of Agriculture, 2014), 635

p. According to this source, the US has about 5.7 million farmers, including 3 million farm operators and 2.7 million hired workers, out of a total US population of 308 million.

9 US Fish and Wildlife Service, 2012.

CHAPTER 16: START A NEW FOREST

1 Kurt VerCauteren and Scott Hygnstrom, "Managing White-tailed Deer: Midwest North America," *Papers in Natural Resources*, digitalcommons.unl.edu/cgi/viewcontent.cgi?article=1384&context=natrespapers. See also David Von Drehle, "America's Pest Problem: It's Time to Cull the Herd," *Time*, December 9, 2013, time.com/709/americas-pest-problem-its-time-to-cull-the-herd.

2 Brodie Farquhar, "Wolf Reintroduction Changes Ecosystem," *Yellowstone*, June 21, 2011, yellowstonepark.com/2011/06/wolf-reintroduction-changes-ecosystem. See also the "How Wolves Change Rivers" video in this chapter's "Beyond the Book."

3 David King and Scott Schlossberg, "Synthesis of the Conservation Value of the Early-Successional Stage in Forests of Eastern North America," *Forest Ecology and Management* 324, (2014), 186–195. See also Mark Swanson, "Early Seral Forest in the Pacific Northwest: A Literature Review and Synthesis of Current Science," report for the Central Cascades Adaptive Management Partnership, January 11, 2012, ncfp.files.wordpress.com/2012/06/swanson_20120111.pdf.

4 Katie Frerker and others, "Long-Term Regional Shifts in Plant Community Composition Are Largely Explained by Local Deer Impact Experiments," *PLOS ONE* 9, no. 12, (2014), journals.plos.org/plosone/article?id=10.1371/journal.pone.0115843.

5 Anne Eschtruth and John Battles, "Acceleration of Exotic Plant Invasion in a Forested Ecosystem by a Generalist Herbivore," *Conservation Biology* 23, no. 2 (2008), 388–399.

6 Susan Kalisz and others, "In a Long-Term Experimental Demography Study, Excluding Ungulates Reversed Invader's Explosive Population Growth Rate and Restored Natives," *Proceedings of the National Academy of Sciences* 111, no. 12 (2014), 4501–4506.

7 See, for instance, Jason Boulanger and others, "Use of 'Earn-a-Buck' Hunting to Manage Local Deer Overabundance," *Northeastern Naturalist* 19, (2012), 159–172.

CHAPTER 17: KEEP YOUR WOODS AS WOODS

1 Natural Resources Conservation Service, *Summary Report: 2010 National Resources Inventory*, (Washington, DC: US Department of Agriculture and Ames, IA: Iowa State University, 2013), 163.

2 Brett Butler and others, *Research Supporting Stemming the Loss of Family Forests across the United States*, Family Forest Research Center, May 16, 2014, forestfoundation.org/stuff/contentmgr/files/1/f733d4713abc573991af9ec86720b712/misc/section_ii__spatial_analysis__of_stem_the_loss_report_05_16_14.pdf.

3 World Wide Fund for Nature, "Impact of Habitat Loss on Species," accessed September 8, 2015,

http://wwf.panda.org/about_our_earth/species
/problems/habitat_loss_degradation.

CHAPTER 18: LEAVE A LEGACY
1   Data for this graph comes from Brett Butler, *Family Forest Owners of the United States, 2006*, (Newtown Square, PA: US Forest Service, 2008), 72.

Italicized pages refer to photos or charts.